Another Five Big Mountains and Treks

MERCER UNIVERSITY PRESS

Endowed by

TOM WATSON BROWN
and
THE WATSON-BROWN FOUNDATION, INC.

Another Five Big Mountains and Treks

A Regular Guy's Guide to Climbing Mt. Rainier, Everest Base Camp, Mt. Fuji, the Inca Trail / Machu Picchu, and Cho Oyu

DAVID N. SCHAEFFER

Mercer University Press
Macon, Georgia
2018

MUP
H954 PRINTED
IN CANADA
© 2018 by Mercer University Press
Published by Mercer University Press
1501 Mercer University Drive Macon, Georgia
3 1 2 0 7. All rights reserved 9 8 7 6 5 4 3 2 1. Books
published by Mercer University Press are printed on acid-
free paper that meets the requirements of the American National
Standard for Information Sciences—Permanence of Paper for Printed
Library Materials. ISBN 978-0-88146-673-7 ISBN eBook 978-0-88146-
674-4. Cataloging in Publication Data is readily available at Library of Congress.

Contents

Acknowledgments vi

Preface vii

1. Mt. Rainier: Third Time's a Charm 1

2. Everest Base Camp: Avoiding the Yak Dung 37

3. Mt. Fuji: Sunrise with the Masses 99

4. Inca Trail/Machu Picchu: A Rocky Road 121

5. Cho Oyu at 60: The Final Chapter 163

Afterword 235

Index 237

Acknowledgments

This book is dedicated to every cancer survivor who refuses to accept defeat. The author is grateful for his urologist, Dr. Mark Haber, and his radiation oncologist, Dr. Peter Rossi, who have made it possible for the author to keep climbing after a PSA count of 115.5 and a rather aggressive form of prostate cancer. Dr. Haber allowed the author to climb Mount Rainier a week before performing the biopsy to confirm the cancer. Dr. Rossi did not hesitate to allow the author to travel to Nepal for the Everest base camp trek five months after 34 days of radiation treatments were completed.

The author also acknowledges the great guidance and friendship of his fellow climbers and especially guides Sherpa Lakpa Rita, Sherpa Lakpa Gelu, Sarah Montgomery, and Ben Jones, who have provided encouragement, expertise, and safety along the way.

Finally, the author dedicates this book to his wife, Kim, who is letting the author retire at age 62; to his son and daughter, Daniel and Lora, who inspire the author to greater heights; and to his hiking buddies, Jim, Lee, Rick, and Richard, who have endured many training hikes and the author's endless storytelling in preparation for his bigger climbs.

Preface

This is the author's second book on mountain climbing. The first, *Five Big Mountains*, told the stories of the author's climbs of Pico de Orizaba, the highest volcano in Mexico and third-highest mountain in North America; Mt. Elbrus, the highest mountain in Europe (in Southern Russia); Kilimanjaro, the top of Africa, Aconcagua, at 22,840 feet, the highest point in South America; and Mt. Vinson, the highest mountain in Antarctica, approximately 500 miles from the South Pole.

The author started his climbing career at age 44 and never expected it to progress to some of the highest mountains in the world. He is an attorney from Atlanta and considers himself to be a regular guy who likes to try to do extraordinary things. The author's writing about his climbs from a regular guy's perspective gives the reader a real insight into the training, preparation, and actual mountaineering experience on a day-by-day and sometimes a moment-by-moment basis. He describes the thrills and the agonies, the triumphs and the failures. The author's intent in writing these books is to share what the climbs are really like, so that those adventuresome individuals who want to "go high" know what to expect.

Another Five Big Mountains and Treks covers the author's more recent climbs of Mt. Rainier, which took three tries; a 15-day trek to Everest base camp; a quick climb of Mt. Fuji in Japan; the 4-day hike of the Inca Trail to Machu Picchu in the mountains of Peru; and his attempted climb of Cho Oyu, the sixth-highest mountain in the world, 20 kilometers west of Everest, at age 60.

This book is also written strictly from a regular guy's perspective, with the author struggling to continue climbing even with mid-life problems: age, weight, fatigue, high blood pressure, and cancer. Each of the final four climbs described in this book occurred following the author's diagnosis of prostate cancer, which required one huge surgery, five follow-up surgeries, and 34 radiation treatments. The author now considers himself to be a regular guy who likes to try to do extraordinary things even as a cancer survivor…and he will never consider himself a cancer victim. Life goes on…

Enjoy the read and the adventure, and always aim for the highest heights!

1

Mt. Rainier

Third Time's a Charm

"If you aren't going to climb McKinley or Everest, then I guess you're done," my sister-in-law announced hopefully after I returned from my successful climb of Mt. Vinson in Antarctica.

I wondered if my wife had put her up to that comment.

"Oh, I don't know about that. I might have to climb some more 14,000ers here in the good ol' U.S.A.," I responded.

"Like what?"

"Well, there are some nice peaks in Colorado that I have my eye on, and of course, there is Rainier. I completely missed that one."

"Rainier? That's the one up near Seattle, right? I've heard it's got a lot of snowstorms, glaciers, and crevasses."

"Yep—that's the one."

"Kim's not going to like that."

"It's only a three-day climb. Thousands of people do it every year. She's got nothing to worry about," I said confidently.

FIRST ATTEMPT

I dilly-dallied around long enough during the first part of 2009 until all the Alpine Ascents-guided Rainier 3-day trips in the prime times of July and August were booked solid. Ultimately, I had to settle for a single slot left during the first weekend of September, over Labor Day weekend. Still, I thought the weather should be fine and the climb would be relatively easy compared to my prior adventures on higher peaks. I had climbed 14,000ers in one day several times, so I thought a three-day trip should be a "piece of cake."

I devoted three months of a moderate training regimen during summer 2009. The time went quickly, and soon I was getting excited about scaling another famous mountain.

When flying into Seattle, it is hard not to stare at Mt. Rainier, its peak gleaming in the sunlight high above the surrounding clouds. My heart started pumping just a bit faster as soon as I saw it from the left side of the plane. I snapped a few photos and mentioned to the guy next to me that I was climbing Rainier this weekend.

Rather than being excited for me, he frowned. "Isn't there a storm coming in?"

"Yes, but I checked with the guides, and the climb's still on. They're hoping the weather will clear before we have to make our summit bid."

"Good luck and be safe," he responded just as the pilot announced our descent into Seattle.

Unfamiliar with the Seattle airport, I followed the crowd and the signs to baggage claim. The fact that my backpack and gear bag had not arrived after thirty minutes was an ominous sign, but I ignored it and headed for the customer service desk. Somehow my checked baggage had ended up on the next plane from Atlanta.

Three hours later, after my bags arrived, followed by a rushed taxi ride into town, I found myself lugging my gear down some steep steps to the basement of Alpine Ascents International's offices near the Space Needle. I was only ten minutes late. Four other guys were already at AAI, with their gear spread out all over the floor. Three more climbers joined us a few minutes later. By then I had caught my breath and relaxed my shoulders.

I hate not being on time—just ask my beloved wife who generally likes to be "socially" late to almost everything.

We would have eight climbers and four guides on this mountain. But for now, our attention was turned to a very fit young lady whose job was to give us our orientation and perform the requisite gear check.

I couldn't help but notice that the girl, while attractive in a tomboyish way, had stronger calves and shoulders than I did. Her muscles were accompanied by a "no-nonsense" attitude. She had an air of cool "dudette-ness" about her, but today she was all business.

At her direction, we first went around the room introducing ourselves and disclosing our mountaineering experience. A couple of the guys had done Whitney and Baker, but none of them had climbed any of the high-altitude peaks. As usual, I was the oldest of the group, but had the most experience. When my turn came, I pointed to the large photos of Kilimanjaro, Aconcagua, Elbrus, and Vinson that adorned the walls of the room.

"I've climbed to the top of that one, that one, that one, and that one. But I am getting older now, so I am working on some 14,000ers I missed on the way."

Everyone was dutifully impressed except the young lady, who looked at my not-so-slim gut and gave me that "I'm not sure I believe you" look.

For the next two hours, she talked about the route, the meals, the snow-safety school at Camp Muir on the second morning of the climb, the need to take it slow and keep hydrated, and more details than I wanted to hear. But there were a lot of questions from the group, so she was obviously covering the right topics.

When it came time for the gear check, I learned that most of the guys did not have their own double plastic boots, crampons, or appropriate outer shells and down jackets. AAI had plenty of them to rent—for a moderate price. Fortunately, I had all the required gear and did not need to spend any additional money.

One would think that I should have the easiest time of all the climbers on this mountain....

The alarm clock woke me from a deep sleep early the next morning at 5:15 A.M. I had to store luggage, check out of the hotel, and hike a few blocks with my backpack to get to the AAI office by 6 A.M. This time I arrived five minutes early. Two guides were there to meet the eight climbers and assured us that our ride was on its way. We were told we would pick up the other two guides at a location nearer the mountain.

AAI's white van, pulling a trailer with a mountain scene painted on its side, arrived shortly thereafter. After our gear was stashed in the trailer for the ride to Mt. Rainier, all ten of us crammed into the van, like sardines. I squeezed in next to the window on the far side of the second bench seat and soon we were off, navigating the streets of Seattle.

From the plane, Rainier looked very close. By road it is several hours, about a third on expressways, a third on a seemingly endless four-lane road surrounded by strip malls, and the final third on winding, single-lane country and mountain roads. Every few miles we could see glimpses of Rainier off to our left on the hazy horizon. But most of it was covered in clouds.

After an almost three-hour drive, we stopped at the famous Whitaker Café at the headquarters for RMI, the original guide group for Rainier. I had to stretch my legs as soon as I tumbled out of the van. The two other guides appeared and greeted the group. I did not catch their names. Inside, the coffee aroma was strong and the sausage, egg, and cheese croissants were particularly tasty. I opted for a final Coke, knowing that I would not have another for the next three days. As I waited for the others to finish eating, I enjoyed the numerous wall-mounted photos of the Whitaker brothers climbing various mountains and thumbed through some of their books.

Soon we climbed back in the van, this time loaded with a total of twelve guys. Luckily, it was a short ride from there. About fifteen minutes later, we pulled into the main trailhead location at an area called Paradise. It was around 10:15 A.M.

On a nice day, we would have been able to see that Paradise is a huge parking lot with a dark-brown lodge hotel on the far right and a chalet-shaped ranger station, museum, and gift shop on the left. The trailhead and a low concrete building with restrooms and showers are in between. However, that day the parking lot was covered with a thick misty haze. The fog had settled in and a cold drizzle had begun just before we arrived. There was no visibility up the paved trail towards the mountain. As I got out of the van, I felt the freezing, damp air and knew we were in for a nasty day.

"Two layers under your outer shell and make sure you have Gore-Tex all over," our head guide said in a British-sounding accent as we climbed out of the van. "You can use the restrooms, get your water bottles filled, and change over there," he added, pointing towards the ranger station on the left side of the parking lot.

I grabbed my backpack, boots, crampons, ice axe, and ski poles from the trailer behind the van and quickly moved everything over to the sheltered edge of the building. I plopped my gear down by some water fountains outside the restrooms. My hands were already soaking wet and stone cold by the time I got there.

This is going to be a nightmare.

Ten minutes later, we headed up the asphalt-paved path leading from the parking lot, twelve in a row. I filed in directly behind the lead guide, a fortyish guy with the British accent. He had met us at Whitaker's Café, so I had not had a chance to talk mountains with him. For the first half hour or so, he and I shared common experiences on some of our climbs. I almost forgot how cold and wet it was. But then we hit some steep sections with multiple sections of high rocky steps. Proper breathing was required to make it up these sections, so I cut off the chit-chat and focused on the climb. I usually make good time up these types of rocky steps, but this time it seriously worked my calves until they were aching. Not much further, the drizzle became flurries and the muddy ground turned to slushy snow.

Just great.

The guides had been smart when they required us to wear our double plastic boots and full Gore-Tex waterproof jackets and pants from the start, but I was already wondering what we were getting ourselves into.

Almost exactly one hour into the climb, we reached a prominent point where we were supposed to have incredible views of the Nasqually Glacier to our left and Mt. Baker and Mt. St. Helen behind us. But gazing through the increasingly thick snowfall, we could see only a waterfall at the bottom of the glacier and clouds in the direction of the nearby volcanoes.

The guides reminded us to get food and water quickly and make sure we did not get too cold while resting. Then, much too soon for me, the lead guide announced the two-minute warning.

For the next section, I settled into the middle of the pack. I felt fine, but the pace for the first hour was just a little faster than I was used to. So, I let a few of the younger guys go ahead.

The second hour of the approximately five-hour climb to our destination, the John Muir Camp, is the toughest and steepest. There was little talking. I found myself listening to my own breathing and just putting one foot in front of the other, trying to keep up with the pace of the guy ahead of me. However, after about twenty minutes, he was falling behind the climbers in front of him. Normally, I would have stepped around him and caught up with the first group, but on this day, my legs wouldn't cooperate. Slowly but surely, the rest of the climbers passed us. I and the guy in front of me were now last, with just one guide behind us. I did not worry about it too much as the first group was only twenty to thirty feet ahead of us, but the gap slowly widened over the next fifteen minutes. Then we hit the steepest section of the day, a near-endless snow "escalator" of kicked-in steps as far up as we could see.

Just keep going, David—slow and steady. Don't worry about the others. Just don't stop.

I was sweating and needed a rest by the time we finally got to what I thought was the top of the tortuous snow staircase, but the guide behind us told us to keep moving. The rest of the climbers had already disappeared above the next ridge above us. I caught my breath on a less-steep section before hitting another nearly vertical section. I pressed forward and upward, feeling my thighs burn.

At the top, I could see the first group huddled in the snow, taking a break.

Thank God!

They had stopped for the second rest of the day. With renewed vigor, I marched up the remaining slope and collapsed next to them, panting like a wounded dog.

Wind added to our misery as we headed up the mountain after too short of a rest. Wet, heavy snowflakes covered our goggles and faces. I pulled my neck fleece up over my chin, almost up to my nose. Now, nothing was exposed except the very bottom of my nostrils.

This time I was able to keep up with the first group of climbers for only about ten minutes before they started pulling away. Within fifteen minutes they were out of sight, up into the blizzard, their young legs undeterred by the conditions.

Three of the eight climbers, including me, fell behind. Stupidly, I led the group, thereby taking the brunt of the whipping wind, now reaching thirty to forty miles an hour. Sometimes it swept down on us, blasting snow into my goggles. The crosswinds shifted to one side or the

MT. RAINIER

other, throwing us off balance. At this point, I completely gave up trying to keep contact with the first group and just concentrated on moving at any pace possible and on just staying upright.

Occasionally, one of the guides would appear by my side and ask if I was alright. I always nodded and gave a "high" sign with one of my poles. Truth be told, I was seriously struggling.

Come on, David. It's just a 14,000er and you're only at 8,000 feet. Suck it up and get going!

The first group was just leaving the next rest stop when our "slow" group arrived. I noticed that they were now wearing crampons.

"Do we need crampons at this point?" I asked our lead guide.

"Yeah, it's getting a bit treacherous up there. A bunch of open crevasses, and visibility is not good, so get your spikes on during this stop," he replied. "And we're falling behind schedule so let's try to keep this stop short. The longer we're out in this stuff, the worse it'll be."

Great. I'm dying here, you're cutting my rest stop short, and it's worse ahead.

I thought about turning back—only for a second. I knew it was closer to the Muir Huts than back to the trailhead at this point and I was not about to embarrass myself by not even making it to the first camp. So, I attached my crampons, managing to secure the straps while my hands froze. Then I stuffed my cold, wet hands into my gloves and headed up the mountain again.

The next two hours were completely surreal. I could barely see the guide who was about five feet in front of me. My goggles were clouding over, so my vision was even further obscured. The wind and an absence of snow on the mountain for several weeks had caused dozens of deep crevasses to open. Normally, the crevasses are covered by five to ten feet of snow and the path just goes diagonally up over them all the way up to the Muir huts. However, since the open crevasses were too wide to jump over in most places, we had to detour sideways for fifty feet, or sometimes more than a hundred yards, to find narrow spots where we could leap over and beyond each crevasse.

This caused the climb to be much longer. Much of the time, we were laterally working our way directly into the crosswinds. Worse yet, the terrain along the lower side of each crevasse was severely bumpy and uneven, like the moguls one sees in the Winter Olympics, except they were completely icy. I found myself tripping and going down on one knee more times than I would like to admit.

But I endured. There was no fourth rest stop on this day, and I had no choice but to almost crawl up the mountain. The other two "slow" climbers eventually moved ahead and I was left with one guide encouraging me to keep going. What a lousy assignment for him! As soon as we finally got above the last crevasse and could see a glimmer of the huts above, he, too, left me behind.

At 4:45 P.M., over six hours after we had left the trailhead, and almost an hour after the first group arrived, I plodded into the John Muir Camp, embarrassed to be the last one in. All I remember seeing was a couple of stone walls and boarded-up huts amid a large outcropping of rocks. Luckily, a guide was there to wave me into one of the huts to the left. I stepped down into the cement prison filled with stinky climbers, managed to peel off my pack, chugged the rest of my water bottle, and collapsed onto one of the wooden platforms covered with vinyl bedrolls.

"Nice climb," I muttered to my comrades before I passed out for the next thirty minutes. Truth be told, there was an expletive between the words "nice" and "climb."

"Burritos are up. Time to feed those tired muscles," one of the guides announced as he plunged down the two steep steps into the hut where we were confined.

I had not moved in over a half hour, but I quickly grabbed a bowl and cup from my backpack and held the bowl out for the grub. In the last two hours of the climb, I had not been able to stop for any food, so I was famished.

The burritos were cool on the outside, but still hot inside. I didn't care. I just wanted to get something into my system.

I took a big bite.

Yuck!

I instantaneously recognized that the burrito was filled with guacamole, a substance I particularly detest. I gagged, but miraculously avoided throwing up. There was nowhere to spit out the foul green paste, so I just had to swallow it. My stomach would churn for hours.

I washed down the green, gunky residue with some hot chocolate. But the aftertaste lingered. The only thing that saved me was a nice spicy meat stick followed by a Snickers bar from my private stash.

The rest of the burrito somehow found itself entombed in the snow at the bottom of the steps into the hut. A fitting burial.

"Get some good rest tonight," the lead guide said after dinner. "Tomorrow we will do the snow school after some breakfast and then see what the weather looks like. Maybe we will be able to go up to high camp in the afternoon."

Surprisingly, I woke at dawn, fresh and ready to go. My legs were only mildly sore and I felt great.

But there was nowhere to go. Overnight, twenty-four inches of snow had fallen. An eight-foot drift had formed just outside our hut, and the outhouses just twenty feet away were almost completely buried in the snow.

One of the assistant guides gave us the bad news.

"It's pretty bad out there, boys. Lots of wind, cold, and a helluva lot of fresh snow out there. Get dressed in full snow gear and follow the red flags over to the mess tent over the hill. We'll have some breakfast and then see if things lighten up enough to do the snow school."

"Any chance we will be going to high camp today?" one of the climbers asked him.

"Let's just see how the day goes," he responded.

"That's a no," I said quietly to myself.

Indeed, our second day on the mountain consisted of eating a very tasty breakfast with lots of bacon, pancakes, and hot chocolate, getting blasted by snow and wind as we moved our gear from our hut on the left side of the camp to another narrower hut on the right side, and then being stranded for the next twenty-four hours. We had to move over to the other hut because theoretically another group would be coming up from Paradise to stay in the first hut that night. Later, we learned that all three groups attempting to come up to the Muir camp from Paradise that second day had to turn around.

We had moved for nothing.

Our snow school consisted of a "guide talk" inside the narrow hut, including a demonstration of how to hold an ice axe while climbing and self-arresting, along with a few crampon-stepping techniques. However, without practicing these techniques on the side of a snowy hill, I'm not sure how much we learned. For me, there was nothing new in the lesson, and I missed the opportunity to polish up my skills.

After that, we were not even allowed to go outside to use the outhouses. The winds whipped up to eighty miles per hour. The snow kept coming down and blasting against the hut. The guides periodically shoveled out in front of the hut door to avoid our being completely blocked in. But we were trapped. So, the pee bottles came out and the card games began.

After a while we didn't even notice the smell.

I chose to sleep most of the day, frequently interrupted by a few of the guys telling me to stop snoring. We munched on two days' worth of snacks throughout the day, saving enough in case we were stranded another day.

It was a helpless feeling to be holed up with no escape route and no summit bid on this trip.

I was stiff, bored, and frustrated by the time dawn's light filtered through the snow-encrusted windows of the narrow hut on the morning of the third day. The snow had stopped and the winds had dwindled to a manageable thirty miles an hour. The sun was fighting its way through the clouds.

"Maybe we will get out of here today," I said to the rest of the guys.

No one responded. They were all zombies.

The door opened, bringing with it our British guide and a cold blast of wind. He had a large Ziploc full of breakfast bars.

"No hot breakfast today, gentlemen," he announced. "Looks like we've got a short window of good weather to get out of here. Munch on these chewies or snack on your own food, then get everything packed up. We'll be leaving in forty-five minutes. Sorry we can't go any further up the mountain this time, but your safety comes first."

An hour later, we stood outside the hut, shivering in the cold breeze as the guides roped us up to go back down through the crevasse field. I looked down in the direction from which we had come up thirty-six hours before. Where we had jumped over dozens of open crevasses thirty-six hours earlier, there was nothing but smooth, fresh snow below us.

Christ almighty. Where did the crevasses go—and do they expect us to just walk down through them?

"I don't want to be an alarmist or anything, but aren't we going to drop into the crevasses if we go straight down?" I asked the lead guide.

"That's why we have this," he said as he held up an eight-foot pole, demonstrating how he would probe the snow for crevasses. "And that's why we're roping everyone up."

He then instructed us how to brace and dig in with our ice axes if anyone plunged down through the snow bridges into a crevasse.

"With all twelve of us roped up, no one'll go very far. Nothing to worry about."

Right. That makes me feel a lot safer.

Moments later we were plowing down through knee- and thigh-high snow, just trying to keep up with the climber in front without pulling the climber behind down. It was a brutal exercise at a brisk pace. Fortunately, the lead guide stopped several times to probe with the long stick. Then we were off again. After about forty minutes, we cleared the crevasse fields without anyone falling in. Now that we were out of danger, the ropes were removed from our carabiners.

The rest of the climb down was a slog through fresh snow and renewed foggy conditions. Uneventful, but very tiring.

The only redeeming part of the entire trip were the incredibly large and delicious hamburgers and beers we had at a small restaurant a few miles outside the Rainier National Park boundaries on the way back to Seattle.

I could not believe that after the high-altitude mountains I had climbed all over the world, on this trip to climb a mere 14,000er in Washington State, I was unable to go above the 10,500-foot base camp. And I barely made it there.

I pledged to myself that I would try again the next year.

SECOND ATTEMPT

Five days before my second scheduled attempt to climb Rainier in June 2010, I picked up the *Atlanta Journal Constitution* and read about an avalanche burying eleven climbers on Rainier's Ingraham Glacier.

What the (expletive deleted)! That's the glacier we climb across to go to the summit!

I read on, quickly learning that ten of the eleven buried climbers had been rescued alive. One solo climber with no guide support had been lost. Two of the ten were in critical condition at the hospital in Seattle, but were expected to recover. I later learned that Eric Remza, my guide on Aconcagua, had been instrumental in saving some of the avalanche victims that day.

As soon as I got to my office, I emailed AAI to see if our trip was still on and whether this would affect our ability to summit Rainier on this trip. The response was more positive than I expected. Yes, the climb was still on. Whether we would be able to go above high camp to the summit depended on the weather, but the guides hoped that cold weather would return and solidify the snow, making passage safe.

There would be no refunds or opt-outs for the trip.

My wife was, to say the least, concerned. She worries about me incessantly when I am climbing, even when conditions are ideal.

"You're not going up through that avalanche, are you?" she asked.

"That's the glacier we go up through, but I'm sure AAI will not let us go if it's not safe," I responded.

"They better not—I want you back in one piece and not in a body bag."

"Don't worry. They take way more precautions than I would if I was going alone."

"Exactly. That's why you don't go solo anymore—not since your admittedly reckless solo climb down in Mexico."

She was referring to my very first high-altitude climb of Pico de Orizaba, where my brother turned back and I climbed to the top by myself despite a defective, duct-taped crampon.

"I know that was stupid, but I haven't climbed without a guide since. I'm sure the guides at Rainier won't put us in danger. I mean, look what they did last year. They wouldn't let us go above the John Muir huts."

"Well, I hope so. Don't do anything stupid, and just come home to me."

She kissed me, then turned and walked back to her office.

Five days later, in Seattle, I learned that AAI had just moved into a new space a few blocks from the basement location we used the year before. A temporary sign was out front and I could smell fresh paint as I worked my way inside with my backpack and gear bag.

The gear check room was much nicer, but it had the same bench seats. The walls were still bare, so this time there were no photos for me to point out which mountains I had climbed.

Gear check was "déjà vu all over again." The same strong-legged female guide led the orientation and gear-check session. A bunch of young guys with limited climbing experience, but a lot of enthusiasm, filled the room. And one local sports-radio celebrity announced that he was climbing the mountain on a dare. Most of them had to rent gear.

As usual I had everything I needed, plus a few extra items, the most precious of which was a bumper sticker for my campaign for Georgia Court of Appeals. Believe it or not, I was in the middle of a statewide campaign for appellate judge. Forty to fifty of my supporters had pledged a penny a foot, risking a campaign donation of $144.10 each. One enthusiastic supporter e-mailed me, mistakenly promising he would pledge a dollar a foot, but quickly rescinded the offer once he did the math. That pledge would have paid for a lot of campaign signs!

Anyway, I wanted to hold up my campaign bumper sticker on the summit and put the photo on my election website when I returned, so I carefully packed it where I could readily pull it out once we reached the summit.

Some of the guys saw the blue bumper sticker and immediately started calling me "Judge"—a moniker that lasted the rest of the trip. Unfortunately, calling a candidate by the name of the position for which he or she is running is considered a jinx. That jinx came true when I narrowly missed the election runoff five months later.

Unlike the year before, the sun was out and Paradise was completely clear of fog and clouds when we arrived the next morning. The mountain was gloriously shining above us. As it was only mid-June, the snow reached all the way down to the parking lot. Just a few feet deep at the edge of the parking lot, the accumulation grew to more than fifteen feet deep almost immediately. I loved it. Alpine climbing with crampons and ice axes from the start, under perfectly blue skies.

Our guide team was a very experienced group. The lead guide, Sarah Montgomery, was the founder of an avalanche safety school in Jackson Hole. Impressive, especially with the uncertainty of conditions due to the recent avalanche. She also looked very fit and outdoorsy, and had a confident aura about her.

Another of our guides was one of two Sherpas on AAI's staff. I had met the other of the two, Sherpa Lakpa Rita, the diminutive but excellent guide who had filled in on my climb of Aconcagua several years before. However, this Sherpa was much taller and looked like a stud. Named Sherpa Lakpa Gelu, he had climbed to the top of Everest "only" thirteen times! But he seemed happy to be climbing a mere 14,000er in the United States with a bunch of amateurs on this occasion. The other two guides were young studs who looked like they had plenty of energy.

This time, the trip up to the Muir huts was a relaxing stroll. We enjoyed a beautiful day, with not a cloud in the sky, and just a gentle breeze to keep us cool. The snow was deep and well-packed from other climbers going up and down. There were no crevasses anywhere to be seen except way up on the Nasqually Glacier a half mile away.

Our rest stops were warm and casual. No rushing, and everyone kept together.

Some of the younger guides and climbers moved up the final straightaway at a faster pace once the huts were in sight. I knew better, keeping a nice, slow and steady pace all the way to the camp. There was absolutely no reason to hurry on such a gorgeous day. We had plenty of time to rest before dinner and bedtime, so I took my time and enjoyed talking with Sherpa Lakpa Gelu most of the final hour.

What a difference from the climb the year before!

This time, we could relax outside the huts, enjoy the views as the sun set, and feast on a nice meal before calling it a night.

MT. RAINIER

Thankfully we had no burritos for dinner.

We awoke to another beautiful morning. It was interesting to be able to explore the camp that had been buried in the blizzard and drifts the year before. This time, a whole line of tents ran along an area between the two huts. These were the non-guided climbers who carried their own tents and food up with them, hoping to follow the same path up to the summit as the guided groups, but with no real experience or back-up if weather descended on them or they got in trouble. Others, the brighter ones, were just spending the night at Camp Muir and then would return to Paradise the next day.

After a great breakfast of more pancakes and bacon than we could possibly eat, we put on our gear and practiced climbing up a steep hill on the left side of the camp. There we learned and re-learned self-arrest techniques led by our lead guide, Sarah, who was all business.

We practiced self-arrest falling forward feet first, falling backward headfirst, falling sideways, and falling fast and slow, until we all had snow down our jackets and pants and were thoroughly soaked through with sweat. Then we practiced crampon and rope team techniques for another hour in the hot sun. After about three hours, snow school was finally over. I realized then how glad I was that we had not done outside snow school the year before.

After a quick lunch, we packed and headed for the high camp up on the Ingraham Glacier. We could see the path leading diagonally up a steep hill to a rocky ridge on the back side of Camp Muir. It looked treacherous towards the top, but as we were lining up into four rope teams, I could see several other groups successfully zigzagging their way to the top of the ridge before disappearing from our view.

To my surprise, I was chosen for the lead rope team, immediately behind one of the young guides. I instantly focused my attention on the task at hand, deciding that I would keep a very strong pace for the one-and-a-half-hour trek up to the high camp on the Ingraham Glacier "Flats." I did not want to slow anyone down or embarrass myself.

The climb to the ridge was a challenge, but very doable. It looked steeper from the camp. A few sections were a bit dicey, clear of snow, with loose rocks and scree. But within about thirty minutes, we were standing up on the narrow ridge, sipping water while waiting for the other teams to join us.

The view from the ridge was outstanding. Most of the mountain's central volcanic peak was now in view, with the dreaded Disappointment Cleaver above a rocky outcropping to the right side of the mountain. If we went to the summit, that would be our pathway to the top, in the middle of the night.

"Let's get going," my guide said as he moved away and the rope between us spread out the requisite fifteen feet.

The next section was the hardest of the short trip to high camp. We climbed up three successive very steep, narrow paths, with the mountain sloping off precipitously to our right.

Just before we reached the third steep spot, we heard a roar beyond the ridge above us to our left almost like a jet going overhead. But there was no plane in the sky. The roar increased in volume and filled our ears. We stopped dead in our tracks.

"What the hell is that?" I asked the guide in front of me.

"Avalanche on the other side of the ridge. Nothing to worry about over on this side. But let's keep moving."

My thighs were burning by the time we reached the top of the third incline. In our nervousness, our pace had quickened. I wanted to get away from that avalanche as rapidly as possible even though it was clearly on the other side of the mountain.

The whole group was rattled, but as soon as we reached the crest of the hill, our spirits were buoyed by the sight of the colorful tents at the high camp, another twenty minutes or so ahead of us.

We skirted a few crevasses on our way up the gentle incline to the tents, reminding us that we were now on a slowly moving glacier with a lot of hidden dangers. As we reached the high camp, I looked up the mountain, trying to determine where the big avalanche had occurred six days earlier. But it all looked like undisturbed snow.

Maybe we can dodge any more avalanches and go for the summit after all!

By 4 P.M., we were already getting restless. No climbers had tried to summit since the avalanche. Several other groups at high camp were weighing their options and the risks of going up through what could still be unstable sections of snow. We wondered what the chances were that we might be able to "go for it" that night.

Our guides sensed our level of uncertainty and called a short meeting in front of the tents.

"Here's the story," Sarah said. "Lakpa, John, and I are going to climb five or six hundred feet up towards Disappointment Cleaver and dig down six to eight feet to see whether the snow is stable enough to safely head up the mountain. It depends on whether the snow has melted then frozen enough to create a solid base with firm snow. Then if the temperature drops to 24 or 25 degrees by midnight. Maybe we'll get lucky."

"What's the temperature now?" someone asked.

"It's about 34 degrees right now—still above freezing. But they're expecting it to drop."

"So, when will we know and what do we need to do to be ready?" another climber asked.

"The best thing you can do right now is to get a bite to eat and then get some rest. If we are going for it, we'll wake you up at midnight, and you'll need to be ready to go within thirty minutes. So, get back in your tents and rest your legs. You need to be fresh if we go."

The meeting was over. Some of the guys were convinced that we would be climbing in another eight hours and on the top of Rainier by daybreak. I was more skeptical. Our lead guide was an avalanche-safety expert from Jackson Hole, Wyoming, with a school dedicated to that subject. Would she risk her reputation and a major source of revenue to take a few guys up under dicey conditions?

Not likely.

However, after the guides returned from digging the hole a few hours later, they told us to be ready to go by midnight. "It all depends on if the temperature drops enough tonight. Keep your fingers crossed and get some sleep."

I did as I was told and within a few minutes I was fast asleep, probably keeping the rest up with my snoring. I have rarely had any problem sleeping at high altitudes, and this was no exception.

Something woke me up long after the tent was pitch black. I wrestled with my cheap Timex digital watch, which had a button that could be pushed to illuminate the numerals. Finally, the green light came on and I squinted at the watch face.

"Damn…it's 1:15. They didn't wake us up," I mumbled.

For a moment, I panicked, thinking that somehow everyone else had left without me. But then I turned and saw that my tentmate, a young college student on his first big climb, was still in his sleeping bag, fast asleep.

I knew they were bullshitting us about going for it tonight.

Just to make sure, I slipped on the inner boots of my double plastic mountaineering boots, unzipped the tent netting, and worked my way through the narrow vestibule to the outside.

It was dark, but the sky was clear and full of stars. A perfect night. Except that it was not cold enough. I could tell that it was not below freezing. In fact, it felt warmer than it had at 4 P.M.

I looked down the row of tents. All the ice axes, crampons, and extra gear were lined up outside the tents. Everyone was still here, cozy in their sleeping bags.

We are going nowhere.

The sun woke us up the next morning, and soon the guides were rustling around outside the tents.

"Sorry we didn't get to go for the summit, guys, but we've got a beautiful day to hike back down to Paradise," one of the younger guides announced. "Let's get packed up. We'll have a hot breakfast down at Camp Muir, then have a casual climb down from there. We should be back to Seattle by four, maybe stop for lunch on the way."

"Great," I said to myself. "Another wasted trip to Rainier. What is it with this mountain?"

I had my tentmate take some photos of me holding my campaign bumper sticker in front of the tents with the summit in the background so that I could hope to collect on some of the pledges from my supporters, but my heart was not in it.

As it turned out, most of my supporters who joined the Rainier "dollar-a-foot" pledge later contributed $115, as the high camp was at about 11,500 feet. But I was terribly disappointed they were not having to pay $144.50 each.

As we formed some lines to be roped up for the hike down to Camp Muir, we noticed that, despite the prior avalanche, another guided group had started up the mountain and were perhaps five hundred vertical feet above us, just about to head right towards Disappointment Cleaver. I cursed to myself, thinking if they could do, why couldn't we?

But my disgust disappeared quickly as I watched two climbers in one of the two four-man rope teams above us collapse and start sliding down the mountain at an alarming speed as the snow moved under them. The other two climbers in that rope team dropped and dug in with their ice axes, perfectly executing the self-arrest technique we had practiced the day before. The two sliding climbers reached the end of the slack in their ropes and came to an abrupt halt.

"Oooh, that must have hurt," one of our group said, giggling nervously. But no one was laughing.

"Now you see why we didn't try it," Sarah responded. "The snow is too unstable. They're lucky they didn't drop into a crevasse. Hopefully they didn't break any bones."

Moments later, we watched the fallen climbers get back on their feet and regroup. Then they started back down the mountain. They had learned their lesson and were turning back.

We later learned that three crazy, unguided climbers risked their lives and made it to the summit that day. But I for one know that our guides made the right decision.

The only redeeming value in the descent that day was my chance meeting of Phil Erschler, a famous guide and climber who, with his wife, became the first couple to climb all seven continental summits. He and his wife had written a book called *Together at the Top of the World*, which I had read the year before. Phil suffers from a malady called Crohn's Disease, but even with the pain and multiple surgeries that accompany that medical condition, he had continued to guide and climb many of the highest mountains on the planet. A friend of my son, an athlete with a college football placekicking scholarship, had developed the same disease and I had loaned him the book for inspiration when he was confined in a hospital only a few months before my trip to Rainier. I told Phil how much his book had meant to a young man facing the same disease.

ANOTHER FIVE BIG MOUNTAINS AND TREKS

The climbing community is small and it is amazing how many of the top climbers in the world I have met in just a few years climbing mountains as a rank amateur.

But the summit of Rainier would have to wait for another time. Little did I know that the next time I would return to Rainier, I would be facing the biggest medical issue of my life.

THIRD ATTEMPT

July 2011 is a month I will never forget. Having changed law firms after my judicial election loss, I needed to apply for a new "key man" insurance policy. In my law firm's conference room, I joked with the insurance agent and the medical tech as they took my vital signs and drew blood for the labs, telling them that except for one infected inner-ear episode, I had not seen any doctor in fifteen years. I had not ventured into a doctor's office since a routine physical at age forty, which had turned into an unnecessary heart catheterization due to a false-positive EKG reading on a treadmill test.

The agent called me a few days later with the results.

"David, I'm sorry to tell you that your life insurance application has been declined by the underwriters," he said.

"You're kidding me, right? What's goin' on?"

"Well, I'm not supposed to discuss blood test results with you over the phone."

"What results?"

"Have you had problems with your prostate, peeing, that sort of thing?"

"No, why?"

"Because your PSA is very high."

I felt a pit in my stomach.

"How high?"

"Let me just have them send you the lab results," he said. "I'm not supposed to tell you that over the phone."

"Look, I waive any privacy—just tell me already!"

"Okay...okay...your PSA is 115. They're concerned you have prostate cancer."

MT. RAINIER

"What? That's impossible. PSA readings are supposed to be less than 4.0. People get concerned if they reach 7.0 or 8.0. That must be a mistake."

"You better see a urologist and get another blood test to make sure."

"You're damned right I will. I'll call for an appointment today."

The urologist's test the next week came back at 112.5, not much better.

"The bad news is that you have prostate cancer—almost certainly," he told me. "The good news is that it's treatable. You'll probably die from some other disease or old age before you would die from prostate cancer. That is, if you do the right things now."

I stared at him in disbelief.

"How can this be possible? I have no symptoms. I climb mountains, big ones. In fact, I have another climb planned for later this month. This isn't going to interfere with that, is it?"

"Hopefully not. Let's just take it one step at a time. First, we need to do a biopsy and determine whether, in fact, your prostate has cancer cells, where they are, and how aggressive they are. Then we can take it from there. Prostate cancer is generally a very slow-growing cancer, so there is no immediate urgency, but I recommend that you have the biopsy in the next two or three weeks at the latest."

"Fine, that's perfect," I said. "Let's do it the last week of July."

I had already booked my flights and paid my deposit for my third attempt to climb Mt. Rainier on July 23–25, 2011. Now I would just have to do it with suspected but unconfirmed prostate cancer. The biopsy would have to wait until I got back.

Late July and early August are the best times to climb Rainier. May and June are a little dicey as the mountain shifts from freezing temperatures to the warmer season, creating more risk of avalanches. By the end of August and into September, serious storms are more likely. Having unsuccessfully tried to climb Rainier once in June and once in September, this time I had nailed a spot on a group right in the middle of the sweet spot—the end of July. This was my best chance of making it to the top. I was not about to miss it for a little biopsy.

This time, I had persuaded a young lawyer and friend, Bert, to join me on my quest. He had climbed Mt. Baker a few years earlier and was still in his late twenties. He did not have much experience, but was very gung-ho about going higher than he had ever been before. Bert was a former Buzz mascot at Georgia Tech. Suffice it to say, he is a high-energy, always-positive, Type-A personality.

AAI's place in Seattle had been seriously upgraded since the prior year. The gear room was fully painted and outfitted with large photos and a big flat-screen TV. Completely new was a huge gear and clothing shop in the adjoining space to the left. When I walked in, I hoped it would be my last visit.

Third time's a charm, David. Third time's a charm.

I plunked my burgundy backpack and yellow North Face gear bag on the floor, introduced Bert and myself to another batch of young climbers, and sat down at the bench with my name tag on it. Bert was across the room with some guys his age. A few minutes later, a girl in her mid-twenties, carrying an identical burgundy backpack to mine, arrived and sat down on the bench next to mine. Dressed in light blue from head to toe, she looked a bit awkward. She quickly announced that she had never climbed anything like Rainier before, but had been training with friends in New England for six months and was really looking forward to climbing with "you guys."

"Nice backpack," I told her, pointing to her identical red pack.

"Yeah, I just bought it for this trip. I hope it's okay."

"It's an excellent bag," I assured her. "You must be Dorothy?"

"How did you know?"

I pointed at her name tag on her bench. "I'm David, welcome to Rainier. It's a fun mountain. I've tried it twice but got turned back by weather and an avalanche the first two times. But this time we're gonna make it to the top."

Our gear guy was our lead guide for the climb. He was about my age, but with extremely thin and gnarly legs and a weathered face. He had well-worn climbing shorts and a faded T-shirt, knobby knees, and a bandanna around his neck.

I instantly liked him.

MT. RAINIER

The gear check was much more relaxed this time. What had taken three hours the prior two years, took only just over an hour. Our guide spent more time talking about the weather.

"The meteorologist is saying that the next two days look very good, but the third day may have some weather coming in," he said. "How would you guys...and gal...feel about possibly moving our summit attempt up about twelve hours and going up on the afternoon of the second day?"

"Will they allow that?" I asked. "I thought they were pretty strict about doing snow school and using the second day to get up to high camp and resting before heading up to the top. Not that I am objecting at all. If it gets us to the top, I would be all for it."

"Yes. We can use our discretion. We moved the summit attempt up a few times earlier this year successfully. It makes for a harder second day, but you're back at high camp having already gone to the top, so you can get a nice night's sleep at high camp. But no need for us to decide today. I just want you to think about it and discuss it among yourselves. We'll only change the plan if everyone unanimously agrees to it."

"Sounds good to me," I said.

Some of the others nodded in agreement. Others looked bewildered.

"Let's hope the weather holds," I said, "but if it looks bad for the third day, I say we go for it early."

On my way out, I pulled out a copy of my book, *Five Big Mountains: A Regular Guy's Guide to Orizaba, Elbrus, Kilimanjaro, Aconcagua, and Vinson*, and showed it to the guys manning the reception counter at AAI.

"Thought you guys might like to add this to your mountain-climbing book collection. Two of the chapters are climbs I made with AAI."

The younger of the two guys took the book from my hands and immediately began thumbing through it, quickly coming to the color photos.

"You've climbed all these?"

"Yes. Had to go to Russia twice to get Elbrus. Went to Aconcagua and Vinson with AAI—great trips."

"Who were your guides on those trips?" he asked.

"Eric Remza, Sherpa Lakpa Rita, and Dave-something on Aconcagua, and Vern Tejas on Vinson. Now there's an interesting guy."

"Yeah, Vern's a legend."

"You'll have to read Chapter 5 then. He and I got a little sideways on summit day down in Antarctica, but we made it up and back just fine. He's an awesome guide and climber—sung his way almost all the way up the headwall."

"Thanks for the book," one of them responded. "We'll definitely put it in our collection."

That evening, my friend Bert and another climber in the group, a guy from Boston, had dinner together. We asked him what mountains he had climbed.

"Nothing much. Some peaks in Maine and Vermont. Thought this would be a good trip to see the west," he said.

"I'm not sure about seeing the west, but you picked a big mountain to climb. It's a good challenge," I replied.

"That's what I understand," he stated matter-of-factly, then barely said anything else the rest of the meal as Bert and I chatted away.

Later, Bert and I both looked at each other and wondered out loud why the guy was even on this trip. He seemed so noticeably unenthusiastic about the climb.

"Maybe he's just quiet and will surprise us," I said. "Anyway, let's get some sleep. We've got to be up early in the morning, and the first day's climb is a bear."

Morning came early and soon we were back at the AAI offices, waiting for the white van and trailer. I could tell it was going to be a beautiful day.

I felt great.

The others arrived, but the van was nowhere to be seen.

Dorothy tapped me on the shoulder. "I borrowed the book you left with the guys at the counter and read half of it last night. I couldn't put it down. Can I get an autographed copy when we come back from the mountain?"

"Yeah, sure, I have one more copy with me in my bag inside. Remind me when we get back. I can't believe you spent the night reading instead of sleeping!"

"I didn't plan to, but the solo climb on that Mexican volcano got me hooked. I wanted to read more. Plus, I plan to climb Kilimanjaro someday. I almost finished that chapter."

"Glad you liked it. Kilimanjaro was a lot of fun. Not too bad to climb if the weather is good…and we had perfect weather the whole time. But you must train or you will end up being carried down like my sister-in-law. I'll bet you could do it."

"Maybe. Some friends of mine have been talking about trying to climb it next year."

"February's the best time to do it. We didn't hit any snow at all."

"Sounds good. If only I can get time off from IBM that early in the year."

Dorothy had introduced herself as a computer software engineer from New York the day before, but had not mentioned she worked for IBM.

"You don't happen to know a couple of guys named Paul and Tom that are software engineers with IBM in Burlington, Vermont, do you?"

"Yeah, I was in a meeting with them a few months ago. Why?"

"They climbed Aconcagua with me. I guess you haven't made it to that chapter yet. I shared a tent with them a couple of nights high up on that mountain. Paul was a very strong climber and Tom made it to the top even though he was a bit sick by summit day. Paul's in the summit group photo in my book."

"Small world, isn't it?"

"Yes."

What's up with so many brainy software engineers wanting to climb mountains?

Just then, the van arrived and we began loading our gear into the trailer. The protocol was the same as the first and second trips to Rainier. This time, however, I had a good feeling.

Under glorious skies, the climb up to the Muir huts was uneventful—except for one thing. The guy from Boston fell behind in the second hour and looked a bit out of it as he finally made it to our second rest stop at the top of the steepest section.

"That's as far as I'm going," he said.

One of the guides walked over to him and put his arm around his shoulders. "Hey, you just made it through the roughest part of today's climb. Get a good rest here, eat some food, and you'll feel much better in a few minutes. You can take your time."

"Maybe you didn't hear me. I'm done. I'm going back down. This is not for me," the Bostonian said.

"Okay," the guide said, quickly turning and starting a hushed conversation with our lead guide.

The lead guide then walked over and talked to the Bostonian in quiet tones that we could not make out. However, from the reaction of the erstwhile climber, we could tell that there was no talking him out of turning back.

"I can't believe he's giving up only two hours into the climb after flying here from the East Coast and paying $1,500," I said to Bert.

"Yeah. Crazy. But he didn't seem too excited last night either," Bert responded.

Within minutes, it was decided. One guide would stay with the guy until another group of climbers from AAI came down from Camp Muir on their way out. He could join them and ride back to Seattle that afternoon.

Just like that, we were down to seven climbers. Frankly, I had thought that if anyone would drop out, it might be Parag, a gentleman of Indian descent from New York. Clearly overweight, he was one of those guys who likes to carry all the extra gadgets and heavy camera equipment on the climb. But through the first two hours, he had shown considerable grit, managing to keep up with the rest of us.

The afternoon climb to Camp Muir was a relaxed, but still tiring affair. No one was in a hurry, so the group stayed together. The toughest part was avoiding getting sunburned as there was not a cloud in the sky and almost no breeze. I kept it in low gear, concerned that my ailing prostate might somehow prevent me from completing the climb if I pushed it too hard. However, it did not seem to affect me at all.

MT. RAINIER

Towards the end, Bert and some of the younger guys pushed ahead by a few hundred yards. I found myself ascending at a nice, moderate pace alongside Sherpa Lakpa Gelu, with Dorothy close behind. We made it to the huts in good time. I immediately noticed that the whole area was much more crowded with climbers and tents than was the case the last two times I had reached that point.

After resting and rejuvenating with some hot chocolate, I managed to find a spot just below and to the left of our hut where I could get a cell phone signal and called my wife for a few minutes. Kim was surprised to hear from me, as usually telephone signals on mountains are absent without a satellite phone.

As usual, things were chaotic in my absence. City workers supposedly fixing a small sinkhole in front of our house had caused a sewer line under the road to collapse and she had been told that because the sewer from our house ran through that line, we had to hire and pay for a private plumber to repair the line. I told her to tell them they should fix it themselves because the broken line was not on our property. But the work had already been done at a cost of almost $5,000, which she had paid.

How I would like to sue the city over that dispute!

She then brought me up-to-date on the latest from our daughter, Lora, who was interning in Hollywood. Lora had just got nabbed by the camera cop while making a right turn on red, thereby receiving a stiff $475 fine for the offense.

Geez, how much money are we spending this week?

Now you know why I like to get away and go climb a mountain. It helps to get away from the everyday aggravations. I would rather spend some money to take in some breathtaking scenery and to enjoy the exhilaration of hiking. Rainier is not too shabby on the former. That evening's view, looking out at St. Helen and Mt. Baker from the Muir huts as the sun began to set, was priceless.

In the morning, after Parag had kept us awake all night with his snoring (this time I was not the worst offender), our lead guide woke us up early. He told us the weather report was beginning to look even more dicey for the next day. He recommended that we cut snow school short and head up to high camp before lunch, then try to summit in the afternoon. A quick show of hands revealed unanimous agreement.

"Okay. We'll get a good breakfast in thirty minutes, do an abbreviated snow school, then leave for high camp by nine-thirty. That should get us up to high camp by eleven and we can leave for the summit by one."

"Sounds good," I replied. "What time does that mean we'll get to the summit?"

"Probably around five-thirty or six. Then we'll hustle back down to high camp before it gets dark."

Though it was six-thirty in the morning, everyone immediately perked up. Having been given our marching orders for summit day, we instantly began packing and reorganizing our gear. We did not have time for any delays.

Two hours later, with our stomachs full and our self-arrest skills honed, we stood waiting to be assigned rope teams for the hike to high camp. I was very pleased to be assigned to Sherpa Lakpa Gelu's rope team. Dorothy was the third climber on the team, right behind me. The guides must have determined that we hiked at about the same pace.

Bert was paired with one of the "younger-guy" teams in front, both of which took off at a rather quick pace. Fortunately, Lakpa Gelu did not feel the need to stay up with them. We proceeded out the back of Camp Muir and towards the steep ridge behind it at a reasonable pace. For obvious reasons, I felt I was in very good hands with a Sherpa who had climbed to the top of Everest fourteen times at the front of my rope team. Having a somewhat gangly, inexperienced girl on the team gave me some concern. But Dorothy had shown no signs of fatigue on the way to the Muir huts, and while she was inexperienced, she looked strong and determined.

We had no significant problems getting to the Ingraham Flats, with the colorful tents at high camp greeting us a little more than an hour later.

When we arrived, I was a bit surprised that Bert had already set up his gear in a tent with one of the young guys, leaving two tents left for three climbers. Normally, I would have suggested that Dorothy take a tent for herself and I would share a tent with Parag, who was still about twenty minutes behind us. But Dorothy immediately said that she did not want to be in a single tent and asked if I minded sharing one with her.

My initial reaction was that this was not a good idea. A married guy sleeping in a tent with a single girl high on a mountain might be hard to explain. However, I was not too thrilled about sharing a tent with Parag snoring all night, and I had no romantic inclinations towards Dorothy. I weighed the options and decided that a good night's sleep outweighed the dangers. I agreed to share a tent with her, but only after insisting that if she needed privacy, she should just tell me and I would go outside whenever necessary.

As it turned out, it was never necessary as neither of us ever removed any clothing for the next twenty-four hours.

We barely got our sleeping bags situated in the tent when our lead guide announced that we would be leaving for the summit in twenty minutes.

"Change in plans. We need to go now. Get a quick snack, go to the bathroom, and pack plenty of water," he said. "Make sure you have your down jackets for rest stops handy as it will get cold up there. But don't put on too many layers now or you will overheat on the way up to Disappointment Cleaver. Stay in the same teams that you were roped up in on the way up here. We'll have to make good time to reach the summit and get back here this evening before the storms roll in."

Suddenly, what had been a relaxing, jovial day turned into a serious job at hand. Half of us began scurrying for backpacks and gear. The other half formed a line at the designated pee hole.

Fortunately, I had just used the "facilities" and was still wearing the proper clothing. After tossing a few unnecessary items out of my pack and into the tent, I stepped into my double plastic boots, strapped on my crampons and harness, and clipped on my climbing helmet.

I was ready.

I started to adjust my ski poles, but our lead guide told us to leave our ski poles behind and use ice axes from this point on, a telltale indication that we were about to be climbing some steep slopes.

The climb above Ingraham Flats involves a steady fifteen minutes of slogging straight up to avoid a large crevasse that runs upwards from the camp. As soon as we finally passed the end of the crevasse, we turned sharply to the right, over a steep notch, and then traversed straight across the mountain. In another twenty minutes or so, we came to a rocky outcropping, with loose scree and some exposed areas in which the mountain dropped off precipitously to our right. There, ropes had been affixed to the walls to our left to hold onto as we worked our way around the rocks on some narrow ledges.

Once through the rocky section, the real climb started—seemingly straight up. This was the hike up to Disappointment Cleaver. Up to this point, we were still close behind the first two rope teams. But soon they scooted ahead, making zigzags in the switchbacks above us, barely visible in the rapidly descending mist. Lakpa Gelu demonstrated proper ice axe and rope technique on the upper end of each switchback, and soon we were marching upward at a steady gait.

Several minutes into the steep climb, I turned my focus inward and concentrated solely on the steps ahead, one by one, becoming oblivious to the progress of the other climbers above us. Visibility was already down to about one hundred feet, so there was not much to see anyway.

Occasionally, we slowed momentarily for Dorothy when she took a misstep, or for me when my ice axe plunged downward to the hilt instead of finding solid snow for an anchor. This turned out to be a constant problem all the way up the mountain. Preferably, unless the slope is very, very steep, the ice axe is supposed to stick in a few inches to provide balance and just enough traction to avoid slipping or falling. However, in the afternoons when the snow is soft, the point of the axe goes all the way in sixteen to eighteen inches, causing the climber to plunge down with it, throwing him or her off balance. This defeats the purpose of the axe. On this afternoon, the temperature was not cold enough to keep the sides of the switchback paths icy and solid. So, my ice axe plunged in deeply, over and over, making progress that much more difficult. That is one of the reasons why most of the time, summit bids are made in the early morning before the snow melts and becomes slushy.

Though the side of the mountain was very steep, the many switchbacks made the path a lot more manageable. I found myself just carrying the ice axe rather than plunging it in except when we reached the end of that switchback and had to maneuver around the corner to go up in the other direction. There some ice axe traction was essential.

Normally, Alpine Ascent guides take breaks every hour, and I usually need them at least that often. The trek up to Disappointment Cleaver was no exception as far as my needs. It was tough going and I felt myself tiring as we approached the one-hour mark. However, there was nowhere to stop or rest until we got to the top of the cleaver, which from the high camp was at least an hour and forty-five minutes. I sucked it up, followed one steep switchback after another, working my way up the never-ending-slope.

Not being able to see anything above us because the mountain was completely shrouded in clouds, I began measuring our progress solely by the amount of time that elapsed on my watch. As we reached the one-and-a-half-hour mark, I asked Lakpa Gelu how much farther to the cleaver.

"Ten or fifteen minutes, give or take...," he said.

"Sounds good," I responded, and dug in for another twenty minutes.

"Give or take," my ass! They always underestimate.

When we reached the top of Disappointment Cleaver, I was so zoned in on the path that I barely noticed we were there. Lakpa Gelu stepped off the main path and into some deeper snow to our right. I followed without question. For the first time, I noticed we were on a shoulder-like flatter area and there was visibility away from the mountain to our right. We could see down to the shining valley below, but above us, the mountain was still completely shrouded in clouds.

The first two rope teams had already left this spot. I figured they must be at least ten minutes ahead of us. I wasn't really worried about them, though. Instead, I focused on getting some food and water in me before the next section. It was a five-hour ascent to the summit so we still had more than three hours left. I knew I would need plenty of fuel for the climb.

Dorothy looked a bit weary, but said she felt fine and asked Lakpa Gelu if he thought we were still on track for the summit.

"Yes, yes, of course," he responded. "We just have to keep moving and hopefully the weather will hold off."

As it turned out, the spot where we sat was a windy one. Within five minutes I was shivering. Like a complete amateur, I had been so happy to make it to where we could sit down that I had forgotten to pull out my down jacket to stay warm. Fortunately, just as I began to reach into my bag for the jacket, Lakpa Gelu gave the two-minute warning and I knew we would be back climbing before I got too cold.

For the next half hour, we worked our way around a very deep, gaping crevasse, then along the right side of the mountain, mostly at a very gradual incline. The clouds were thin and every few minutes we could see out of the mist and down to the green valleys below. Somehow plenty of light was hitting those valleys, but no sun was visible to us.

This section was a nice respite, but it did not last long.

Soon we turned left and started up another steep section of switchbacks, not much different from the first set up Disappointment Cleaver. I was grateful that Lakpa Gelu did not rush us. Despite some fatigue, I could keep up, using about eighty percent of my maximum effort. It helped that Dorothy asked to take a photo or two whenever the clouds to our right cleared, giving me a chance to rest.

After about another hour, we reached the top of that section and took a second rest stop. But this time, the break was short and Lakpa Gelu told us we needed to pick up the pace. Surprisingly, as we worked our way up a flatter straight section, I realized that Parag and his guide had almost caught up with us. He was doing a lot better than I expected.

The path turned left and Lakpa Gelu picked up the pace noticeably as we zoomed across an almost horizontal section for about ten minutes. Just before we reached the end of that section, the clouds cleared above. For a few seconds, I could see what looked like the top of Mt. Rainier. I am sure it was not the top, as we still had over an hour to go, but I took it as a good sign.

Little did I know that we were about to reach the third vertical set of switchbacks up to the crater rim and summit. We turned abruptly to our right and instantaneously I had to shift into fourth gear. I looked at my watch. It was ten after four.

Only fifty minutes to the top. Give or take…

MT. RAINIER

And Lakpa Gelu was picking up the pace. Now I was working hard to earn the right to stand on top of Mt. Rainier. My calves began to burn as we quickened our steps, ever upwards. I could not see anything ahead of or behind us, but that was not necessary. I zoned in on Lakpa Gelu's steps and tried to match them. By now, the temperature had dropped significantly enough that my ice axe was gripping the upper side of the snow on the switchbacks firmly, so I felt very comfortable and balanced. My leg muscles were working overtime and I knew that I would be seriously sore for a couple of days. But when I know I am getting close to the top, things get a lot easier.

"Woo-hoo! You've made it!" I heard as I looked up and noticed the two rope teams ahead of us, their packs strewn on the ground. I looked around. After three tries in three different years, I was finally atop Mt. Rainier, looking down across its crater. Not that we could see much over the edge. The visibility was no more than thirty feet in any direction.

I looked at my watch. Four fifty-seven.

"Made it with three minutes to spare," I announced loudly. "How long have you guys been up here?"

"About twenty minutes," one of them said.

"You guys suck," I said. "But congratulations. That was a heckuva climb! Too bad there's nothing to see up here."

"Yeah, it's like we're on another planet."

We unclipped from the rope and hugged everyone in sight, celebrating our victory. I felt good. But, perhaps because of the limited view or the fact that I had not suffered that much getting there, I was not as ecstatic as usual. Or maybe it was because the guides quickly explained that we were at the crater rim, but not at the highest point, which was not much higher, but was approximately a third of the way around the crater.

"This counts as a successful summit," they said, "but it's too socked in to risk going around the rim today."

Bullshit. Are you kidding me? I want to go to the top!

But I said nothing, as no one else was complaining and I did not want to rock the boat.

I looked for Bert, and to my surprise, he was sitting to the side, moaning and rubbing his shins. Apparently, his rental boots were too tight and he had not worn two pairs of thick socks, so the boots had dug into his shins all the way up. Now he was in agony. Nevertheless, he got up for pictures and gave me a bear hug.

"I thought I would never make it," he said, almost choking with emotion. "My shins are killing me. I don't know if I can make it down."

"You don't have any choice, Bert. You just have to suck it up."

"I know, but it really hurts…really bad."

"Sorry, man. I feel for you, but you've just got to get back down to camp. No one is going to carry you."

About ten minutes later, Parag made it to the top, collapsing in a pile. He immediately pulled out his camera and began snapping photos right and left from his sitting position.

All seven of us made it to the top—well, almost to the top. Now all we had to do was make it down.

Less than fifteen minutes after my rope team arrived, we started to retrace our steps, this time downward. Lakpa Gelu led the way down the upper section, then about halfway down, reversed the rope team and directed Dorothy to lead the way while he anchored us from above. I was a bit skeptical about that decision at first due to her inexperience at these elevations, but Dorothy did a great job of keeping the pace up and working her way down the toughest and steepest sections.

I always seem to do fine going down. This time, the only problem was the ever-plunging ice axe, which was even more irritating on the way down than on the way up. Several times I almost flipped forward, keeping my balance only because we were still roped up.

But, all in all, we had a pleasant trip down the mountain, arriving back at high camp just before eight o'clock. Parag arrived well after dark, an hour and a half later.

We were all back safe.

Our final day began with complete cloud cover, stormy conditions above, and snow flurries at high camp and Camp Muir, followed by a pleasant three-hour stroll back down to Paradise. That is, except for Bert, whose shins had gotten even worse overnight. He was in serious *extremis* on the way down, uttering the deepest moans of pain I can ever remember hearing. Every step was a sharp dig and it just kept getting worse the entire time. All because of wrong-sized boots and insufficient sock padding.

I think that will be the last time Bert uses tight boots and only one pair of socks on any climb.

Back at the Alpine Ascents office in Seattle, I signed my other copy of *Five Big Mountains* for Dorothy, who later wrote a nice review of my book on Amazon. I understand that she started training to climb Cotopaxi, a 20,000-foot volcano in Ecuador.

Sounds good. Maybe I should add that one to my bucket list. Except, Cotopaxi unexpectedly erupted a few years later and no one is permitted to climb it at this point.

A horrible biopsy, three operations, a lot of catheters, and 34 radiation treatments later, my PSA was almost back to zero, and I hope I am cured of prostate cancer forever. The urologist was right. I will die of something else and am told this should not interfere with my ability to climb mountains.

At least, not for a long time!

CHAPTER 2

Everest Base Camp

Avoiding the Yak Dung

Vertical. That is the only word that came to my mind when I stepped off the plane in Lukla, Nepal. It was my first trip to see the Himalayas, and I had just survived landing at the tiny Tenzing-Hillary Airport tucked into the side of the mountain, which purportedly is the most dangerous airport in the world. The asphalt strip, barely 460 meters long, requires the pilot of the Twin Otter aircraft to slam its landing gear down just a few feet beyond a sheer cliff, apply the brakes sharply, and quickly turn right into a small taxi area. The alternative is to crash into the side of the mountain at the end of the abbreviated runway.

Obviously, no Boeing 747s or 777s land in Lukla.

To the left of the airport was a colorful village with an alley full of shops and cafés, including, as I would later find out, a Starbucks and a multitude of other knock-off coffee shops offering Starbucks coffees. There was also a YakDonald's, though no golden arches, sesame-seed buns, or actual corn-fed beef products could be found. Peeking out above the clouds beyond the shops was the first of many 20,000-foot snow-capped peaks I would see that day, almost forcing me to crane my neck upwards.

Vertical.

The mountain, Gongla, was small compared to those we would see during our next ten days, but nevertheless, it soared above Lukla like a giant watchtower. To the right of the runway and at its end, the mountain also went almost straight up.

We were shuttled through a small building and out into an alley, which led up and around the airport over to the village. Instantly, we were working our way up stone steps, a task we would "enjoy" many times for the next fifteen days.

As I reached the top of the stairs and turned left, one of the airplanes that had just landed was preparing to take off for the flight back to Kathmandu. I hustled up to where I could take some photos of the takeoff.

The plane revved its propellers and began accelerating down the sloped runway. It had only about 1,500 feet to create sufficient speed and lift to take off. It swooped down and towards the end of the runway, which ended with the edge of the mountain. Like a fighter jet leaving an aircraft carrier, it went airborne just as the runway ran out. Everyone cheered.

Crazy-ass airport—who the hell designed it?

After three straight years devoted to reaching the summit of Mt. Rainier near Seattle, Washington, I was ready for a little more exotic mountain adventure. With five of the seven summits under my belt and my wife vetoing Everest and Denali, I decided on the next best thing. An Everest base-camp trek. I had never seen the Himalayas or traveled to Nepal, and the price tag for the Alpine Ascents trek was only $3,900. With round-trip tickets from Atlanta to Kathmandu and back, and some spending money and tips for the guides and porters, the whole trip could be completed for less than $6,500.

A bigger concern was my fitness level. After two surgeries related to my prostate cancer, followed by thirty-four radiation treatments in April and May 2012, my training was seriously deficient and my weight had ballooned to record levels. I was concerned I might be too weak to handle the steep slopes and altitude. However, I threw caution to the wind and sent in my deposit.

What better incentive to get back into shape than a trip to see the world's highest mountain?

And, more importantly, I wanted to be a cancer survivor and not a cancer victim.

My wife, upon learning of my plans, immediately renewed her vow to go to Tuscany if I was going to climb another "stupid mountain."

"Stop threatening," I responded. "Just do it!"

Apologies to Nike for the plagiarism.

This time she did. With her sister. So, while I flew around the world and hiked trails filled with yak dung every day for fifteen days, staying in Sherpa villages with limited shower facilities and nasty toilets and outhouses, she bathed in the luxury of a nicely appointed apartment in Soriano, drinking wine and ogling the dark-haired Italian stallions while getting cooking lessons.

What's wrong with this picture?

I was surprised to learn that I could get to Kathmandu from Atlanta on just two flights, the first a fourteen-hour leg to Seoul, Korea, and the second a seven-hour flight across China to Kathmandu. With both flights on Korean Airlines and a four-hour layover in Seoul, I figured there was at least some chance that my bags would make it all the way through without being lost. Just to be safe, I filled my carry-on daypack with my hiking boots, a pair of trekking pants, a couple of Patagonia wicking shirts, my outer Gore-Tex shell jacket, and extra pairs of socks and underwear.

The worst thing about the flights was the timing. Apparently, Korean Airlines does not have much pull at Hartsfield-Jackson International Airport in Atlanta, as the departure time was 12:30 A.M. Yes, thirty minutes after midnight. And the arrival time in Seoul was 4:30 A.M., when all shops were closed and no drinks or food were available. On the bright side, the new international terminal in Atlanta was practically deserted except for passengers on our flight, so the security lines were almost non-existent. I went directly to the gate with no delay.

Despite the late hour, the plane was filled up to capacity. I found myself stuck in the middle seat in the middle row of the coach section between two Korean gentlemen who did not speak any English.

So much for some friendly, idle chitchat to pass away the fourteen-hour flight!

I noticed that the Korean Airline flight attendants were very polite and well-groomed, right down to their fitted green silk blouses, their tightly-bunned hair, and their starched scarves which flew up near their ears. Identical and perfect.

I wondered if they were permitted to have any personality.

As we crossed the Pacific, I partially slept through six terrible movies showing on the small touch-screen in front of me. The worst of the bunch was *Rock of Ages*, an ill-casted musical featuring Tom Cruise as a drunken rock star. Really!

By the time the plane landed in Seoul, I was almost comatose. Once off, I followed the "in transit" transfer signs until someone pointed down a hall to my right, where another security line led to an escalator to the next floor up. Hand inspections of bags and rather comprehensive and intrusive pat-downs were part of the screening, in addition to the usual metal detector. At the top of the escalator, I entered a magnificent international terminal, wide and spacious, with a multitude of gates and upscale shops. Seoul must have built the terminal for the Olympics because it was huge and impressive.

But everything was closed at 4:30 A.M.

On the way to my gate, I saw signs for an airport hotel up to my right. For a moment, I thought about getting a room for a few hours. However, I opted to save the money and tried to sleep on some seats close to the gate. I snoozed off and on, waking up periodically whenever Manchester United scored a goal on the nearby TV.

Mercifully, at 6:30 A.M., a Starbucks opened a few gates down the concourse. I bought a Coke and a sandwich for breakfast with American dollars, getting some Korean bills and coins in return for change. I didn't care how much it cost. I was thirsty and starving.

Back at the gate, I talked to a gentleman from Kentucky who had also flown in from Atlanta and was heading for Nepal with a trekking group sponsored by National Geographic. We shared some war stories about climbing, including guys getting sick from food and messy toilets. When I advised him to take Cipro prophylactically to avoid intestinal problems in Nepal, he looked at me skeptically. I wished him luck, suspecting that he would not heed my advice.

Before we boarded, he bought me an apple pie for a breakfast dessert from the nearby concessionaire—the best thing I had eaten since leaving Atlanta.

Nice guy.

EVEREST BASE CAMP

We landed in Kathmandu about noon, having lost three hours and fifteen minutes in the time zones. Why Nepal is off by fifteen minutes was not explained, but after twenty-one hours on two planes with almost no sleep, I didn't really care. I adjusted my watch, walked down the roll-up stairs to get off the plane, and crammed into a bus, which took us to a small international arrival terminal.

In the hallway into the terminal, a sign mentioned that Nepal had 250 mountains over 6,000 meters, which equates to about 19,800 feet. That's higher than Kilimanjaro. For those who think that Kilimanjaro is one of the highest mountains in the world, think again. It is not even in the top 300!

The first thing I noticed about Nepal is that I could barely breathe. Kathmandu is extremely smoggy; its air is brown and arid. I thought that Kathmandu was a small city with a few mountaineering hotels and shops. But I soon learned that Kathmandu is a bustling metropolis spread across a sprawling valley with three to four million people—most of whom rely on motorcycles for transportation. Some streets are paved, but many are not, leading to a lot of fumes and dust constantly being spewed into the sky. It does not help that many people burn their garbage in the streets just after dawn, adding to the filthy air. The smog permeates everything. Even indoors. By the time I headed to baggage claim after managing to work my way through the visa line in about thirty-five minutes, I was already coughing.

I was relieved to find my yellow North Face duffel bag on the far side of the crowded baggage area. I grabbed a luggage cart, struggled to maneuver it through the mass of people, and headed outside. There, I expected to find a sign from Alpine Ascents prominently displayed. However, about a hundred signs were held up by representatives of dozens of guide groups. I could not find the right one. I crossed the road towards the parking area and was instantly surrounded by very short taxi-cab drivers vying for my fare. It seemed like everyone there was barely five feet tall. I felt like a giant at six feet one inch. Fortunately, the Alpine Ascents "local" representative, Jiban, spotted me—I don't know how—and quickly escorted me to a gray Toyota tourist van where two or three more climbers were waiting. They mumbled their names, but looked as tired as I felt.

Traffic in Kathmandu is essentially a game of "chicken." Motorcycles are everywhere, most loaded with at least two people. Mixed in are regular bicycles and some rickshaws. The cars and vans are crammed with people, all going somewhere. There are no lanes on the roads, few traffic lights, and drivers are forced to push through gaps to make turns and squeeze between motorcycles, other vehicles, and pedestrians.

Progress was extremely slow. It took us forty-five minutes to drive the six miles to our hotel, even using "shortcuts" through unpaved, curvy, and uphill roads filled with motorcycles and pedestrians. Most of the latter were wearing masks to avoid breathing in the crud, while trying to avoid getting hit by the crazy motorcyclists.

The streets were lined with little narrow shops displaying wares of various kinds. Most of them had women sitting out front, inhaling dust and fumes from the congested traffic, hoping for someone to stop and buy something…anything.

We turned off a main street just before we reached a KFC and Pizza Hut up on our right. Another left, then right, and suddenly we were at the Yak & Yeti Hotel, a pleasant haven from the dirty city.

Very nice-looking place.

I stepped off the bus, quickly entered the spacious marble and hardwood lobby, and breathed cool, air-conditioned oxygen for the first time in almost two hours.

Excellent, in fact.

In the lobby, I instantly recognized two faces—our guides. Sherpa Lakpa Rita, who I had met on Aconcagua in Argentina five years earlier, was our lead guide. At that time, he had reached the summit of Everest only a mere sixteen times! Lakpa greeted me warmly, instantly recognizing me from the prior climb. The other friendly face was that of Sarah Montgomery, who had guided me on my second Mt. Rainier attempt two years before.

"Judge," she called me, referring to my nickname from that climb, which took place during my campaign for Georgia Court of Appeals.

"Not 'Judge,' unfortunately," I said. "Kind of a sore subject, so maybe we can forget about that nickname this time."

"Gotcha," she responded. "Good to see you again, David."

EVEREST BASE CAMP

Later that afternoon, our team met around a table on the lawn in the back of the hotel. The back of the hotel was like a mini-oasis. There were clay tennis courts and a blue swimming pool to the left and a large expanse of grass to the right, interrupted by a few white tables with partial tents over them, and a large pond on the far end. In the middle, just to the right of the swimming pool was a set of steps, which went up to a small temple of sorts. The hill next to the steps was filled with yellow and orange flowers. A gaggle of geese strolled along the grass in front of the flowers. The whole area was ringed with a gravel running track, which went around the pond, gradually rose to the top of the stairs, went behind the "temple," and descended back to the grassy area near the tennis courts.

I can get used to this.

Lakpa and Sarah introduced themselves first and gave us a short outline of the trek to come. First, they told us what we would be doing for the next twenty-four hours. Then each of us had the opportunity to introduce ourselves.

There were five women and four guys besides myself.

Kiyoko, a 67-year-old retired professor from Calgary, but of Japanese descent, and Kamila, a woman from England, were friends who had traveled and hiked together, including conquering Kilimanjaro. Kiyoko looked very slim and fit; Kamila was slightly less trim, but made up for it in enthusiasm and a positive attitude. Yvan and Sylvie were a French-Canadian brother and sister combo from Montreal. Both looked thin and athletic. Yvan quickly explained that Sylvie did not speak English and that he would have to translate for her. Sarah instantly interrupted him with some almost fluent French, offering to help Sylvie learn and understand English as needed. Apparently, Sarah had majored in French at college and had spent a year in France, so she could speak the language.

Next was George, a urological oncologist from Indiana, who had climbed some peaks in Ecuador and was a former world-class cyclist. Tall and gray-haired, he was the oldest guy in the group at age 62. The youngest in the group was Andrew, a 35-year-old Aussie who was at the time stationed in Beirut on a United Nations peacekeeping force. He had not done much climbing before, but looked burly and fit enough to handle this trek. Crystal, a dark-haired mother of two from North Carolina, had contacted me by e-mail before the trip and flew in from Seoul on the same flight as I did. She had an interesting background as an international flight attendant, but now was an architect/interior designer. She also knew a lot about NASCAR races, as her husband worked on a pit crew for some of the drivers. She looked solid and ready for the climb.

I introduced myself, mentioned the mountains I had previously climbed, and noted that I had already had Lakpa and Sarah as guides. But I quickly pointed out that I was recovering from two surgeries and some radiation treatments, so they should not overestimate my abilities on this trip. Since I still had a nice pooch above my beltline, they were probably wondering how I managed to climb Aconcagua and other continental summits in the first place.

The final climber in the group was a freckled divorcee from California named Corrina. She had flown in through Hong Kong a few days early and already was familiar with some of the locales in Kathmandu. She did not look like a climber, but seemed gung-ho about the prospect of heavy-duty exploring.

All in all, we had a very diverse group, with people from all walks of life, ages ranging from 35 to 67, and varied climbing experience. I had the most mountaineering experience, but I was clearly not in as good a shape as some of the rest. But everyone had a good rapport from the start.

Lakpa led the way to dinner that night, showing us how to cross roads in the dark and not get killed by the multitude of cars and motorcycles still zipping through the city. We walked and walked and walked, finally entering the very narrow streets of the Thamel tourist district, which was filled with tiny shops and restaurants. Though they should have been pedestrian-only streets, as they had no sidewalks and were only about ten feet wide, cars and motorcycles pushed their way through the crowds, constantly tooting their horns and barely missing oncoming cars, bikes, or pedestrians on either side.

We hugged the buildings on the left side, and, after about a twenty-minute walk, turned into a small courtyard, which was the entry into a "safe" restaurant, which Lakpa explained meant it serves food that would not make you sick or give you diarrhea.

EVEREST BASE CAMP

Lakpa ordered three different types of appetizers, all of which looked a bit suspicious, but he assured us that they were okay to eat. They were tasty, though a bit spicier than I would prefer. They just made the beer taste even better. Dinner turned out to be delicious, with several good choices of fish, chicken, and beef entrées. More importantly, the group interacted and started building camaraderie that would carry us through the next two weeks of climbing. It also gave me an opportunity to present Lakpa with a signed copy of my book, *Five Big Mountains*, which had a chapter on Aconcagua and mentioned Lakpa several times.

The walk back to the Yak & Yeti was a little easier, as the traffic had finally eased. But I kept a constant hand on my wallet in case pickpockets were hanging around just waiting to prey on some unsuspecting and rather conspicuous foreigners.

The next day, we got to see the key sights of Kathmandu up close. That meant going to the Monkey Palace, the crematorium platforms at the river, and Little Tibet.

It also meant breathing in a lot more rancid air.

The Monkey Palace, named for a huge stupa that had become infested with monkeys, sits high on a hill overlooking Kathmandu—or what you can see of it through the brown haze. As we got out of our gray Toyota tourist van, prayer flags seemed to be strung from every tree, creating a colorful scene that begged for photos to be taken right away. Monkeys ran around on the platforms and jumped through the trees at will.

A long set of steps went upwards to our right. Soon we were working our way up them, passing very sad-looking beggars strategically positioned at each landing. At the top of the steps was a huge white dome-like structure, with a square tower with "all-knowing" eyes painted in all four directions under a gold-colored steeple of sorts. The "stupa." More prayer flags were flying in all directions. Completely surrounding the stupa were cylindrical metal containers on spinners, our first view of prayer wheels. Our guide told us each wheel contained multiple written prayers and that spinning the wheel credited the spinner with saying all the prayers in the wheel. We watched as locals walked clockwise around the stupa, spinning every prayer wheel in sight.

Not long after that, we, too, walked clockwise around the stupa and started spinning wheels as well, not knowing what we were praying for, but joining in the tradition. We tried to avoid the monkeys and the mangy stray dogs that seemed to fill the place.

There were children selling candles or incense, a bunch of souvenir shops surrounding the area, and a couple of Buddhist temples to the left and behind the stupa. So there was plenty to see. On the far right was a balcony overlooking the city, but the view was almost totally obscured by the smog. The guide told us that, less than ten years ago, the area of sprawling tenements below us was all farmland. Apparently, families in Kathmandu were having five or six children each. The population, especially under the age of 14, had exploded. Now, the entire valley was covered in houses and buildings, and more were on the way. It certainly looked like there had been no urban planning involved in the process.

Our next stop was to the Bogmati riverbank where the local Hindus publicly burn and cremate bodies on concrete platforms or "ghats" and dump all the ashy remains in the river. I had seen this on a Discovery Channel special so I was not too surprised at the spectacle. However, I was not prepared for the smell. Smoke from burning flesh was added to the dust and smoggy air. Incense was used to try to cover the smell. The combination just made my stomach heave. I pulled my shirt up over my mouth and nose most of the time, but still felt nauseous the entire time we were there.

It didn't help that small children were wading in the river directly under the funeral platforms, diving for jewelry or other valuable items swept into the river at the end of the cremations.

Not far from where the children were wading, a body wrapped up in a red and yellow cloth had been laid a few steps up from the river's edge, apparently waiting to be burned. However, for the thirty or more minutes we were there, no one did anything with that lonely body as it was left roasting in the hot sun.

One thing was for sure—I needed to get out of that place.

The only way out was along an alley on the far side of the river where a series of shops and souvenir stands were set up. But while we waited for one of our group to take some final gruesome photos of the burning bodies, various vendors surrounded us, trying to sell us cheap-looking postcards, purses, and coins. Regardless of how many times we said, "No, not interested, no thanks, sorry," the men, women, and children persisted in thrusting their trinkets into our faces or pawing at our arms. They had no hesitancy in invading our personal space.

"Only one dollar," one child kept saying as he held up his dusty postcards, nudging them toward each of us. "One dollar."

I wanted to give him something, but knew that if I got out my money I would be mobbed.

Finally, the last photo was taken and we started down the souvenir alley. I kept walking without stopping at a single booth until I reached the end of the booths. There, a makeshift parking lot was filled with dozens of identical gray Toyota tourist vans. Our bus driver was not in sight and I could not distinguish our bus from the others.

Great! I'm sick to my stomach, I need to go to the bathroom, my throat feels like I just swallowed chalk dust from a blackboard, and I'm stuck on the side of the road with no idea which bus to get on. I'm a mess and I haven't yet left Kathmandu.

Luckily, I found a nearby port-a-potty to take care of my most urgent need, the bus driver eventually arrived, and I held on until we arrived back at the hotel. There I went straight to my room, jumped in the shower, changed clothes, and headed to the lobby bar for a beer.

Beers in Kathmandu are very good...and large. Gorkha had a nice taste, but my favorite was Everest beer. The bottles are about twenty-two ounces and the hotel served them with Spanish-style peanuts still with the brown skins on them. I quenched my thirst and nibbled away until dinnertime.

Very early the next morning, we checked our city clothes in small duffels with the hotel valet and toted our backpacks and large gear bags to a bus already waiting outside. This time the drive to the airport took only about fifteen minutes, as rush hour had not yet materialized. The bus pulled up to the much smaller domestic terminal where Lakpa and our cook, Gopal, took charge of getting all of us and our bags through the security checks. Soon we were in a square room with four airline counters and a couple of snack shops. It seemed like the entire place was filled with trekkers waiting to fly to Lukla.

I recognized the name of the airline company whose plane had gone down the week before, killing all nineteen on board after hitting some birds as it took off from Kathmandu. Apparently, a huge garbage dump was situated near the end of the Kathmandu runway, attracting numerous vultures to the area. Not an ideal setting for planes flying overhead. I was relieved when I saw that Lakpa was not heading to that counter.

Our boarding passes indicated we were #2 in line on Sita Air to Lukla, so I assumed that we would be taking off quickly. However, we sat and waited for over an hour before we were finally called to the gate and placed on a rather cold bus. We sat and waited another half hour for the bus to take us down to the Twin Otter plane down the tarmac to our left. We chatted nervously and began studying the map of the Khumbu Valley that Andrew, the Aussie, had picked up in Kathmandu. I wondered if we would ever be hiking anywhere that day.

Finally, the bus doors closed and we headed to the plane. There was no waiting once there. We stepped up a few rungs onto the small plane, ducked our heads, and found a seat. I grabbed a seat on the left side of the plane. Lakpa had told me the mountains would be on that side as we approached Lukla. However, the plane was so narrow, it really did not matter which side we were on.

This time the plane avoided any vultures and soon we were soaring above the outskirts of the city and into the vast ranges of green mountains. I expected the mountainsides to be uninhabited, but every one of them was lined with terraced gardens and small abodes. The Nepalis use every bit of space that can handle plants, and hundreds of little villages were dotted across the landscape.

Every few minutes we were wowed by a glimpse of snowcapped peaks between the clouds to our left. They were so far up in the sky that they did not look real. However, none of them were Everest. We were still too far south to see the tallest mountain on the planet. Still, I could feel my stomach tighten with excitement as the enormous, glimmering peaks kept popping up on the horizon.

"There's the runway," one of our group said from up near the cockpit after about forty-five minutes.

"Where?"

"Right there in front of us."

From my vantage point, all I could see was the side of a large mountain ahead of us. Then the runway came into view. It was perched on a shelf just to the right of what looked like a tiny village hugging the side of the mountain.

"Shit," I said, "you've got to be kidding me. My driveway's longer than that."

The runway really looked short, and at the end, it went straight into the mountain.

"I sure hope they have some good brakes on this thing," I said to no one in particular.

I knew that dozens of planes had already landed safely in Lukla that day, so I should not have been nervous. Still, as Andrew unabashedly videotaped the whole thing, I held my breath as the plane descended and approached the asphalt strip, which seemed to hang over the cliff.

There was no margin for error, so the pilot did not attempt to touch down smoothly. Rather, the plane dropped quickly, immediately banging the wheels down onto the tarmac as soon as we crossed the edge of the cliff. The wing flaps engaged and whatever brakes were available slammed on as the plane careened up what I could now see was a sloped runway, inclined upwards at about ten degrees. The mountain in front of us looked like it was about to come right through the windshield just as we swung right into a small, square parking area next to a tiny terminal.

"That was fun," I muttered facetiously.

But I did not have time to worry, as we were rushed off the plane. Our bags were just as quickly removed from the hold, loaded on handtrucks, and brought into the building. Trekkers returning to Kathmandu and their gear were rapidly packed onto the plane and within minutes of our landing, the plane was ready to take off. More planes were coming and they had to make space for them.

I looked over at the village of Lukla and looked up. The snowcapped peak of a mountain named Gongla stuck out above the clouds way up above the horizon.

Vertical. Now we're talking mountains!

After a short snack and rest stop at a tiny teahouse/bunkhouse on the main drag in Lukla, we donned our daypacks and sunglasses and started hiking north along the path towards Everest base camp along the east side of the Dudh Kosi River. Our duffels would follow on the backs of yaks.

I would not really describe the trail as a path. For miles and miles, it was more like the Appian way or a "grey-brick road," lined with cobblestones or, in many places, flagstones. For the first few miles, the trail was filled with shops and small lodges. And rather than going up, we were going slightly down most of the afternoon. As we left Lukla, a series of rock steps led us down hundreds of feet vertically. I watched as hikers coming back to Lukla struggled to ascend the steps. Sunburned and grizzly, they looked completely whipped.

What am I getting myself into?

But with the path steadily descending, it was easy going for us. After about a mile, we encountered a steep downward set of rock steps and a very rugged descent to the first of many suspension bridges swinging across tributaries flowing into the Dudh Kosi River below. I quickly learned that the hardest climbing would always be going down to bridges and then having to climb up on the other side. Both sides were tough—going down worked on the knees and thighs and going up on the calves. But there was no other way to get across the tributary chasms. So up and down we went.

The suspension bridges, made from parallel strips of metal fastened alongside each other every four or five feet and lined with metal guide wires on each side, were a bit intimidating as they swung sideways in the wind and bounced up and down above the crashing rapids a hundred or more feet below. Looking down while on the bridges is not recommended. I felt a little more confident about the safeness of the bridges after I watched three yaks cross one without it collapsing under them. However, the fact that all the bridges were lined with prayer flags made me wonder whether I should be praying every time I crossed one.

After about five bridges, we all started having fun on them, bouncing along and taking pictures of each other as we crossed.

EVEREST BASE CAMP

Not long after we got started that day, I realized that one of the biggest challenges on this trip was to avoid the yak dung. Yaks and dzos, which are yak/cow hybrids, are the main transport vehicles of the Himalayas. There are no semis or pickup trucks or ATVs along the way. But there are plenty of yaks—everywhere. Whether technically they were yaks or dzos, they were all yaks to me. And yaks poop all the time, on the trail, on the rocky steps, in the dirt, and on the bridges. There was no part of the trail that was safe from the dung.

Fresh dung appeared in round, moist piles three or four inches deep. Not-so-fresh dung was drier and had usually been stepped on and flattened into brown pancakes or smears. Days-old dung was almost like straw on the path, still best to avoid it, but not a problem if it got under foot.

We were walking through it for fifteen days. And breathing it at every teahouse. You see, dried yak dung is also used as charcoal for the potbellied heaters in the main teahouse rooms and frequently the smoke going out the top of the roof would blow into the bunk rooms, making it almost impossible to breathe as we slept. Yak dung apparently is also used to clean floors in Sherpa houses and we frequently saw it plastered onto walls either to insulate or to caulk cracks between stones or wood.

According to Lakpa, who would definitely know, yaks cost about $1,000 apiece. Two years' worth of fees for yak transport of mountaineer duffels, food, and supplies would usually pay off the original cost. Then the yak would be pure profit for about twenty more years. So, wealth in the mountains of Nepal and in the Sherpa villages is sometimes measured by how many yaks are owned. And yaks were taken care of by their owners, even living in the lower sections of their houses when not working. We were happy to have three yaks or dzos carrying our gear, but unhappy about breathing the dust as they went by. And even more unhappy about having to step lightly around a pile of dung every few feet.

Around three in the afternoon, we arrived in Phakding, a small village at approximately 8,800 feet altitude. I thought we would be staying there for the night, but after passing several teahouses and bars, we kept walking out the other end of the town.

Where the hell are we going?

We hiked up a steep hill, around a corner, and through some dense trees before coming to an opening. There across another suspension bridge over the Dudh Kosi was what looked like a brand new, blue-trimmed lodge/teahouse, with its orange marigolds basking in the late-afternoon sun.

The Sunrise Lodge.

Sweet!

Just as we got across the bridge and were about to relax, a whole herd of yaks or dzos came rushing through the gap on the other side of the hotel, making us squeeze into the wall to our right as they passed by. I tried to get a close-up picture of one, but it just came out as a massive fuzzy blur.

After about a dozen of the big animals passed, the path was clear to the flagstone patio amidst the shoulder-high marigolds. I was not that tired, as most of the hike that day had been slightly downhill and my legs were still fresh. Still, it felt good to ditch the daypacks and sit with the sun on our faces and shoulders, enjoying the warm, orangey mango drinks served shortly after we arrived by Lakpa's interns. This would become a routine for the next fifteen days, one I never actually got used to. The cups were always ice-cold and I expected a refreshing, cool drink inside, but the juice had been heated and was always warm, if not too hot to drink. Nevertheless, any flavored liquids were good and I found myself asking for seconds. The guides were constantly pushing drinks to avoid dehydration and to help us acclimatize.

Not long after arriving, we were assigned roommates and were led into a narrow dark hall to find our gear bags, which had been placed in our rooms by the porters. My roommate was George, the urologist from Indiana. I guess they decided to put the two old guys together! We had the first room on the left and were surprised to find that we had our own private bathroom with a sit-down toilet. The shower was just a spigot with a drain below it, but this was luxurious by Nepali standards. The only thing that was missing was toilet paper.

George came with an enormous Eddie Bauer First Ascent gear bag, complete with almost a full pharmacy. Anything anyone needed could be obtained from George. That is, if George did not need it himself. I had

Cipro, some Tylenol, and some sunscreen in a pint-sized Ziploc bag. George would have needed a backpack to carry all the medicines, bandages, and medical paraphernalia in his bag. At least he was a physician and knew what to take for what ailment.

We had a couple of hours to kill, so George, Andrew, and I headed back into Phakding to see if we could find some beers. I purchased some Everest playing cards from a young Nepali girl at a souvenir stand along the main strip, then watched as some local Sherpa boys played a Nepali version of caroms, except with smaller "pockets" and rings to shoot at. The boards were coated with flour or talcum powder to make the rings slide with less friction. After watching about three games, we decided that they were too good to dare challenging them. The safer entertainment choice was the reggae bar from which we could hear music blaring about a block away.

Inside the bar was a pool table, a bar, and some bench seats with a low table in front of them on the far-right corner. We ordered Everest beers from the lady behind the bar as we saw bottles with the Everest labels at one end of the bar.

"No Everest. Tuborg only," she replied.

The Tuborgs were just twelve-ounce cans, so I repeated, "Everest beer, please, we are very thirsty."

"No Everest. Tuborg only."

"Okay. Three Tuborgs then—on a tab."

We grabbed some seats in the corner and after about ten minutes the bar girl brought us three Tuborgs. They were lukewarm, but there was some popcorn to eat with them, so we didn't complain. The music was lively and we had beer to soothe our tired leg muscles. But there was nothing much going on.

After a while, a couple local guys came in who clearly knew the bargirl. Within minutes, they were drinking nice, big, cold Everest beers.

No Everest beer? Bullshit!

It wasn't long before the reggae bar was picking up steam. A few girls came in, some young guys started to play pool, and we ordered some more beers. Suddenly Everest beers were unavailable again, and we again had to settle for Tuborgs.

Then a guy who looked American walked in with another fellow and asked if they could join us on the corner seats. It turns out he was a writer/editor for *Outdoor* magazine named Grayson Schaefer and was heading up the Khumbu Valley looking for climbers recovering from some of the earlier disasters on Everest that spring. It turned out that he was good friends with Lakpa, Sarah, a former Alpine Ascents guide named David Morton, and another young guide named Melissa Arnot, who had climbed to the top of Everest four times, more than any other American female.

Grayson filled us in with information about who was currently in the Khumbu Valley working the treks. Apparently, Melissa was guiding a solo climber somewhere in the vicinity and would be up in the Everest base camp region in about a week. David Morton was also trekking with his wife and baby boy—just for kicks. I quickly realized that the climbing community in Nepal was a very close-knit group. Everyone knew everyone. And the reggae bar in Phakding was a great place to swap mountain-climbing tales.

Back at the teahouse, we met a young guy who was on his way to climb Ama Dablam, a spectacular and dangerous mountain with a notorious "hanging glacier." I wondered if that meant a lot of people had died trying to climb it or whether it just appeared to hang from the mountain. The young guy, who looked like he was about twenty-five years old, was very nonchalant when he described having climbed all seven continental summits and a couple of the fourteen peaks higher than 8,000 meters, but he certainly looked the part. Trim and sinewy. I guess he should be thin and strong, since he said his regular job was working in the oil fields in North Dakota.

My regular job is sitting on my butt in a law office most of the day, so I have an excuse for not looking the part!

Dinner that night was obviously forgettable, as I cannot remember a thing about it. However, it inevitably included soup with bok choy or noodles, followed by a rice-based dish with little or no meat and plenty more bok choy and cooked carrots, which I hate. Dessert probably included an apple pie or apple tart or apple crumble of some sort, another staple of the Sherpa diet. I supplemented the meal with nuts, a Coke, and some Pringles potato chips, another surprisingly available product for sale at all the teahouses.

That night, George and I took turns keeping everyone else awake with our snoring. With only a half-inch piece of plywood between rooms, every sound passed through to the adjacent sleepers.

Our destination on Day 2 of the trek was Namche Bazaar, a larger Sherpa town nestled in a notched semi-circle in the mountain at about 12,000 feet. To get there, Lakpa told us we would steadily climb upwards on a very well-traveled trail for about three hours, crossing the Dudh Kosi several times on suspension bridges, then walking along a flat section of the riverbed for another half hour. There, we would climb up to and across the Lorje Bridge, a particularly high suspension bridge over a narrow gorge through which the river violently crashed. On the other side of the bridge, we would ascend about two thousand feet almost straight up through a forest until we reached Namche Bazaar. What he did not tell us was that the last section would involve an endless series of switchbacks and high, rocky steps for about two hours straight.

The highlights of the morning were the views of the sharp-peaked Thamserku mountain, which loomed up above us to our right, at one place appearing to be guarded by King Kong sitting on a ridge to the right. Of course, King Kong was just a well-shaped rock outcropping, probably five thousand feet below the towering summit, but it was an impressive sight. Our group spent almost five minutes taking pictures from that spot on the trail. I took at least ten shots of the giant gorilla protecting the snowcapped peak.

We stopped at a tiny place called Monjo for lunch in the bright and warm sunshine at some tables set out on a small lawn. About halfway through our lunch, the National Geographic group with my airplane friend from Kentucky arrived. He was in good spirits, feeling well and having a great time. It looked like they would be on the same schedule as our group.

After crossing the Lorje Bridge, the long suspension bridge covered in prayer flags, the trail immediately got serious. Lakpa took the lead at a very slow but steady pace. I felt strong when we started, but after about thirty switchbacks and a dozen or more sets of steep stone stairways, I needed a break.

But Lakpa did not stop for a minute. We kept pushing up and up, our calves straining with each step for about forty-five minutes.

Not exactly torture, but certainly enhanced muscle strain.

"Lakpa!" I yelled up towards him at one point. "Can we take a few minutes to catch our breaths and regroup?"

Kamila and Kiyoko had fallen back a few minutes behind the main group and I thought maybe Lakpa would be conducive to a short rest stop. However, he knew that his young Sherpa assistants were back with Kamila. He shook his head and said there was a rest stop "a bit further up."

I knew that "a bit further up" did not mean "soon," so I sucked it up and just kept going, gradually falling a switchback or two behind the leaders as we pushed up the mountain.

One step at a time, David. Disregard the others. Just do what you can do and keep going. Don't stop.

Fifteen minutes of serious pain later, Lakpa stopped at a crowded landing up on the right side of the trail.

Damn. There were three or four nice places to stop in the last ten minutes with no people in the way. Why is he stopping here?

Sadly, I was so tired, I resorted to expletives in my mind rather than appreciating the fact that we were stopping. More importantly, I did not realize that the reason there were so many people stopped at that landing was because, from that vantage point, we had our first clear view of Everest through the trees to the right of the trail.

"Woah," I said audibly with a dry throat as I saw Everest for the first time. "Unbelievable."

Though Everest was way off in the distance, still an eight-day trek away, it was impressive just in the way it, along with the neighboring peaks of Lhotse and Nuptse, stood out as steep, gray sentinels with very little snow on them, above and beyond the other mountains. In a word, they looked ominous. I snapped a few photos, but knew they would not come out as the mountains blended into the sky beyond the dark trees. Still, the view of Everest instantly raised my spirits and eased the pain of the previous forty-five minutes of climbing.

EVEREST BASE CAMP

The rest of the climb up to Namche Bazaar, though still a steep, dusty climb through thick forests, was anticlimactic. I fell in behind Corrina, who was in fact a pretty good climber. I just matched her step after step, avoiding the increasingly frequent yak dung. Lakpa stayed in the lead and kept the pace moderate, so we all kept together except Kamila, who, with assistant guides Nima and Subash, brought up the rear about ten minutes back.

I was very impressed by Kamila's ability to keep on going, even when she was not up with the leaders. As I grow older myself, I have become even more awed by her performance on this trek.

As we approached the village, we stopped at a checkpoint for permits to be checked. Our cook handled the registration with the policia. Directly across from the checkpoint was a little shop with sodas and candy bars and a nice, cool wall on which to sit. George immediately bought a Fanta and I figured we were close enough to our destination to indulge in a Coke. After all, we had been climbing almost non-stop up and through some steep shit for two hours straight.

Unfortunately, after I downed about three quarters of the Coke, I realized that the checkpoint was just around the corner from the next section of trail—an endless staircase from hell. Leading up to Namche Bazaar was a long series of stone steps, starting with a long, gradual climb with steps every couple of yards to steep, high stairs requiring knee-bending "Stairmaster" steps, then ascending trails to the next series and the next. We finally emerged from the trees to see the town spread out around the semi-circled gouge in the mountainside, then climbed four more steep steps up to a courtyard on our right.

Lakpa congratulated me for making it to Namche. I stopped and relaxed for a moment, thinking we had reached our destination.

But he kept on walking.

We climbed three or four more short, but steep sections of stone steps to get through or around several hotels, one called the "HillTen Hotel." Not exactly a Hilton.

Then we started up a cobbled path, which kept getting steeper and steeper up the right side of the village. The views were astoundingly beautiful, but my calves were practically groaning and about to surrender.

As I plodded up and up, the lead group pulled away and I felt like I was walking in quicksand.

Sarah, our second guide, suddenly appeared at my left shoulder. "How're you doing, David?"

"Okay, but I'm about done with this climbing today," I said breathlessly.

"It's just up at the top of the hill on the right."

"Yeah. The same thing they said at the checkpoint. I'll make it, but I'm glad tomorrow is a rest day."

I lowered my head and kept going. I couldn't help but notice that Sarah was trekking in a pair of sneakers. She obviously has tough feet and even tougher ankles as we had walked on a lot of uneven rocks and cobblestone for two straight days.

A few minutes later, we turned right through a gateway, walked around to the back of the building, through a few doors, and into a teahouse at the Panorama Lodge, not surprisingly, a hotel with an awesome view. I collapsed on a padded bench seat behind the tables at the end of the room and chugged the last quarter of my Coke.

"I need another!" I exclaimed.

Of course, the next day was only partially a rest day. After a breakfast of some sort of white paste, fried eggs, and potatoes, washed down with hot chocolate for me and various types of tea for the others, we headed out for a purportedly restful hike up to the Everest View Hotel about a thousand feet above us.

After a short uphill stint, we crossed over above Namche Bazaar, in front of its small hospital. For some reason, medical facilities at these Sherpa villages are all at the top of the hill above the villages, making it a nice climb to get to them. In this case, a heliport was situated up the hill from the hospital, so its location made some sense, but if anyone in the village got sick, they had a steep climb to get serious medical treatment.

Once past the hospital, we turned back to our right and immediately started climbing switchbacks up the remaining hill above the village. Luckily, we were fresh, so the ascent was not too bad. Eventually, we found ourselves climbing through more gradual slopes that resembled sand dunes of sorts. Because we were on a casual "rest-day" climb, Lakpa made no effort to keep the group together.

The sand dunes did not last very long, and I soon noticed that we were approaching a steep ridge with a stupa at the top almost straight above us.

Damn—what type of rest day is this?

For the next twenty minutes, I labored again up switchback after switchback, interrupted only by sets of stone steps even steeper than the path. The stupa slowly got closer and closer until I was right below it. A building to the right and another to the left came into view as I crested the hill. Beyond them was a rocky, dirt runway—the Namche airstrip. Apparently, it is used only once a week for a supply plane. I would not want to try to land on it. Rocks, yaks, and crossing trekkers were plenty for a pilot to have to avoid, let alone trying to land and take off at that altitude.

We regrouped next to some large yellow signs on the far side of the runway. One of them announced the entry into the Sagarmatha National Park—the park and World Heritage Natural Site in which Everest is located on the far north end.

After a short water break, we headed further up the trail as a group. This trail worked its way up and over to the right, near another stupa marking the top of a very, very steep trail up from the village. Unbeknownst to us, Lakpa had given us a break by taking a longer but more gradual ascent.

We passed a small farmhouse and turned left along a nice flat section.

I was now enjoying myself completely. The path was level and was covered in soft dirt. Easy on the feet. The sun was shining. The temperature was rising.

What a day in the Himalayas!

I was looking to my right at the deep chasm that led down to the river and almost ran into the climber in front of me as everyone suddenly stopped in their tracks at the next left turn in the trail.

Why is everyone stopping?

I looked up at the most magnificent view I had ever seen in my life.

Everest in all its steely grey glory under completely still blue skies was right in front of us, flanked by the sharp-peaked Lhotse on the right and bumpy ridges of Nuptse to its left. Further right was Ama Dablam, with its block-shaped peak and hanging glacier shining in the sun. Silently, I stood there, staring and marveling along with my fellow climbers. All of us were practically frozen in place, stunned by the beauty of the scene.

Slowly, we started to mumble words or phrases like "unbelievable," "magnificent," "I can't believe it looks so close," "awesome," "the most beautiful view ever," etc.

Then the cameras came out. For the next ten minutes, shutters clicked and we posed for pictures with Everest in the background. Lakpa stood on the side watching us with amusement. He had seen this view a hundred times, but he knew the effect it had on novices like us.

After a while, Lakpa said, "Time to move on. The view is even better from the hotel." He pointed towards the ridge in front of us where we could just see the roof of a large building.

We practically skipped down a short downhill stretch, across a field and up to the hotel. Of course, just to test us, the hotel had a set of about forty steps up to its main entrance. We worked our way through the hotel to the rear balconies where people were gathered, eating and drinking wine or sodas. Sure enough, the view was amazing from that vantage point, totally unobscured by any trees, rock outcroppings, or other obstacles.

Wow! This is perfect.

I pulled two small, round tables together to accommodate our group, sat back in a plastic chair, and put my feet up on the short rock wall on the outside of the balcony. Then, in total comfort, I just admired the view.

The cameras came out again. I took a bunch of shots—wide-angle, zoomed-in, vertical, horizontal, several framed on the left by the branches of a nice green-needled pine tree. It was hard to stop clicking.

However, I saw the opportunity to take the photo of the day after I turned around and saw a perfect reflection of Everest, Lhotse, and Nuptse framed in a section of the windows of the hotel. I kneeled carefully on the rock wall, positioning myself so that my reflection would also be in the shot without blocking the view of the mountains. It came out perfectly. Everest in a mirror with David Schaeffer superimposed in the left corner, taking the picture.

What a masterpiece!

The hike back from the Everest View Hotel was a cakewalk...until we reached the stupa on the other side of the dumpy airport strip and Lakpa decided to take the shortcut down the mountain instead of the gradual way we came up that morning. Suddenly we were descending a series of very sharp switchbacks and steep rock steps with the rooftops of Namche Bazaar straight below us. Prayer flags were strewn across our vision, making it a nightmare for anyone with a fear of heights. Luckily, I am not stricken with that malady. I pulled out my second hiking pole for extra balance and embraced the challenge.

About twenty-five minutes later, with knees and thigh muscles aching, we reached the bottom of the steep ridge and found ourselves at the hill just above our teahouse. A huge, colorful prayer wheel was situated at the bottom of the path, with three small Sherpa children guarding it (or more likely sitting in the cool shade beneath it). I stopped to take a photo and to rest my knees, then followed the rest of the gang down the cobbled hill. I was still excited about seeing Everest so vividly, but was ready for some food and relaxation.

That afternoon, we strolled down the hill and into Namche Bazaar. It was a pretty hopping place with jewelry and mountain-clothing stores, several bars, and many souvenir shops with Yak-Yak-Yak-Yak t-shirts, yak bells, yak scarves, yak shawls, yak blankets, and yak poop in the alleyways. I bought a few yak scarves and five yak bells for Christmas presents and some extra nuts for the trail before joining the others at a very nice German bakery with a beautiful second-story balcony overlooking most of the town. A chocolate croissant washed down with a nice, cold Coke was a pleasant end to an extraordinarily wonderful day in the Khumbu Valley. Even the climb back up to the teahouse could not ruin it.

We left Namche Bazaar early the next morning with Lakpa's hometown, Thame, as our destination. He told us it would be an easy three- to four-hour gradual climb.

Right. Maybe for him.

The first few hours were not too bad. We briefly visited a museum with Sherpa artifacts and photos, including several photos of Lakpa in the section of successful Everest summiteers. Once on the trail, my attention was first distracted by colorfully painted rocks on a hill below the "sacred" grey mountain, which loomed above us to the right. Then there was a snowcapped mountain ahead of us with a black-colored mountain in front of it. As we worked our way up the path, the black mountain slowly began to block the view of the snowcapped mountain, like an eclipse. We were constantly ascending, working our way up some steep spots to more stupas and keeping to the left of the muni walls filled with tablets etched with mantras. But I kept looking at the map and it did not look like we were making much progress.

Three hours into the hike, we arrived at a village I thought was Lakpa's hometown, but it turned out to be Thamo, not Thame. Silly me; I thought it was just a typo on the map, like "Roma" instead of "Rome."

We stopped there for a lunch break. As we drank our warm orange juice and slurped up another bowl of noodle and vegetable soup, some locals were constructing new steps and a wall nearby. So we got a chance to see their rudimentary, but amazing rock chiseling and stone laying techniques "up close and personal."

After lunch, the hiking was much harder. Supposedly we had only another hour to Thame. However, it seemed like we would never get there. We went up and up and up and then further up, steadily gaining altitude. Somewhere between Thamo and Thame, we stopped for a well-deserved rest and Lakpa told us to look back from whence we had come.

Wow!

The valley behind us, still lush with greenery, lay tranquil in front of a series of snowcapped mountains across the entire far horizon. In my tunnel-vision concentration, I had not bothered to look back for the last hour, so I had missed the view. Thamserku and Kantega dominated the right side of the picture and Tabuche Peak stood out on the left, with a dozen more peaks I could not name scattered in between.

"Breathtaking" hardly describes it.

Lakpa clearly was proud to be showing us the view he grew up seeing every day.

"Lakpa," I said with a smile, "are there any good views around here? I thought we would see some really amazing mountains today."

He instantly recognized that I was teasing him and told me to "have another meat stick, David."

"Only about thirty minutes more to Thame," he continued as he shouldered his backpack, indicating our rest stop was over.

The last thirty minutes took us up and then way down to a small non-suspension bridge across a violently rushing gorge of water between two steep walls of granite. It was one of the steepest descents yet. On the way down we looked across to the path on the other side and winced at what lay before us. On the other side was a sheer rock with a narrow path going diagonally up at what looked like about forty degrees. It was probably only twenty-five degrees, but once we crossed the bridge, we were really gaining altitude with every painful step. As I started to fall behind the lead group about halfway up the steep slope, Sarah again magically showed up at my left shoulder, encouraging me along.

"How ya doing, David?" she asked.

"Okay…just taking my time…at my own pace," I managed to respond without sounding too out of breath. "I wish my ankles would allow me to walk in light sneakers, like you do."

"No problem. It's not far now."

"Pol-y, pol-y," I said, remembering the instructions from my Kilimanjaro guide to go slowly on the steepest parts. "I'll make it, don't worry about me."

And I did make it, with a few carefully timed stops to take photos of some yaks grazing at a farm at the edge of the village. Sarah and I were probably five minutes behind the lead group as we arrived at Lakpa's sister's teahouse. Kiyoko and Kamila arrived not too long after that. They were constant troopers.

And I thought our hiking was done for the day…

But, no, next we had to go see the famous Thame monastery, which conveniently sat way up the hill above the town.

Shit.

Thirty minutes of tortuous traipsing up what seemed like goat tracks up a ridge behind the village brought us to two major stupas in the windy mist above. I was relieved to reach what I thought was the level of the monastery, but quickly realized that we still had several hundred vertical feet to go. Thank goodness, the last section was not as steep, but the high stone steps to reach the courtyard in front of the monastery's main building sapped the remaining energy from my legs. I collapsed on some cold stone seats along the outside of what really served as a large balcony overlooking the town.

I was not the only one who was gassed by the climb. Most of our group looked whipped, and at the other end of the balcony, another couple rested from the climb.

The two-story main monastery building was painted red with two levels of yellow windows. The windows were framed with bluish stone and covered by frilly white canopies. Pink cloths were hung from some of the windows and a white line crossed at the second level of windows. At the top of the wall was a dotted white line, just under overhanging eaves, which were also painted red. The bottom five feet of the building was sheer stone and it looked like the only way into the building was to climb four or five very large, steep steps on the right up to a double wooden door, which was still open. A few children dressed like monks came in and out, handling the large steps as if they were nothing. They disappeared into a smaller, lighter-colored building with brown windows to our right.

We sat, not knowing whether we could or should venture in or not.

After I recovered, I decided that I would check it out. I worked my way slowly up the steps and saw that people had left their shoes in a little ante-chamber just inside the wooden doors. A man with a broom of sorts in one hand waved me up and motioned with an arm, signaling that I could go in through a curtain. I removed my hiking boots (which felt good) and stuck my head inside a slit in the curtain separating the ante-chamber from a large room filled with chanting Buddhist monks and their trainees.

Inside, an older monk waved me in. I positioned myself a few feet inside the curtain in the corner of the colorful room, which was filled with instruments and paintings and flowers. The whole place reeked of incense. Frankly, it was almost too much to take in. Every inch of the room was covered with some artifact, painting, flower, or something. Soon a few more from our group joined me in the corner of the room.

Just then, the chanting stopped and the entire room erupted in music as the monks each played a different instrument, some with strings and some with wind instruments.

During this musical frenzy, the older monk motioned me forward, walking clockwise around a central column of paintings and flowers until I was almost right in front of the head lama, who was sitting cross-legged at a central "throne" in the front of the room. I felt out of place...a lot out of place...and nervously looked around. Surprisingly, to my right, just in front of the grand lama, was a platter of candy bars and snacks.

I guess these guys get hungry for chocolate and Pringles while chanting and playing instruments all day long.

Apparently, I had gotten too close, as a young man appeared in front of me and quite casually pulled some twine out from the wall to my right and pulled it across the aisle, blocking me from going further—like yellow police tape to seal off a crime scene.

I got the hint and slowly retreated to the corner of the room, where most of our group had gathered. Rather than wait with them to listen to more chanting, I kept going, grabbed my boots, and bounded down the stone steps into the safety of the courtyard below.

The couple, a dark-haired guy and a pretty blonde, was still sitting below, seemingly unsure of what to do. They looked European, and I wasn't sure they spoke English.

"You can go in...it's pretty cool...worth seeing," I said to them. "Just don't get too close to the guy in front."

"Are you sure...it's alright? How much to go in?" the girl asked in very good English.

"Nothing. It's free. You just have to take your shoes off to get inside."

"Thanks, we probably would have just sat out here if you hadn't gone in first."

They headed up the steps and went into the main room, just as the rest of our group was coming out.

When we headed back down to the village, the clouds and mist had come in, making the descent a bit nasty. We quickly passed the two lower stupas and worked our way down the steep ridge. I noticed that the area immediately below the path was heavily fenced in with some barbed wire.

"Why is this barbed-wire fence here?" I asked one of Lakpa's interns.

"It's a nursery," he responded.

"A nursery?" I said, confused.

"Yes...a tree nursery. Not many trees up here. We have to protect them."

I had not noticed that we had reached almost the tree line at this point. Lakpa had told us earlier that wood was one of the scarce resources. They had plenty of rocks and water, but hardly any wood. This explained why all the buildings were made of stone and only the windows and doors were made from wood. Putting the few remaining trees behind barbed wire nailed the point home. No wonder they used yak dung for their fuel. Wood was too valuable to burn.

Dinner that night was the same old rice and soup, bok choy, and carrots. I was more interested in the pizza the European couple from the monastery had ordered a la carte. Plus, I was tired of talking to our same group about all the same things. We had been together for every meal for about six days and I was aching for some new conversation.

So, I pulled up a chair across from the young couple and asked if they minded if I joined them for a bit.

"Delighted if you would," the girl replied, again in perfect English.

"Where are you guys from?" I asked. "You speak English very well."

"Actually, we're from Holland," the guy responded. "But I do a lot of business in England."

"Ah, that explains it."

"And I studied in England, but now work in Switzerland," the blonde added.

"What do you do in Switzerland?"

"I'm in healthcare—an emergency-room doctor—in Geneva," she said with a smile.

For the next thirty minutes, we covered a lot of current issues, including universal healthcare pros and cons, medical malpractice, and Obamacare. For the record, they thought not having universal health care was barbaric and did not understand what all the fuss was about Obamacare. I guess Europeans have a completely different attitude, as they have grown up with universal healthcare provided by the government. They really take it for granted and think it works very well.

We finished our conversation with the couple showing me on a map the trail they had taken up to the Goyko lakes near Cho Oyu, one of the fourteen peaks over 8,000 meters. They had been climbing with no guide and no itinerary, just showing up at villages and looking around for the best place to spend the night. They had been out for about ten days and were now heading back towards Namche Bazaar and Lukla before heading down to Thailand for some beach time before returning to Holland and Geneva.

These Europeans know how to vacation.

I excused myself to get a Coke and rejoin our table. The couple headed to their room, removing the main distraction for the evening. Sarah was off in a corner typing something on her iPad, probably the cybercast for the day. The rest of our group was divided up, with a few reading books, Crystal trying to Skype with her kids, four playing a game of hearts, and Lakpa and our cook quietly battling it out over the chess board. George stood above them near the chess board, shaking his head, and rolling his eyes at their every move. Before he got too frustrated, he decided it was time to pack it in for the night. Five minutes after George left the room, I joined him. I was dead tired and ready for bed.

After breakfast the next morning, Lakpa walked us over to his parents' house, a two-story rock structure built in the Sherpa tradition. Along a narrow corridor, we turned left through a door I had to duck down to enter. We stepped down into a damp room with ground beneath our feet. Ahead of us was a rough wooden ladder up to a second story. To our left was a large room, essentially a barn for the yaks. In cold weather, the "basement" of the house was used as a shelter for the yaks, which were the most valuable assets of the family.

Besides Lakpa Rita, of course.

We climbed up the ladder to the second story of the house, entering the kitchen area first. Lakpa's mother and one or two other women were working over the cooking area. Lakpa led us into the next spacious room with a vaulted ceiling lined with fabric as insulation, which covered the entire rest of the second story of the house. The room was similar to the teahouses in that it had a row of narrow tables along the left side with padded bench seats along that entire side. But the right side was lined from floor to ceiling with shelves containing virtually every size and shape vessel for carrying water, a section full of blankets, supplies, and various tools—everything the household needed for everyday life in the Sherpa lifestyle. At the other end of the room was their Buddhist prayer center with altar, paintings, and flowers. In this one room, Lakpa's entire family ate, slept, worshipped, socialized, and spent their time.

I will never again complain about not having my own bedroom or bathroom when I was growing up. At least I only had to share a room with my brother.

Needless to say, no television was in sight.

Lakpa's mother and father welcomed us to their home not only with a bite to eat and a hot tea drink, but also blessed us each individually with light-colored, long and frayed woven scarves for good luck, which Lakpa's father placed around our necks. This was a traditional Sherpa blessing, but it was even more special because Lakpa's own family was doing the honors. We proudly wore them around our necks most of the rest of the day on the trail before storing them for safekeeping in our packs for the rest of the trip.

Unfortunately, several years later, Thame was severely damaged by earthquakes and Lakpa's family home was destroyed. I understand that they are in the process of rebuilding.

Khumjung, a village about two hours north of Namche Bazaar by foot, was our next destination. Incredibly, Lakpa went to school there for three years, from when he was eight years old to eleven. That required him to hike four hours each way from Thame. Obviously, they did not have school buses or "school yaks" to get him there. Counting the eight hours in the classroom and the round-trip hikes, his school days were sixteen hours long. He said that most of those days he left the house long before sunrise and came back after dark, so he knew the route like the "back of his hand."

That route took us on the same path two-thirds of the way back to Namche Bazaar, then made a sharp left up the mountain and across to Khumjung. What took four hours for Lakpa at age eight took us six hours. The final two hours were the toughest, pushing up steep slopes to the airstrip above Namche, then slogging up multiple switchbacks to a stupa above that, before plunging down an even-steeper descent paved with deep rock steps to Khumjung. I lost some ground to the lead group of George, Yvan, and Sylvie on the way up to the stupa, but hustled down the steep steps and caught them just as we reached the long, flat playing fields of the school on the outskirts of the town. Sarah had no need to catch up and encourage me that day! Maybe I was finally getting in shape…

As we marched down the path with one field on our right and the other on our left, we were rewarded with stunning views of Ama Dablam, the "Matterhorn" of the Himalayas, with its hanging glacier and block-like peak glistening in the sunlight at around 23,000 feet in elevation.

No way to climb that monstrosity! Not me, anyway.

Not surprisingly, that night we stayed at a teahouse appropriately called the Ama Dablam View Hotel. By then, we had been in so many look-alike teahouses that I cannot recall any distinguishing aspect of the place except that, once outside, I could only look to the east and stare at Ama Dablam. I do recall everybody commenting about how astonished they were that Lakpa, as a boy, hiked back and forth every weekday for three years from where we slept the prior night. No wonder he has been able to accomplish so much as a Sherpa and mountaineer. That type of dedication is unheard of in the Western world. I used to brag about walking a mile each way to primary school in London as a child…

The next day was one of the most pleasant of the trek. We started out with an easy fifteen-minute jaunt over to the town of Khunde, famous for its hospital and nursing center, built by Sir Edmund Hillary. I kept turning around to take early-morning pictures of a perfectly clear Ama Dablam, so I was last arriving at the hospital, which was up the hill on the right side of the village. The morning sun was so hot that we all stripped down to a single shirt layer as soon as we arrived.

Unfortunately, we were there too early for the tour, and Lakpa did not want to wait for an hour before heading down the trail. So, we did not get to see any part of the inside of the hospital. I didn't really mind as it looked to be very small and rudimentary from the outside. I couldn't imagine it being very impressive inside.

We backtracked through Khumjung and out the other side, passing some nice souvenir tables set up by the locals. Corrina stopped for a moment, but just a moment, as Lakpa kept walking as if to tell us not to waste our time on the trinkets being offered. I would have liked to linger over some unique items we had not seen in Namche Bazaar, but I was not going to fall behind that early in the morning. So, I just kept walking as well.

Basically, from Khumjung, we were going on level paths or even a bit downhill most of the early morning, working our way over to the main drag from Namche to Tengboche, an elevated ridge in the middle of the Khumbu Valley. At the top of the ridge was a large monastery, reportedly with brilliant views of Everest from its doorsteps. To get there, however, we had to first drop down to the river, cross a bridge, and go even higher back up to Tengboche.

Almost as soon as we merged into the main drag coming from Namche, Lakpa led us down a path to our right. It went straight down.

I pulled out my second hiking stick for balance. For the next forty-five minutes, we worked our way down the steepest switchbacks and series of rock steps yet. The people coming up this section were chugging for breath and taking frequent rest stops. Several times the trail got so clogged that we had to wait a few minutes for groups to work their way slowly around the rocky corners of the switchbacks. I was glad we were going down…until at a clearing in the trees I saw how much farther we had to go down to the river and, worse yet, how steep the trail looked going up on the other side.

Damn! Why don't they build a long suspension bridge from right here and save us all the trouble?

It seemed like forever, but we finally reached the bottom, crossed a small bridge, and, without a break, started up the other side. I instantly switched into a slow third gear for the ascent. Luckily, Lakpa was in the lead and he, too, slowed down to a snail's pace.

EVEREST BASE CAMP

Wow! If he is going this slow, we're in for a tough climb…

Amazingly, for the first time since we left Lukla, I felt strong going up this hill. Maybe I was acclimatizing; maybe my legs were just getting stronger as the days went on; maybe the meat stick I had snuck in on a short water break that morning was giving me unusual energy. I don't know. But what I do know is that I stayed up with Lakpa all the way up to the monastery.

The hour-long uphill trek to Tengboche seemed to be over quickly and soon we found ourselves almost floating down a grassy knoll, with the monastery to our left and a teahouse and bakery at the end of the field in front of us. We knew it was a bakery because it said so on its roof. Several stray horses were grazing or cantering about in a very surreal fashion. But I didn't focus on the monastery or the teahouse or the horses.

Rather, my eyes were glued to the north. Nuptse, Everest, and Lhotse filled the horizon above and beyond the bakery, creating what looked to me like the perfect jigsaw puzzle photo. The scene was straight out of a picture book. I stopped, stared, and pulled out my camera and took a great picture of Everest and its surrounding peaks in the sky above the green roof of the bakery, which had yellow letters—B-A-K-E-R-Y—painted on it.

After washing down another very nice chocolate croissant with a cold Coke and relaxing in the warm sun on the stone porch in front of the bakery, a group of us decided to explore the monastery. As usual, there was an ornate entryway into the monastery complex followed by a series of steep steps up to a large set of double wooden doors. This time I bounded up the steps almost in a full run. Where I got the energy that day, I'm not sure.

Once inside the wooden doors, we turned left up another set of even steeper steps up to an open courtyard where young monks were performing some sort of exercise or dance. One monk demonstrated a dance move and then all of them joined in. Soon the whole courtyard was filled with dancing and prancing monks, obviously enjoying the afternoon. I could not tell if they were performing a religious ritual or just goofing off. Whatever it was, we all enjoyed their enthusiasm.

After a while, it seemed clear we would not be able to go inside the monastery itself, so I excused myself and circled back behind the whole monastery complex near where we had reached the top of the ridge. I wanted to get a picture of Everest with the monastery roofline in the foreground. Unfortunately, when I got back behind the place, there was no hill or vantage point from which I could get a good photo. I was able only to hold my camera way up above my head to get a sliver of the summits of Everest and Lhotse in the sky above the monastery wall and rooftop.

Not exactly a masterpiece.

So, I headed back down to the bakery, where Lakpa and a few others were still relaxing in the sun. Our respite was interrupted by a mangy, stray horse, which kept approaching and nibbling on backpacks. Our cook, Gopal, kept chasing it away, but it kept coming back for more. A slap with a strap from Gopal finally got the message through to the horse that its presence was not wanted, and it galloped away, only to start bothering some other climbers at the nearby teahouse.

As soon as the horse left, some very large hawks landed on the bakery roof just above our heads, waiting for some scraps of pastry to become available for scavenging. Lakpa shooed a few away, but they kept circling and landing like vultures above until Lakpa signaled that it was time to leave.

Several hours later, after we descended about a half mile to a small village further north, I watched mesmerized as the summit of Everest slowly became enveloped and blocked by the afternoon clouds filling the lower Khumbu Valley. As the clouds encircled the summit and the daylight waned, I took a final picture of the disappearing summit.

Then I went inside for another dinner of soup, rice, and bok choy. My friend from the National Geographic group was there that night, but he was not eating. Three or four of his group had gotten a stomach bug and had been throwing up for a few days. I resisted the temptation to tell him "I told you so," before he quickly told me he had started to take Cipro and was feeling better.

Our next stop would be the village of Periche, famous for its high-altitude sickness education and treatment center. Climbers with high-altitude sickness—whether pulmonary or cerebral edema or less serious dizziness, nausea, and vomiting—are evacuated from high elevations by helicopter and brought to Periche. Several doctors, purportedly with expertise in this area, man the treatment center and give daily lectures.

The climb up to Periche was long, gradual, and uneventful. We were treated to multiple views of Everest, Lhotse, and Nuptse every time we reached the crest of a ridge or turned a corner to our left. Each time, the summit of Everest got closer to being fully obscured by the bumpy Nuptse peaks in front of it. By the time we reached Periche, Everest had fully dropped behind Nuptse. We would not see it again for three more days.

The biggest change on this day of hiking is that we left the woods behind and were now hiking in the stark mountain landscapes above the tree line. We were not yet in the glacial murrains, but we were getting a lot closer to serious mountain terrain.

The lecture on high-altitude sickness at Periche turned out to be essentially an advertisement for the use of Diamox, a drug many climbers use to build up red blood cells and make acclimatization easier. The English-sounding physician, who said he was in his second three-month stint volunteering at the high-altitude treatment center, spent a few minutes describing the process of acclimatization and the symptoms of the various high-altitude sicknesses. He then proceeded to advocate for the use of Diamox for anyone going over 10,000 feet. He made it sound as if anyone who did not use it was an idiot.

I was a bit offended by the guy's attitude. I had been taught that Diamox, while helpful for many climbers, can make a climber feel artificially stronger than they really are and may mislead climbers into going higher before they are carefully acclimatized. Diamox is not for everyone...and not for me. I had been to almost 23,000 feet in altitude at Aconcagua without Diamox and had no symptoms of high-altitude sickness. Plus, some say that it causes more frequent urination during the night. With my urinary frequency already accelerated following my prostate surgery, that would not be welcome. Our guides on the Nepal trek had Diamox with them, but indicated from the start that they would use it only as needed in individual cases. I agree with that approach, though I am no expert on the drug.

Nevertheless, after the lecture, several of our team members started taking Diamox, having been scared to death by the mountain doc. Whether they were peeing more, I'm not sure, but it seemed that the outhouses got more crowded at night from that point on.

We had another day in Periche, so we washed some stinky socks and underwear and hung them out to dry the next day. I wish we had been able to get some extended sleep the first night there, but the wind was perfectly designed to cause the yak-dung smoke coming out of the heater in the teahouse to fumigate each of the bunk rooms along the side of the building as we tried to get to sleep. The fumes made it almost impossible to breathe in normal air. The only way to avoid it was to cover my head with my sleeping bag and suffocate from within. Sometime long after midnight, the smoke finally stopped and I was finally able to doze off without gagging.

Then, on our "rest day," Lakpa took us on a "short" day-hike to get additional acclimatization. Since I have placed these words in quotes, you can be sure that the day hike was neither short nor restful. We climbed up a bare ridge, across a plateau, and up another steep ridge to a stupa with a magnificent view of the town of Dengboche on the other side. Behind Dengboche was a valley leading up to a series of mountains, including Makalu, the fourth-highest mountain in the world, and Island Peak, a 21,000-foot peak that could have been climbed if we had opted to spend four of five more days on this trek. I had considered doing that climb as an extension, but ultimately did not feel I could add another week to the trip.

The views from the first stupa were gorgeous and resulted in another frenzy of photo-taking. Had we stopped there, I would have been more than pleased with our day trip. However, there was another stupa with impressive prayer flags and two large white flags a bit further up the steep ridge above us. This quickly became our next destination. The altitude gain was relentless as we struggled up and up, or more accurately, as I, David Schaeffer, struggled up and up. Somehow, most of the rest of our group seemed to be moving faster and easier up the switchbacks.

Maybe they are all on Diamox now!

EVEREST BASE CAMP

As usual, as I started to lag, Sarah appeared beside me in her sneakers, asking me if I felt okay and encouraging me to keep going.

"I'm fine, but I thought this was supposed to be a rest day," I replied. "Haven't we already gained about fifteen hundred feet? That should be enough for one day's acclimatization."

"Nah, we've only gained about 1,100 feet so far."

"Well, I know I can make it up to the white flags up there. I'm just going to take it at my own pace. What's with those guys? They seem like they are racing up the mountain today."

"I guess everyone's feeling good today."

"Yeah, but let's not forget that we have a long climb tomorrow."

Sarah set a nice pace in front of me that I matched almost all the way up to the next stupa. Just before we reached them, she veered off slightly to the left, but I saw a well-worn switchback straight up to the white flags up to the right. I chose the right fork and put it into high gear, just to show her that I still had some climb left in me.

Dumb move.

I made it to the white flags, barely, then collapsed beneath them. As I pulled out my water bottle, I looked around and none of our group was near the flags. They were stopped a little bit above and to the left of the stupa, exactly in the direction Sarah had gone. As I sat down, I saw Sarah join the rest and look back at me with an "I told you so" look on her face.

Even though I was out of breath from my foolish spurt up the hill, I sucked it up and slowly covered the distance up to the group, only to learn that we were still not done for the day.

I looked up. Above us, there were no more stupas or flags, only periodic rocks and some paths that looked less than well-worn. But Lakpa announced that we would go a few hundred feet further to maximize our acclimatization.

"Phakding," I said under my breath.

About twenty minutes later and after some serious calf strain, we reached a large rock with some nice pads of grass below it. Lakpa pulled off his pack and untied his boots, his signal for a longer rest stop. I found a rock to sit on and unclipped my daypack. Moments later I was munching on a Snickers bar, trying to regain some energy.

"I think we have gone far enough today," Lakpa said. "I will head back down in a few minutes for those who want to go back."

"I plan to go a little further up," Sarah said. "Who wants to join me?"

Yvan, Sylvie, Andrew, and Corrina instantly volunteered. I was too tired to remember if George and Crystal eventually joined them. All I knew was that I had clearly had enough.

"I'm going down with Lakpa," I said with no hesitation.

Later that evening, after everyone returned to the teahouse in Periche, Andrew revealed that the volunteer climbing group had gone as far as they could, to the top of the ridge.

"There was nothing beyond it. We had to go down from there," he explained.

"Were you able to see any additional mountains from up there?" I asked.

"Well, no, but it was really windy up there," he replied.

"Excellent. Then I didn't miss a thing."

Dinner was interesting on the second evening in Periche not because of the food, but because of two groups that showed up to spend the night. The first was a group of three Korean guys, who were back down at Periche for a final rest and recuperation in advance of an Everest summit attempt. They had been in Nepal for almost two months, working their way up to Everest base camp, then making trips across the ice fall to ferry food and equipment to the four camps above base camp. That much time at altitudes over 18,000 feet takes its toll. So, many groups, including this Korean team, descend to the villages below to regain their strength with some good food and more restful sleep before heading back up for the final push to the top. Unfortunately, the Koreans did not seem to speak much English and kept to themselves, so we did not get an opportunity to find out what it was like going through the ice fall and climbing above it.

The second group was a British group of young guys and gals in their twenties. They had just been to Everest base camp the day before and had descended that day all the way from Gorek Shep, the last teahouse before Everest base camp, and Kala Pattar, a small nearby peak, that day. They looked whipped and cold. Several of the girls had very red noses and cheeks, another indicator of cold weather further up the mountain. However, after a few beers they all were in good spirits. One of them said they had endured a long day, starting at 4 A.M. to climb Kala Pattar and then hiking all the way down to Periche throughout the day. But none of them had any high-altitude sickness Soon they were chattering away in their British accents, happy to be back in a warm teahouse at lower altitudes.

That night, I went to sleep tired but excited about the prospect of being at Everest base camp in two days.

For the first two hours, the trail up from Periche gradually ascended alongside the river, in a wide greenish valley. Lakpa told us that the whole expanse was sometimes flooded with water during the rainy seasons, so the paths along this section were winding and intermingled, with no main well-worn sections. We hopped over marshy areas and enjoyed the scenery since the hiking was easy.

As we worked our way up the valley, two mountains ahead of us on our left dominated the view. One was Taboche and the other Cholotse, both around 22,000 feet high. Cholotse looked particularly impressive as it shot up almost vertical on the sides with a sharp, spiral peak at the top. I could not imagine anyone being able to climb it. But, of course, Lakpa had climbed it, along with a few others.

"It's not for everyone," he said.

"Definitely not for me," I responded. "Way too technical."

At the top end of the long wide valley, the terrain shifted dramatically. We turned a corner to our right and started up a steeper incline. Then, just as our legs were getting used to the increased slope, we looked up and saw prayer flags almost vertically above us, way up the mountain. Lakpa had warned us that there was one tough section on today's climb. This was clearly it.

I first saw the prayer flags, but then as my eyes focused, I could see dozens of people working their way up this slope, disappearing behind huge rocks and then appearing further up. The rocks looked like they had collapsed from above and slid down, creating a steep mess of meandering switchbacks. Some areas had been stabilized with stone steps.

Other areas were simply steep bare patches of yellowish, gritty soil, which made footing treacherous, especially for those coming down towards us.

Slowly but surely the prayer flags kept getting closer as we headed up the hill. Apparently, Lakpa did not intend to stop until we got to the top, and this time his pace was quicker. Maybe he was testing us. More likely, he knew that the slope looked worse than it really was and there was a special place awaiting our arrival above. Within forty-five minutes, we crossed under the prayer flags suspended from two large rock pillars and entered a plateau surrounded by snowcapped peaks. I looked around, three hundred sixty degrees, and saw nothing but jagged white peaks.

What a tranquil, beautiful place.

I suddenly realized that we were standing in the middle of a graveyard.

On our left was a series of stone cairns along a ridge with Cholotse in the background. That was where the Sherpas who had died on Everest were buried. To our right were stone or cement pillars with painted names and dates on them. One was "Scott Fisher," a guide who died in the 1996 Everest disaster chronicled later by Jon Krakauer in his book, *Into Thin Air*. Another had a fresh coat of stucco and a picture of a young lady who had apparently died earlier that spring. These above-ground burial spots were dotted across the landscape, a final resting place for those who had lost their lives in the pursuit of glory on Everest.

"Well, if you have to go, this is a helluva place to hang out for eternity," I said to George.

"I think I would rather die of old age," he said.

"Me, too, but there are not many cemeteries like this one," I replied.

George chuckled and said, "Check this out."

He lay down in front of a few of the pillars, pulled his blue hood over his head, spread his legs, and pretended to be dead. Or maybe he was just dead tired from the climb to this spot. Either way, he did not move for about ten minutes.

I took a photo of my comatose roommate and some photos of the graves and then sat nearby, re-energizing with a meat stick and another Snickers bar. I did not know whether it was rude to eat in the middle of a burial plot, but I was famished. I also needed to replenish for the next three hours of climbing.

The stop at the graveyards was the longest non-meal stop we had anytime during the trip. But soon we were back on the trail, working our way up a much more rugged valley filled with glacial debris and grayish ridges. We had crossed over into more serious terrain where the land was devoid of any plant life and the only things around us were rocks, gravel, more rocks, bigger rocks, and a slew of enormous peaks. We were only two days away from Everest base camp and were approaching 16,500 feet in altitude.

Early that afternoon, we traipsed over a crest and there, straight ahead, was Pumori, a gigantic peak that I knew was just to the left (west) of Everest base camp. For some reason, Pumori reminded me of a huge spaceship taking off. For the next hour, its peak kept disappearing behind rocky ridges and then reappearing even bigger. But it remained on the launch pad and never took off.

We finally arrived in the little village of Lobuche around 2 P.M. The sun was still out and the air was comfortable, but something told me it was going to be cold that night.

After about an hour of rest and relaxation, Sarah announced that she was going to climb up a ridge to our right to get a good look at the Khumbu glacial murrain…and maybe see some of the Khumbu ice fall. My ears perked up. Yvan and Sylvie immediately volunteered to join Sarah, and Kiyoko said to count her in. Though I was still somewhat tired, I looked over towards the ridge. It did not look too high. So, I surprised myself by agreeing to join them, even though it meant doing completely unnecessary climbing. Not my usual thing! Maybe, just maybe, I felt guilty for having not kept going up the ridge above Periche the day before and wanted Sarah not to think I was totally worthless.

So, we headed across a flat area requiring hopping a few streams on strategically placed rocks, over some dune-like hills, and across another flat area over to the bottom of the steep ridge. There was no clear choice of angles to climb from, but I saw what looked like a less-steep path up to the lowest point of the ridge just to our right and headed in that direction. Yvan, Sylvie, and Sarah kept going straight ahead in the direction of a steeper path just to the left. Kiyoko followed me.

As it turned out, I picked the right trail this time. The dusty path was well-worn and worked itself diagonally up the ridge with only two short switchbacks. It was not as steep as it looked from over at the teahouse, and soon I was near the top. I looked back to see Kiyoko about halfway up, making good time. As I reached the top, I noticed the whole ridge was filled with little cairns or series of rocks balanced on each other, forming little hoodoos everywhere. Beyond the ridge was a deep canyon of grey silt and rocks where the Khumbu glacier had receded. It was a very impressive sight, but we were still way too far down the mountain to see any ice fall.

I looked to my left. Between the hoodoos, I saw Yvan and Sylvie make it to the top about two hundred yards further north. I waved at Kiyoko as she reached the top to let her know I was heading up towards the others. As I went that way, I stopped several times, liberally snapping photos of the void left by the receding glacier.

Within ten minutes of reaching the top of the ridge, clouds started forming in the valleys below us and the wind picked up. We decided not to dilly-dally around any longer. This time, Kiyoko and I descended the steeper path the others had climbed up, then hustled across the dunes and flat areas. Less than twenty minutes later, we were warming ourselves up around the yak-fueled stove in the middle of the teahouse.

As expected, that evening the temperatures dropped rapidly and everyone was glad to be inside. Unfortunately, the latrines at this teahouse were outside, at the end of a windy, exposed strip of concrete, so we enjoyed brisk "potty breaks" that evening.

Not long before dinner that night, Melissa Arnot, with four Everest summits on her résumé, and her client, a guy named Neil, showed up at the teahouse. Neil was wearing a very puffy, blue down parka and looked beat to a pulp. Melissa, sporting a stylish ribbed down jacket and tight pants, looked like she had just come off a model's runway. I later learned that she actually models mountain gear for the Eddie Bauer adventure clothing group, First Ascent.

She greeted Lakpa and Sarah cheerfully, then casually slipped in behind one of the tables beside me, waving at the proprietor for a beer. Neil collapsed in a corner, looking like he would never get up.

"Where'd you guys come from today?" I asked her.

"Across the divide from the Goyko trail—twenty-five miles, most of it uphill," she said nonchalantly.

"How high is that divide?"

"Somewhere between eighteen and nineteen thousand. We had to maneuver around some snow and ice in a couple of places. Nothing serious."

"Sounds pretty serious to me. How's your client doing?"

"Not so good right now, but he'll be okay. He's strong."

I looked over at Neil, who was starting to stretch. With his down parka on, he looked considerably overweight, but when he took it off, I could see that he was fit and trim with well-toned muscles. But he was clearly struggling to recover from the long trek. Minutes later, he left the room without saying boo to anyone.

I quickly learned that wherever Melissa Arnot is in the house, she is the center of attention, not only because she is drop-dead attractive, but because she is outgoing and conversational with everyone, even us peon trekkers. Even though no American woman has climbed Everest as many times as she has, she never put on airs. She seemed completely laid back. But, as I watched, she appeared to be effortlessly prepared for whatever was happening around her, always having the right gear or gadget for the occasion. And she looked fresh even after a twenty-five-mile climb at anywhere from 16,000 to 19,000 feet.

Amazing.

Neil finally made it back for dinner, and after a bowl of warm soup and some tea, he looked a lot better.

"How was it today? I heard you guys did about twenty-five miles," I asked him.

"Tough day."

"Are you heading for Everest base camp?"

"Yeah. Then we're gonna climb Lobuche East."

"To the top?"

"Yeah, if the weather holds."

I had seen Lobuche East, a peak with a summit at over 21,000 feet just to the west of the village. It was not quite as sharp-peaked as some of the other mountains, but it still looked like the only way to the top was a slick-looking slope of about sixty degrees.

"How is it climbing with Melissa?"

"Not bad. Not bad at all," he said with a grin, then added, "Too bad she's married to one of my best friends back in Wyoming...."

"She looks like she has just been on a stroll today."

"Yeah. Doesn't look like it, but she's very strong, very strong."

"Well, if you do go for the top of Lobuche East, be safe. Looks like a pretty good challenge."

"I wouldn't try it by myself, but Melissa says I can do it if we don't get any snow."

"Good luck then."

I went to bed that night thinking Neil must be crazy—or else he just enjoyed climbing with the best-looking guide in the Khumbu Valley.

We left Lobuche on the morning of October 25, 2012, heading to Gorak Shep, the last outpost before Everest base camp, with great anticipation. Although the Alpine Ascents website indicated that we would stay two nights there and visit base camp on October 26, Lakpa spoke about the possibility that we would spend only one night at Gorak Shep and hike up to the base camp in the same afternoon we arrived. So, if the weather held up, there was a strong chance we would make it to our ultimate destination that afternoon.

The hike to Gorak Shep was dry and dusty. Every part of the landscape was glacial murrain, mostly grainy grey sand, dusty rocks, or brown grit, with ridge after ridge after ridge to climb over or around. The whole morning, we kept getting closer and closer to Pumori, which continued to soar into the blue skies in front of us.

At some point, Sarah pointed out Kala Pattar, at 18,200 feet, the highest point of our trek, which she said was the best place to get clear photos of Everest's peak. But it looked like a brown mound of nothing on the low side of Pumori. Hardly an impressive mountain. I was instantly disappointed. Somehow, I thought Kala Pattar would be more of an independent mountain with a clearly defined peak with some snow on it.

This looked more like a large pile of yak poop beneath a huge icy spaceship.

EVEREST BASE CAMP

Every time we reached the crest of a ridge or came around a rocky corner, I expected to see the Gorak Shep outpost. But one time after another, all I could see were more hills and ridges in front of me. Two hours stretched into three, then three into four. We kept going up, down, and around piles of rock. Finally, we came around a ridge and saw the blue, green, and red roofs of Gorak Shep right in front of us. Beyond the buildings was a huge, flat expanse, with the brown base of Kala Pattar on the far side. We practically raced down the slightly downhill trail to the buildings, only to enter one of the teahouses and find that it was already packed with people.

Lakpa spoke to one of the proprietors and shortly thereafter waved us out and up some steep steps to another level on the back of the building. There, only three more wooden steps up, was a back porch of sorts, shielded from the wind by thick sheets of plastic. A large picnic table filled the far end of the small room. To the right were three doors, presumably to bedrooms.

There was barely enough room for all of us, but we didn't have much choice except to crunch together and make the most of it.

Cozy.

As usual, the assistant Sherpas brought us hot orange drinks, this time in nasty-looking, but clean plastic cups. Still, we had been sucking in dust all morning, so we drank heartily.

A German family joined us in the room at a little table closer to the door and soon pulled out aromatic meat and cheese, which the father cut in generous slices for his wife and daughters. George and I salivated, taking in the smells and coveting their meal.

After what seemed like forever, we were served soup and French fries, the usual fare. I was tired of soup and potatoes and wondered if we would ever get any more meat. But my disappointment in the meal quickly disappeared when Lakpa announced that we would be leaving for Everest base camp in ten minutes.

The scurrying began. Andrew and Corrina began checking their cameras. Yvan and Sylvie paced back and forth outside, already strapped up and ready to go. I stepped outside and realized that the wind had picked up and gloves would be needed. I vacillated between two or three layers up top and decided on two, thinking that I could always add a layer later. I popped my wool beanie on to keep my ears warm. Two minutes later, I was freezing and added the third layer.

Surprisingly, Lakpa did not lead us as we left Gorak Shep. For the first time, our cook, Gopal, marched to the front and waved us in behind him. Then he took off like a bat out of hell.

By the time we were halfway across the flat expanse, Crystal, Corrina, and I were about fifty yards behind the lead group. Kamila and Kiyoko were even farther behind.

Slow down, damn it! We've got a long way to go.

But Gopal had set his pace and he was keeping to it.

At the end of the flat section, we worked our way up a ridge or two and could just barely see the top tip of Everest between the side of Nuptse on the right and a large, lower shoulder of Everest on the left. I snapped a quick picture and kept going. We went up and down for about a half hour, periodically getting a glimpse of Everest's peak, but mainly staring across at an enormous glacier coming down from the side of Nuptse, which hung over the edge of the deep chasm where the Khumbu glacier had receded below.

At well over 17,000 feet in altitude, we should have been moving slower, but Gopal's pace never let up. Lakpa had predicted it would take two and a half hours to reach base camp. However, at this pace I had no doubt that we would easily beat that time. And I was getting hot, so I stopped and stripped off one of my three layers.

After about an hour, we worked our way up to the top of a narrow ridge, which stretched out in front of us for what looked to be a mile or more. Beyond it and to the right we could now see the Khumbu ice fall and dozens of people gathered in front of it, maybe hundreds. More people were working their way down from the ridge across a lower section of rocks towards the gathered group. Several hundred yards further north was a smattering of about a dozen yellow tents, presumably for those climbers from the few expeditions still hoping to make a summit attempt.

At the highest point of the ridge, I stopped to take one more photo of Everest's summit, peaking out in the gap to the left of Nuptse. I realized that I was getting cold again, so I pulled out my third layer and pulled it back on.

EVEREST BASE CAMP

Jeez, Louise. Make up your mind, Weather!

Soon we were off the ridge, still trying to catch up with George and the others, who were scrambling to stay up with Gopal.

We plunged down the side of the ridge into a boulder field of slippery and occasionally icy rocks.

Just perfect to turn an ankle on or slip down and crack a skull. That would be great!

As we pushed our way past slower climbers and saw the colorful 2012 Everest base camp banner up the rocky slope in front of us, Lakpa appeared from behind us. He had taken care of some business back at Gorak Shep and had hustled to catch us just before we reached our goal. His pace was obviously even faster than Gopal's.

I looked ahead. Gopal, Yvan, Sylvie, George, and Andrew had reached the crowd surrounding the colorful Everest base camp banner. About five minutes later, Crystal, Corrina, and I joined them. I looked at my watch.

One hour and forty minutes! You've got to be kidding me.

It was supposed to take us two and a half hours. We were fifty minutes ahead of schedule. I sensed that I would pay for it on the way back down, but for now I felt euphoric and surreal just being at Everest base camp, our final destination. I stared down at the ice fall beneath us, then across and up as it disappeared between the mountains in front of us. It was a jumbled mess of giant ice blocks going every which way. I looked for, but I could not see, any of the long ladders tied together across crevasses or gaps in the ice blocks I had heard so much about.

Looking up I tried to see Everest's peak, but it was hidden behind the large shoulder of the mountain in front of us. I turned and scanned the scene. Everyone was excited, milling around, waiting for their turn to have their photo taken in front of the banner. At some point, reality kicked in and we realized where we were. We hugged and slapped each other on the back in celebration.

Once I stopped moving, I noticed just how chilly it was. Cold air was whipping up the valley, sending the wind-chill factor down precipitously. Kiyoko had arrived, and was covering up. George was pulling on his down jacket. Lakpa warned everyone to put on outer shell jackets and gloves while we waited for the banner to clear for group pictures. For the first time on the whole trip, I pulled on my Gore-Tex jacket for a windproof fourth layer, adjusting my beanie under the hood. Before I could start shivering, I decided to walk down to the far-right end of the little plateau on which the banner had been placed to try to get a photo that included a sliver of Everest's peak.

At the very far end, I could just make out Everest's summit at the top of a thin grey line along the side of the large snowy shoulder. I snapped a photo with some piled stones and prayer flags in the foreground, hoping it would come out. Then I rejoined the others.

"Yvan," I shouted over the wind, "can you take a picture of Lakpa and me in front of the banner?" I handed him my camera.

"Absolutely," he replied.

I motioned to Lakpa and proudly put my arm over his shoulders and posed in front of the banner. What an honor to be at Everest base camp with a man who has been to the top sixteen times!

Yvan held up my camera, began to adjust the zoom, and suddenly the lens whirled and receded back into the body of the camera. Yvan pressed the power button on the top of the camera with no luck.

"Battery's dead," he announced glumly.

You've got to be kidding me.

"Are you serious?" I yelled over the wind.

"Don't worry, David. I'll take one with my camera," he said.

"Thanks—you're the man!" I replied, smiling as he snapped the ultimate photo of me and Lakpa at the pinnacle of our trip.

Just in case, I had George take another picture on his camera. God knows whether I would ever receive either shot, but I wanted to double my chances.

Everyone wanted to do a group photo, but Kamila had not yet arrived.

It's getting cold out here. Let's go!

But we waited for the whole team to be complete.

Exactly two hours after we had left Gorak Shep and twenty minutes after most of us had arrived, Kamila appeared and was embraced by the group.

"Two hours exactly," she said. "We made great time!"

EVEREST BASE CAMP

And she was right. Even though she was the slowest in the group, she still beat Lakpa's estimate by thirty minutes. What an incredible feat for her. I was so proud of her. Some of us wondered whether she would make it all the way, especially after she looked sickish back in Khumjung. But day after day, she persevered and kept going, until there was nowhere else to go. All nine of us had made it to Everest base camp.

Sweet!

The group photos took a while as everyone wanted one taken with their own camera. Of course, my camera was dead, so I figured I would just get one from another climber later. Andrew sent me two group shots at the base camp banner about four months after the trip, so my photo album is now complete.

After a grand total of thirty minutes at Everest base camp, it was time to go. I would have liked to have had time to walk up to the expedition tents, hike down to where the trail leads to the ice fall, and check out some of the ladders set up across crevasses. But apparently there was no time for that if we were to get back to Gorak Shep before dark. Plus, it was getting very cold and windy. So Lakpa told us to take the return trip at our own pace, but to get going now.

I thought that getting back would be a breeze, since most of the way back would be slightly downhill. However, the climb back up to the narrow ridge sapped some of my energy, and, as we worked our way into the wind along the ridge, most of the rest of my energy reserves rapidly depleted. Maybe hiking up from Lobuche and then adding the climb to the base camp onto the same day was too much. Maybe I had used up my energy in the excitement of the moment. Maybe it was the fact that we were at almost 18,000 feet. Maybe it was just the wind and the cold. I'm not sure.

However, on the way back to Gorak Shep, I felt just a bit off...a misstep here and the catching of the toe of my boot there. Stumbling over a rock. Losing my balance just slightly. Three or four times I had to steady myself with my trekking pole or I might have gone down.

Come on, David. It's all downhill from here. What's wrong with you?

Corrina and Crystal were following me, using my wider body as a shield from the wind. George was a little further behind, gradually catching up with us.

"Do you guys want to go ahead?" I asked the ladies.

"No, you're doing just fine. We'd rather follow right now," Corrina responded.

Great. I'm feeling lousy and they still want me to lead...

"Okay, but I might take it a little slower. It's been a long day," I said as I turned back into the wind.

The rest of the walk back to Gorak Shep was a struggle. I didn't feel nauseous, didn't have a headache, didn't have any injury, and my legs were fine. But I didn't feel right. I had a slight sense of disequilibrium, which caused me to stumble where I would usually never stumble.

George finally caught up and passed me. I moved in right behind him, finally drafting instead of being drafted. Soon he and I were moving at his pace and leaving the girls slightly behind. Sarah caught up with us shortly before we reached the last hill above the flat expanse and, as usual, asked us how we were doing.

"I think I've had enough for today," I said. "I'm a little unsteady for some reason."

George added that he was fine but tired.

"Well, we're almost there, so get some good rest tonight. We've got Kala Pattar to climb at four in the morning," she said as she speed-walked ahead. I noticed that, for the first time, she had real hiking boots on instead of sneakers.

"I'm not sure I'm gonna climb Kala Pattar," I told George. "I'm barely staying on my feet now and it's going to be damned cold tomorrow morning at four. Besides, Kala Pattar is just a brown mound on the side of Pumori. It really doesn't look like a mountain to me."

"I'm going to see how I feel in the morning, then make up my mind," George replied.

"Yeah, but right now, I feel like I am not going to do it. My camera is dead, so I can't take any pictures anyway. Plus, it's a long day's hike down to Dengboche tomorrow as it is."

We walked the rest of the way over to the buildings in silence. We had run out of energy and out of conversation. But we had successfully made it to Everest base camp and nothing could change that.

EVEREST BASE CAMP

The next morning, George, Yvan, Sylvie, Corrina, and Kiyoko, froze their heinies on the way up to the top of Kala Pattar at sunrise, while Crystal, Andrew, Kamila, and I stayed warm in our respective beds and enjoyed a leisurely eight o'clock breakfast. I had not changed my mind about not climbing Kala Pattar. I just didn't want to take any chances.

As I sat down at the breakfast table, I noticed a girl sitting at the next table, looking dazed and frozen. Her cheeks were almost beet red.

"Are you alright?" I asked her.

"Yes," she said in a European accent. "I just came down from Kala Pattar."

"How cold was it up there?"

"I don't know, but I didn't have enough gear to stay warm. My boyfriend stayed to take pictures, but I had to come right back down. It's too cold." She rubbed her hands and took another sip from her hot tea.

"I hope our group is okay up there. I decided not to go this morning," I added.

"They're probably okay. I saw a lot of people going up on my way down. I think I was the first one coming down."

"Well, you should be warm pretty quickly down here. Maybe they will put some more yak dung in the heater."

About ten minutes later, her boyfriend arrived, looking very frosty.

About that same time, Melissa Arnot walked in, dressed warmly.

"Are you guys back from Kala Pattar already?" I asked her.

"No. We're gonna head up there in a few minutes."

"That makes a lot more sense than our group leaving here at four or five in the morning and freezing their butts off," I said.

"I think so, but Neil and I will probably make much better time," she responded. "Why didn't you go?"

"I felt a little unsteady on the way back from base camp yesterday, and decided not to push my luck. I wish they had decided to wait until now to go up in the light and when it's a little warmer. I might have felt better about joining them."

"I'd say you could join us, but Lakpa will want to get you guys going down in the next hour or so, so I don't think that would work."

"That's okay. I'm gonna take it easy today."

Thirty minutes later, Lakpa, George, Yvan, and Sylvie arrived, chattering about how freezing it was at the top. George muttered about having to scramble on icy rocks at the top. He told me that he and Lakpa got there first and he had trouble trying to stay warm while waiting for the others to reach the top. But they were all excited about the views they had seen of Everest at dawn.

Corrina, Kiyoko, and Sarah were not very far behind, and soon our group was reunited in the warm teahouse.

At the time, I was very pleased with my decision not to climb Kala Pattar. Now that I am home and have had time to reflect, I wish I had gone ahead and tried the climb. It was the highest point of our trip and I missed it. Oh, well, I did not feel a hundred percent and by skipping it, I had a very pleasurable downhill hike the rest of the day.

My one negative comment on the post-climb survey for Alpine Ascents was that I felt we were rushed up at Gorak Shep and the base camp. I would have preferred to spend two nights at Gorak Shep as originally scheduled, with a climb of Kala Pattar in the afternoon, and then a full day to spend hiking to the base camp and really inspecting the whole area. Maybe we could have talked to some of the expedition climbers. Certainly, we could have gotten closer to the ice fall.

But Lakpa seemed intent on spending only one night and getting us back down to around 15,000 feet as soon as possible. There is some sense in that, but no one in our group seemed to be having any difficulty with the altitude, so I wish we had stayed two nights and taken our time to explore base camp fully.

After the rest of the group warmed up and enjoyed a quick breakfast, it was time to go. But first, I noticed Sarah using her cell phone and talking to someone far away. I asked her if I could use her phone to call my wife. She obliged. Amazingly, I could talk to Kim in Atlanta on Sarah's cell phone as if I was in the next room.

Gorak Shep obviously has a great cell tower and it was great to hear my wife's voice.

After working our way through the hills and valleys of rock just below Gorak Shep, we zipped down the mountain, bearing left after the graveyard to stay on the ridge above the wide river valley. We made a long gradual descent to the first stupa below the white flags where we had climbed up from Periche on our "rest" day a few days earlier. This time, however, instead of descending west down to Periche, we worked our way down a very steep hill to the little town of Dengboche, which sat at the entrance to the valley leading up to Island Peak and Makalu. Those who had climbed Kala Pattar that morning were pretty wiped out by the time we arrived. I felt fine after six hours of downhill walking.

We were the only ones staying at the teahouse Lakpa chose for the night. And it was a good choice. They had "yak sizzle" and "chicken sizzle" entrées for dinner, a nice change from the usual garlic soup, potatoes, rice, and bok choy! It was the Nepal version of Ruth Chris' Steakhouse!

Just when we thought we were on easy street for the rest of the trip, Lakpa announced that we would be taking a different trail down to Namche Bazaar...a trail off the beaten track. Our destination was Phortse, pronounced more like "fartsy," a remote village above and to the east of Tengboche and Khumjung. It sounded like a good idea to avoid the main trail where so many trekkers were clogging the way. However, Lakpa forgot to tell us why the trail to Phortse was not well-traveled.

I'll tell you. Because it is a narrow, exposed bear of a trail, like a roller coaster running along the almost vertical side of a mountain. In many places, the trail was only two feet wide with a thousand-foot drop-off directly adjacent to the trail. In other places, whoever designed the trail had to build in extremely steep rock steps up and over buttresses and down the other side because the mountain was too vertical for even a two-foot path. All afternoon, we went up and down, over and around, up and down again, all the while looking out at sheer air only two feet to our left.

But the view was worth it. Sometime early that afternoon, we came around a corner and there on a ridge in the middle of the valley way below us was the monastery and bakery at Tengboche, shining in the sun. Ama Dablam remained gloriously majestic above the hills on the far side of the valley. To the south, the whole horizon was filled with snowcapped mountains, including Kantega and Thamserku.

Beautiful.

Late that afternoon, as the sun was beginning to drop behind the mountains, we came to a stupa on the ridge above Phortse. Looking down, we could see the tops of the roofs of the village, which sat on a wide ledge above a deep gorge. On the other side of the gorge we could see a very steep path leading up from the gorge.

"Our way out tomorrow," Lakpa said, pointing at the path.

But for now, it was all downhill to our rest stop for the night. Not a minute too early for me.

The proprietor at the teahouse in Phortse was a Sherpa friend of Lakpa's who had climbed to the top of Everest fourteen times. Lakpa readily acknowledged that his friend would surpass his total in a few years. These days, the quality of the guides seems to be based not on whether they have successfully reached the summit of Everest, but on how many times they have accomplished that feat. Of course, now that many of them are going up twice every year, the numbers are rapidly adding up. It will be hard for Lakpa to keep up with the younger Sherpas who already have a dozen or more summits and are adding to their totals every year.

For the first time in over a week, we ordered beers before dinner. We had only three days left. One short day back to Namche Bazaar, another short day to the town called Monjo, about halfway between Namche and Lukla, and the final day to Lukla. It wasn't exactly party time yet, but the beers tasted good after the difficult and long climb that day.

Our celebration was a bit premature. What we couldn't see from the teahouse was the depth of the gorge we had to cross early the next morning. It was like going down to the Colorado River from the central plateau of the Grand Canyon. We went down, down, and down, then down further for about forty-five minutes before finally reaching the river below and crossing a small bridge to the other side. The steep trail, which looked so brutal from the other side of the mountain, started about eight hundred vertical feet above us and so we had a significant climb just to get to where it started.

By now, I had become accustomed to things being tougher than advertised, so I just lowered my head and got on with the task at hand. George and I were pretty much glued together and took the climb at our own pace, maintaining visibility with the group, but not killing ourselves. I remember reaching one outcropping that had a few prayer flags and thinking that was the top of the trail, only to realize that it was barely above where we saw the trail start from the other side of the mountain. There was nowhere to go but up from that notch.

But about a half hour later we saw a large stupa and some buildings with a lot of prayer flags above us. We picked up the pace to get there just behind the leaders. This time we had reached a divide and the top of the trail. The place looked like a small ski village with chateau-like structures above and to the right of the trail. It had a few shops and a nice patio area to sit and munch on my next-to-last meat stick! The one drawback to this rest stop was the cool wind, which whipped across the divide and threatened to freeze the sweat I had worked up just getting up to this point.

The rest of the morning was a steady descent back to the main path to Namche, interrupted only by two pit stops during which Andrew and I managed to fertilize the local landscape with something other than yak dung. Unlike the yaks, we moved off the main path to make our deposits. George couldn't stop laughing when halfway through my squat, a lady on a mule came down the trail and got a full-moon view from her higher vantage point.

Oh, well, she'll never see me again anyway!

Just before lunch, we hit the main trail between Tengboche and Namche and soon arrived at a very popular spot with several restaurants and a huge patio facing back up towards Ama Dablam. Souvenir vendors were everywhere. Dozens of trekking groups were having lunch, enjoying the warm sun and the jovial atmosphere. It was a beautiful spot at the junction of several trails. We lingered there over lunch for more than an hour.

The afternoon hike was short and easy, along a wide, relatively flat sandy path. Everyone kept together, knowing that Namche Bazaar was only about an hour south and that we would not be doing any more climbing. I wondered why we did not take this easy path out of Namche on the way up the mountain!

There is not much to say about the rest of the trip back to Lukla. We only had to hike down the steep trail to the Lorje Bridge, this time watching dozens of other groups struggling up the hill and the switchbacks, then along the river and down to Phakding. This time we did not stop and just kept going until we reached the little village of Monjo, where I realized we had stopped for lunch on our first day out of Lukla. This time we spent the night there.

The only unique thing about Monjo was that they claimed to have homemade wine and the best apples in the valley. The apples were delicious. But their skins looked so mottled that I spent about fifteen minutes peeling them with a pocket knife before slicing them for the group. They went quickly.

The wine was not drinkable.

The next morning, we hiked for a couple hours back to Lukla. What seemed like a lot of downhill trekking when we left Lukla did not seem so bad on the way back up. Hopefully, we did not look as whipped as the hikers I had seen on the way down two weeks before.

The final push up to Lukla was quite steep, with cobbled paths and several sets of a hundred or more stone stairs. But we almost pranced up them, with George and Andrew vying to be the "first to the top." Before we knew it, we were going under the gateway into Lukla and waltzing down the narrow path through the town, checking out bars and restaurants at which to celebrate.

As it turned out, we ended up eating a yak burger at YakDonald's, having coffee and pastries at Starbucks, and drinking beers at several different bars. By the time we got back to the teahouse, we were blitzed.

Of course, we added another layer of inebriation with two bottles of wine carefully selected by Corrina, our wine expert. Cheese, crackers, and nuts completed our pre-dinner gorging.

That evening, the whole group celebrated dinner together. After the meal, Lakpa praised and handed out our tips to the assistant Sherpas, cook, porter, and yak driver who had made our lives so much easier for the last two weeks. The little porter, who claimed he was seventeen but looked to be barely thirteen, was hoisted horizontally across the table for group photos. Then Lakpa bought beers for the whole group.

"It's on Alpine Ascents," he said.

That night, as we tried to get some sleep, we listened to a cover band with a tone-deaf Nepalese lead singer blasting away at a nearby bar. He sounded like an *American Idol* contestant who most certainly was not going to Hollywood. Corrina must have had a few more glasses of wine that night because the next morning she said she had gone over to the bar and claimed the band singer was great!

The takeoff from Lukla was not half as exciting as the landing. We gathered speed, zoomed down the short strip of asphalt, and lifted off just before running out of runway, soaring out into the air above a two-thousand-foot drop-off.

Just like taking off an aircraft carrier! Not that I have ever done that...

Soon we were cruising at a higher altitude than on the way out, allowing us to see dozens of snowcapped peaks that had been hidden behind hills or obscured by clouds on the way to Lukla. Joining us on this ride was Dave Morton, another famous climber and former Alpine Ascents guide who had his wife and little boy with him. He and Melissa Arnot were both affiliated with Eddie Bauer's First Ascent group. Melissa was not able to get on our flight, but her guided climber, Neil, got the last ticket.

Dave Morton knew almost every peak we could see from the plane and had climbed some of them. As we went along, he gave us the identity, height, and a description of some of the more prominent peaks. There were so many of them, I cannot remember their names. But their shapes and awesomeness are forever etched in my mind.

It turned out that Neil was an excellent golfer, with somewhere around a three handicap. When I mentioned that I had arranged to play golf in Kathmandu when we returned, he immediately said, "I'm in!"

As the plane approached Kathmandu, we searched below for any sign of golf courses. Just before getting to the outskirts of the city, we spied some greens and fairways just to the left. The greens looked nice; the fairways were mostly brown.

Somehow there was something alluring about being able to play golf in Kathmandu. Maybe it was because I never expected Kathmandu to have any golf courses. Or maybe it was because I have never known anyone who claims to have played golf there. In any case, we were going to do it.

Back in Kathmandu, after being told that I would not be able to play golf at the country club unless I had a collared shirt, George and I went shopping. We checked out some shops close to the hotel, but I could not find anything suitable. We had heard that Lakpa was the lead spokesperson and model for the Sherpa mountain-clothing line, the Nepalese version of North Face or Mountain Hardware. So, we headed to its flashy store a few blocks over from the main drag. I figured it was a win-win if I could find a Sherpa shirt that would also serve as a golf shirt.

However, once inside the store, I could find nothing that fit. They had some beautiful collared polo-like shirts, but the XXLs were so tight, I could hardly breathe. Obviously, their sizes are calibrated to the Sherpa people, most of whom are under 5 feet, 6 inches, and weigh less than 145 pounds. Finding a shirt that would fit a somewhat-overweight, 6-foot-1-inch Westerner was a big problem.

I was about to give up when George told me that there were some older vintage shirts on a rack up on the third floor. Finally, I found a striped gray shirt that was big enough to wear. It was not exactly one I would have picked, but I was begging, not choosing, at that point. I also bought a Sherpa baseball cap for my son for Christmas and watched as George spent a fortune on a half dozen Sherpa beanies, shirts, a jacket, and a Sherpa catalog with a photo spread of Lakpa modeling most of the best clothing items.

George was not the only one spending a lot of money at the Sherpa store. Most of our group, and especially Kiyoko, managed to make it over to the Sherpa store and pull out the credit card for some large purchases. The clothes were nice, but I think most of the brisk business was mostly due to our affection for Lakpa.

The next day, I played golf in a pair of sneakers, trekking pants, and my new Sherpa shirt. Neil and Kiyoko joined me. We had a great time. It was an 18-hole layout, but had only sixteen greens, as two very large greens had multiple pins for different fairways, much like St. Andrews' Old Course layout in Scotland. The fairways were a bit rough and the roughs were essentially jungle, but the greens were very smooth and quite nice. Plus, every shot went about fifteen percent further than expected, as we were at over 8,000 feet in altitude. The best thing about the course was that we were one of only three or four groups playing, so we had no waiting on the tees and could play at our own pace.

That was a good thing. Neil was almost a scratch golfer, routinely hitting drives longer than 300 meters and usually hitting the greens in regulation. I used to play golf well, but over the years have gotten steadily worse and worse, since I don't have enough time to play regularly. So, I hoped to shoot in the 90s, with a few scattered pars. But I knew it would be mostly bogeys, double bogeys, or worse. Kiyoko hit the ball straight and short most of the time, occasionally connecting on a drive or fairway wood, but celebrating any hole for which she scored in the single digits.

As it turned out, we got a real workout. Some of the tees were so elevated that they had switchbacks just to get up to them. Four of the holes were in what seemed like another county, on the other side of a forest about a half mile wide. The holes were also a bit longer than traditional American courses, presumably to counteract the thinner air at the higher altitude. And hilly. Up and down all day long. And with monkeys running across the fairways, jumping through the trees, and stealing balls if the forecaddie was not careful.

But it was a lot of fun. Neil finally got a birdie on a long par four with a brilliant five-iron approach shot, and I finished strong with a par on the 18th hole, managing a nice drive and a cruise-missile four-iron up the hill to the elevated green. After watching Neil putt the ball off the green and into a bunker from just beyond me, I overcompensated and left my first putt at least ten feet short. Then with my knees shaking, I sunk my second putt and pumped my arm skyward.

A good thing it hit the hole and dropped or else I would have been in the sand trap as well.

Golf in Kathmandu! Who would have thunk?!

It was a nice finish to an outstanding trip to see the highest mountain in the world—one I will never forget.

3

Mt. Fuji

Sunrise with the Masses

The 5 A.M. alarm on my wristwatch came early on the morning of August 18, 2014. I had flown into Tokyo's Narita Airport non-stop from Atlanta with my family the day before. We arrived at our hotel at about 7 P.M. after an hour-long train ride into town on the Narita Express.

Now, barely twelve hours after arriving in Japan and completely screwed up by the thirteen-hour change in time zones, I had to meet my climbing group for Mt. Fuji in the lobby of the Keio Plaza Hotel in the posh Shinjuku district of Tokyo. Luckily, my wife had booked us into that same hotel, so all I had to do was get up, shower, get dressed, hoist my backpack onto my shoulders, and take an elevator down to the lobby by 6 A.M.

Physically, I was there on time. Mentally, my brain was still somewhere over the Pacific, watching movies on the small screen on the back of the plane seat in front of me.

Seven out of the twelve in my climbing group were already gathered around some chairs in the hotel lobby when I stepped off the elevator. The largest group was a family of five. I assumed they were Japanese, but soon learned that they were Taiwanese and lived in New Jersey—a mother, a father, and three teenage boys. Two of the boys looked to be twins. Then there were two young guys in their late twenties, one from Hungary and one from America. Shortly thereafter, an older couple in their mid-fifties arrived. They apparently had flown in the night before from Phoenix.

Our guide, Miles, of the Fuji Mountain Guides group, was a tall, thin fellow from Colorado, who said he had guided fifteen prior climbs on Fuji that summer. He handed me a standard disclaimer form, absolving him and the guide group from any liability for any injury on this "potentially hazardous" climb. I skimmed and signed the form, knowing that without signing it, I would be left behind.

The last two in our group, a couple of young ladies in their early twenties, arrived just after 6 A.M., frantically explaining that they got lost in the Shinjuku train station. This was a very plausible excuse given the size and scope of that station, which someone told me was the largest in the world. The night before, it had taken us over fifteen minutes to navigate our way through multiple levels and corridors from the arrival tracks for the express train from the airport to the West Gate nearest our hotel.

Very confusing, to say the least.

Once our group was complete, Miles called everyone together and quickly explained our itinerary. We would be traveling by bus for two and a half hours, with one rest stop, to the trailhead for the Subashiri trail on Mt. Fuji, a lesser traveled trail that was not reachable by train. Apparently, there are four major routes up Fuji. We would be taking one of the least-crowded ones—at least up to the huts at the "8th station." There, our path would merge with another major trail. Miles warned us that it may get crowded after that. He said he hoped for us to be on the trail by no later than 10 A.M. and added that it could take anywhere from five to seven hours to climb to the 8th station hut, depending on the fitness of the group. Then we would eat, rest, sleep, and get ready for the final ascent in the middle of the night, with the plan being to reach the crater rim before sunrise on the second day.

That sounded quite reasonable, and from the looks of it, I figured that I could keep up with most of the group. This did not appear to be an experienced group of climbers.

A few minutes later, we were on our way in a moderate-sized bus, which probably could hold up to twenty-four persons. Given that we had only twelve and a guide, we had plenty of room, even with our daypacks. When I climbed into the bus, most of the front seats were taken, so I went all the way back to the rear seats—four across...all to myself.

The young girls, named Duc (pronounced "Duke") and Briana, took the seats immediately in front of me. I quickly learned they were recent college grads from California who were currently teaching English to students in South Korea. They had been to Taiwan, then to Kyoto and

MT. FUJI

Tokyo, and were finishing up their trip with the Fuji climb. Since my daughter was doing essentially the same thing, teaching English to Japanese students in Okinawa, we struck up a good conversation on the long bus ride.

After about an hour, Miles told us to look to our right to see Mt. Fuji peeking out from the clouds. Unfortunately, only a small part of the crater rim was visible for maybe ten seconds before the whole mountain disappeared behind a wall of clouds. I was unable to get my camera out in time for even a "glimpse" shot.

Moments later, we stopped at the "rest stop," which was more like a mini-mall. Miles told us that, on clear days, Mt. Fuji was fully visible from the parking lot. On this occasion, there was nothing to look at but grey clouds.

Miles advised us to get something to eat, so I bought a pre-made sandwich and a Coke in the "Family Mart" and then returned to the bus. The pre-made sandwiches are quite tasty in Japan—white bread with a bit of meat, lettuce, and egg salad or cheese, and no crusts—cut in triangles with either two or three portions in each cellophane-wrapped package.

We turned off the main highway at Gotenba, a town after which one of the trails is named. Gotenba had a main four-lane thoroughfare, complete with a McDonald's, a Big Boy, and, surprisingly, a Denny's restaurant, among many other Japanese shops and businesses.

We did not stop.

Not far beyond Gotenba, we started up the lower regions of the mountain, eventually reaching a series of switchbacks and hairpin curves in the road, which seemed like they would never end. The bus almost conked out on the hills, but finally we reached our destination at the "5th station" trailhead of the Subashiri trail. There, the bus stopped in a parking lot beyond the trailhead and up a steep hill, making us walk down to the shops and cafés marking the beginning of our trek.

Miles led us to some rustic tables under some bamboo-shoot covers for some tea and water before starting out. Also, he had worked out a deal with the owner of the restrooms, allowing us to use them free of charge rather than for the normal fee of 200 yen (approximately $2). I immediately noticed there was a Coke vending machine across the path

from our tables, so I knew instantly that I would be able to quench my thirst adequately as soon as we got back down the mountain.
But first we had to climb it.

For the first quarter of a mile, the "trail" was a paved path with an occasional step up. Then we hit a series of steeper steps before reaching a gateway of sorts where a more natural trail through a dense forest started. At first, the trail was a gradual ascent. The only challenge was avoiding the sharp volcanic rocks poking up everywhere along the dark dirt trail. After about a half hour, the trail got steeper. The chatter among the climbers reduced significantly as we began to work and breathe harder.

Surprisingly, Don and Ann, the older couple from Phoenix, seemed to be the strongest climbers, leading the way through most of the early stages of the climb. I plodded along behind them at a steady pace, keeping my breathing under control and my heartrate relatively low. But, with the humidity high, I began to sweat profusely even though we were in completely shaded conditions under the thick trees. I also quickly realized that I was having to drink a lot of water to make up for the loss of fluids.

As we climbed higher, the group started splitting up. The Hungarian guy, named Victor, pushed ahead with the guide. At some point the girls went ahead of us, but then slowed and fell in behind us. The family from New Jersey and the other young guy were somewhere behind. However, the trail was well-marked and there was nowhere to go but up, so I did not worry that anyone would get lost. Red signs along the way had some English "subtitles" indicating how far we were from the next "station" and arrows pointing in the right direction for the Subashiri trail.

After almost one and a half hours, we reached the hut at the "6th station." The hut had both accommodations and a small café, with a shop selling drinks and small souvenirs. Already getting low on water, I bought a bottle of water for 300 yen and an ice-cold "popsicle" for 100 yen. The frozen treat came in a plastic tube, which could be broken in half so the contents could be sucked out of it. It was worth every yen. The instant thirst-quencher made me temporarily forget the humidity.

MT. FUJI

Duc and Briana arrived not long after me and asked me to take their pictures under the torii gate at the entrance to the 6th station. They saw my popsicle and quickly bought some for themselves.

The remaining members of the group arrived within ten minutes. Some of them had special hiking poles, a favorite souvenir for those climbing Fuji. At each station, climbers can get their prized walking sticks stamped with a burned imprint for that station level.

I preferred my regular hiking poles and knew they would never let me on the return flight with a five-foot-long stick. So, I skipped the ultimate Fuji souvenir.

Miles gave us a nice rest break before advising us to continue to drink plenty of water and to take it "slow and steady" up to the next station.

After adjusting my pack and hiking poles, I looked around for the couple from Phoenix and realized that they had already started up the mountain. Miles told me to go ahead if I wanted, so I gathered my things and headed after them.

But they were already out of sight.

For the next forty-five minutes or so, I hiked alone, working my way up through more trees and then reaching a series of rocky switchbacks. Victor, the Hungarian guy, passed me at some point. Shortly before I reached the 7th station, the girls showed up behind me temporarily before falling back again. They did not seem to keep a steady pace. I never did catch up with Don and Ann, who apparently must have kept up their fast pace all the way to the next station. The girls were close behind me as I reached it.

This time we had a longer rest as the remaining group took quite a while to catch up with us. The mountain and switchbacks were taking their toll.

Sadly, no popsicles were available at this station. So, I walked over to the snack and beverage window and bought a CC Lemon, a yellow-bottled Pepsi product, supposedly with a huge boost of vitamin C.

Very tasty.

Once he arrived, Miles insisted that everyone wait until the whole group was together. The twins from New Jersey arrived soon after the girls and looked no worse for the wear. It was at least fifteen minutes more before everyone else was accounted for. Their mother and the older brother already looked exhausted, but the father looked fine. He, of course, was staying close to his wife and seemed to be a bit frustrated over her pace, but he did not say anything.

After some good encouragement and a warning to make sure everyone had adequate sunscreen on, Miles told us that we would pass by one more hut, then would have a steep climb up to the 8th station. We had already been climbing for about four hours and the climb had been relatively easy except for the last thirty to forty minutes before the 7th station. I could easily see that the toughest part of that day's hike was just ahead—a series of long, steep, and sun-soaked switchbacks heading straight up the mountain on a trail that was all rocks and dust. No shade to be seen. And it was getting quite hot at two o'clock in the afternoon.

Frankly, I don't remember that much detail about the next two hours. It was a monotonous slog upwards on almost identical, dusty switchbacks, one after the other. At the top of each switchback, I would pause to chug a few sips of water to moisten my parched throat temporarily, check ahead to see that I was still within sight distance of Miles and the Phoenix couple, and check behind me to see if the girls were gaining on me. I was not in any hurry, but I wanted to keep a decent pace. Eventually, the trail got steep enough that I put it in low gear and started climbing with the slow rest steps that I had learned in some more serious mountain climbs. It resulted in a plodding pace, but one that I could continue almost indefinitely.

Just keep going, David. Never mind how slowly.

After about an hour, I looked up and could see the large hut at the 8th station, seemingly just ahead. It is always encouraging to get a visual of the day's destination. But in this instance, every time I completed another switchback, the hut looked just as far away. I put my head down and just kept going, one slow step after another. I was getting low on water, my legs ached, and I was ready to be done.

Miles, Don, and Ann slowly moved further ahead towards the end of the ascent to the 8th station. They were within two switchbacks of me for most of the way, but probably ended up four or five switchbacks ahead by the end. Victor was also ahead of me and the girls caught up with me just before we reached the hut. Or, I should say, huts—there was a cluster of at least five or six of them, interlinked by stairs or pathways.

The section right before the hut was almost all scree, followed by a series of steep rock steps up to a landing leading to a balcony in front of the hut.

Miles smiled as he motioned me up. I sighed as I looked at the steep scree and steps between him and me.

Nothing like a little torture on the legs at the end of a long hike.

Once on the balcony, I followed Miles around to the front of our "8th station" hut where I plopped down on a wooden bench across from a drink and snack window. Within seconds of my sitting down, Miles motioned to me from the open door to the hut. I did not want to get up, but apparently, I had no choice. Inside, he showed me a large dining room with three long tables and benches and a door to the sleeping area at the opposite end. There I had to trade my hiking boots for wimpy slippers to wear around the hut. But the slippers had to be immediately removed to enter the sleeping quarters.

Some things in Japan make no sense whatsoever.

A member of the hut's staff escorted me into the sleeping area. It was L-shaped with a series of mats and comforters on the bottom level and another set of mats and comforters on an upper rack. The place was designed to accommodate probably seventy-five climbers on this level. Stairs going up to a second floor presumably led to an equal number of "beds" where climbers could rest or sleep until the ultimate summit push.

The guy in charge of the hut pointed out a two-foot-wide spot on the top rack directly in front of me. Don and Ann and Victor were already lying down in their narrow spots to my right. A few minutes later the girls were assigned two spots beyond them. I was still very sweaty from the climb, so I merely perched my pack up on the rack and returned to the dining area with what was left of my water.

Rather than mess with the slippers, which were way too small, I walked out to the wooden bench in my socks and decided to stretch out. More accurately, I collapsed and napped for about ten minutes. At that spot, a nice breeze appeared. Soon I began to dry out and feel alive again.

A Coke for 400 yen, followed by another CC Lemon at the same price, helped immensely.

I did not really mind the fact that the price for drinks had gone up at each station. Somehow, throwing more yen away did not seem as expensive as spending U.S. dollars. All I know is that the equivalent of nine bucks to quench my thirst after busting my butt up a dry scree hill for the last two hours was worth every penny, a few yen, whatever.

As I sat there, sipping my CC Lemon, I noticed several climbers arriving from the other side of the hut. Then more arrived, dozens of them at a time. I strolled over to the other end of our hut and looked down. Below me was another trail, filled with climbers working their way up switchbacks for as far as I could see. It was the major trail that merged with ours at the 8th station.

For the next two to three hours, hundreds of climbers arrived from the other major trail. Presumably, all would be going for the summit at the same time as our group. Some of them filtered into our hut. Most worked their way up or down to nearby huts and disappeared within.

At around 5:30 P.M. our group gathered for dinner in the main dining room of the hut. The proprietors squeezed us together at one end of the table closest to the back wall, motioning us to move down toward the end near the sleeping room door. Seconds later, another group squeezed in beside us and soon the whole room was crammed with people.

We were given two choices for dinner—miso soup and rice, or curry and rice with a meat patty and "sausages." I opted for the curry, which was delicious but not bountiful enough to moisten all the rice. The meat patty was okay but the "sausages" were little bright-pink wieners that tasted awful. I pushed them aside and somehow convinced the kitchen staff to give me another spoonful of curry gravy to eat with the rest of my rice.

Excellent.

At the end of the meal, Miles announced that sunrise would be precisely at 4:55 A.M, so, we would be sleeping until 2 A.M. and should be prepared to be on the trail by 2:30 A.M. He said that it would take about one and a half hours to two hours to get to the crater rim, so we should have about thirty to forty-five minutes to spare at the top before the sun would come up over the horizon.

With warm food in my stomach and jet lag hitting me like a hammer, I retreated to the sleeping quarters, quickly nestling into my two-foot-wide space on the upper rack. I set my wristwatch alarm for 1:50 A.M. In moments, I was zonked out, probably snoring up a storm. I did not wake up until about 11 P.M., five hours later, when nature called.

Getting to the bathroom was a bit of a challenge. First, I had to scramble down from the upper rack in the dark without waking others up. Then I tiptoed down the narrow hallway to the dining room door. Opening the door, I realized that dozens of people were still up, drinking tea, playing cards, reading, or just talking to their friends. After finding some slippers that did not fit my feet, I maneuvered my way between the people and benches to the far door, then turned right along the windy balcony near the snack and drink window. Just beyond it, I ran into the line to the bathroom, probably thirty people deep.

Shit.

Luckily my body did not follow that thought. I was able to hold on for ten minutes, just long enough to reach the coin slots for the 200 yen coins necessary to enter the restroom before I froze in my thin t-shirt.

Another two bucks just to take a dump.

Once inside, the lady manning the place motioned me to the urinals and said, "Men," or something close to that, in broken English. I shook my head, pointing to the stalls and said I needed to "go #2," holding up two fingers. That completely confused her, but just then a door opened and I rushed in, ready to squat.

I did not sleep much after that, maybe napping for a few minutes at a time.

Beginning just after midnight, shadows started crossing in front of the one window to the sleeping area, and the sleeping room became a hub of activity as climbers with earlier ascent aspirations got up, messed with their gear, and headed out. Soon the line of climbers leaving the hut was non-stop, and the shadows crossing the balcony on the other side of the window became constant.

I hoped Miles was right about the time to get to the crater rim because a lot of people were leaving three or four hours before sunrise.

By 1:30 A.M., I noticed that Don, Ann, Victor, and the young guy next to me were gone, their packs with them. I checked my watch once again to make sure I had not overslept. Fully awake at this point, I figured I might as well get up.

I made another expensive trip to the bathroom, this time in a warmer top. The line to the bathroom was not as bad, but the line of climbers leaving the hut for the summit was crammed from one end of the hut to the other. More troubling, it was not moving.

Thirty minutes later, after downing a few granola bars and water, our team joined that line, ready to climb to the top.

As soon as we made the turn around the far corner of the hut, we instantly realized just how many people had already left for the summit. The entire mountain above us was lit up like a Christmas tree with white lights bobbling along as far up as we could see. The white lights from climbers' headlamps were interrupted periodically by glowing, colored sticks of mountain guides trying to wave people forward and upward at the top of each switchback.

It did not take a genius to figure out that we would be hiking hip-to-hip and backpack-to-chest with other climbers the whole way up. It was a pilgrimage of Japanese climbers with a few scattered foreigners, all with one goal…to reach the crater rim before sunrise.

The trail up to a hut just above the 8th station was not too bad, and we made reasonable time. The path up to the next hut, maybe a hundred vertical feet above that, was so jammed that we could hardly move. Miles moved into narrow gaps and squeezed by climbers, with Don, Ann, and me managing to stay with him. Others in the group who did not move quickly enough soon got cut off from us behind slower climbers.

Victor caught up to us by bounding up the rocks on the side of the trail. He still looked very strong. His strength was waning, however. About a half hour later, at about 12,000 feet altitude, Victor started feeling nauseous. Altitude sickness was taking its toll on the otherwise fittest climber in our group. He struggled the rest of the way, falling further and further back.

MT. FUJI

When we got to the second hut, Miles instructed us to wait in a wide area on the upper side of the hut, while he waited for the rest of the group to arrive. We did as we were told. It was no fun waiting in the dark at the very windy spot beyond the hut. I fully expected our group to regroup within minutes so, at first, I did not worry about the cold. However, it took almost fifteen minutes for the rest of our team to show up, one by one. The New Jersey mother finally arrived with her husband in tow. By then, we had all pulled out Gore-Tex shell jackets to ward off the wind and at least stay relatively warm. I did not realize it at the time, but some of the members of our team besides Victor were also already feeling the altitude. They were struggling to stay up even at the stagnant pace.

I was a bit frustrated by the number of people who passed by us during that fifteen minutes. Several times I considered bolting from the group and just heading up on my own. But I resisted the urge and waited. Finally, all our team members were together. After stuffing my shell jacket back into my backpack, I fell in line once again behind Miles, Don, and Ann as we headed onward and upward.

The next hour and a half was an exercise of sheer patience as we waited, then squeezed through narrow gaps in the crowd, and watched the white lights stream upwards above us in a never-ending series of zigzags. Every ten minutes or so, I checked my watch as we stood waiting for the crowd to inch up to the next switchback. Three-thirty in the morning passed and we were still a long way from the top. Three-forty-five in the morning passed and we had moved only another two switchbacks in fifteen minutes. The white lights still loomed way above us. Four o'clock came and I decided that we probably would not make it to the crater rim for the sunrise. There seemed to be no chance. By 4:30 A.M., I was sure we would not get there in time. We were still mired behind hundreds of climbers crammed in and blocking the trail.

But then Miles said, "We're almost there—one more switchback and a bunch of stairs."

I looked up and could just see the top. Just then a glimmer of light started coming over the horizon and the path became illuminated. The pace of the climbers in front of us picked up, and we made our move. Miles turned the corner at the end of the last switchback and practically bolted through a gap between the climbers. We followed him up the right side of the rocky steps, moving to the left side halfway up. Towards the end, Don, Ann, and I fell a bit behind. We then turned to our left and saw Miles standing on a wall to the right of the last fifteen or twenty steps. We hustled up and soon were standing next to him just beside a grey stone monolith with Japanese writing vertically etched into the sides.

The crater rim. Fujisan.

I looked at my watch. It was 4:48 A.M., seven minutes before the sun was scheduled to rise.

Miles told us to enjoy the sunrise from anywhere we wanted on the crater rim and to meet back at the gray monolith at 5:15 A.M. We would then re-gather as a group and get some breakfast. He would wait for the rest to make it up to the top.

Don took off through an alley of souvenir shops and cafés that lined that part of the crater rim towards a hill at the other end where hundreds of people were gathered to see the sun rise. Ann and I followed in quick pursuit. Soon the three of us were standing on a windy ridge beyond all the buildings where we had a clear view of the horizon, with our cameras poised for the penultimate "dawn at Mt. Fuji's summit" photo.

Below us and just to the left of where we expected the sun to show up was a wooden torii, an entrance gate that reminded me of the signposts for dude ranches out West. I adjusted my camera so that I could get pictures with the torii and the sun when it rose above the horizon.

As I looked around, I realized there were probably a thousand or more climbers just in that small area of the crater rim, all waiting for the same thing.

But before the sun rose, we needed to get our jackets back out to stay warm and shield us from the formidable wind that whipped up across that ridge.

Finally, at precisely 4:55 A.M., a sliver of orange appeared on the horizon and the click of cameras began. For the next five minutes, as the bright orb slowly showed itself against the pink clouds, I snapped photos along with the thousands of other amateur photographers in front of and beside me.

A glorious scene... with more camera clicks than at a Hollywood red carpet event!

Sadly, none of my photos came out well. It is never the best choice to take photos into the sun.

We then agreed that we wanted to do the whole crater rim trail, including to the true summit on the opposite side of the crater rim, where multiple radio antennae and a power station of sorts had been built. The circuit around the crater rim was part of the tour package, and Miles had indicated that if anyone wanted to do it, he would lead the hike after the group had breakfast. As it turned out, we were the only ones who wanted to do it.

When we rejoined Miles a few minutes later at the grey stone pillar, we were surprised to learn that no one else from our group had made it to the crater rim yet. They had all stopped to take photos further below once the sun came over the horizon.

Eventually, all members of our team arrived. The twins showed up shortly after we rejoined Miles. Victor arrived a few minutes later and looked whipped, with his head hanging almost down to his shoulders. He was clearly nauseous and feeling the altitude. The girls and the young American guy arrived tired, but in good spirits. Miles went down to find the others.

About ten minutes later, he returned with the remaining members of the New Jersey family. Miles quickly announced that it was time for breakfast. He led us to the third or fourth café on the right side of the alley, which was starting to clear as climbers headed down the mountain. We pushed through the souvenir shoppers in the front part of the café and sat down on a couple of wooden benches lined up in the back. I looked around and saw that our group was a bedraggled bunch. Victor was clearly under the weather, the girls suddenly looked extremely tired, the New Jersey family was just holding on, and the young American guy looked spent.

I felt fine, but was famished.

A few minutes later, Miles verbally described about eight different choices on the menu, all variations of miso or noodle soup or curry/rice combinations. Still feeling good in my stomach after the evening meal the night before, I opted for curry and rice again. This time the little beef patty with it turned out to be quite tasty. I wolfed down the meal in about three minutes.

After breakfast and our well-deserved rest at the café, most everyone looked better except Victor, who had not been able to eat anything and still was hanging his head.

Miles told everyone where the restrooms were located (at the end of the alley of shops on the left) and how to get to the "down" trail back to the 8th station. The trail going down from the top of the mountain is different than the trail we came up. It starts just beyond the end of the alley of shops and is a wide path consisting entirely of deep scree, with a few loose, larger rocks here and there. The scree trail is lined with ropes on both sides, so no one could get lost on the way down. It looked like a downhill ski slope, except with scree instead of snow.

Miles told the rest of the group that they could check out the souvenir shops for fifteen to twenty minutes, but then they should start down and wait at the hut at the 8th station.

He then turned to me, Don, and Ann and said, "Let's get started around the crater rim. It should take a little over an hour. Then we will hustle down and catch up with the others."

With that, we left the others and headed out beyond the ridge where we had watched the sun rise, and began circling the crater rim clockwise. Miles set a brisk pace, which was very welcome after the plodding ascent all morning.

For me, the walk around the crater rim was the most enjoyable and spectacular part of the climb. We could look down into the crater where large sections were still covered in snow and over the outside of the mountain, straight down seven thousand vertical feet to the valleys below.

On one occasion, we had to wait a few minutes for a huge group of Japanese folks to pass by us on a narrow part of the rim trail as they completed a counterclockwise circuit. Otherwise, the traffic on the trail was sparse.

About a quarter of the way around we came to another major trail near what Miles described as the highest post office in the world. The rim trail dipped down to that structure. Beyond it we could see the power stations and the large radio antennae at the highest point of the crater rim.

Anxious to get to the true summit, Miles, Don, and Ann picked up the pace. I stopped to snap a few photos of the summit and fell about twenty yards behind as they climbed the steep scree-covered path up to the power station. I reverted to my rest-step technique on that section to avoid getting out of breath too badly. Soon we were all at the top of the path.

A series of steps led up to a balcony on the left where climbers were taking pictures next to another grey stone pillar marking the summit. The right side of the steps was covered with climbers waiting in line for "summit" photos.

Don, Ann, and I decided that time was short, so we went up the left side of the stairs to the balcony and tried to take our "summit" photos with the stone pillar in the background. But the sun was behind the pillar and again they did not come out well.

Let's just say that standing at the true summit with a couple dozen people all lined up like shoppers waiting to sit on Santa's lap at a shopping mall was a bit anticlimactic after reaching the crater rim and watching the sunrise.

We rejoined Miles at the bottom of the stairs, then raced around the rest of the crater rim, going slightly downhill most of the way. Just before reaching the alley of shops where we started, we crossed a very windy and cold knoll. I just pushed through it without adding any layers and soon we were back in the sheltered alley of shops. We made a quick stop at the restroom, then headed down the scree trail towards the 8th station.

Downward scree trails are a lot of fun if the scree dust is sufficiently deep. The best technique is to walk briskly and dig in the heels of one's boots. The scree gives way, allowing your boot to slide forward. Each step slides into almost two steps, similar to the accelerated pace on a moving sidewalk. With the right conditions and an energetic stride, one can essentially ski straight down the mountain slope in one's boots.

This works only if the scree dust is deep and soft. Where the underlying trail is rock hard, with only a dusting of scree and gravel on it, the path becomes treacherously slippery. This happened in a couple of places on the way down to the 8th station. I was glad to have two hiking poles to maintain my balance. Those with no poles or just the souvenir wooden poles had a lot more difficulty navigating those areas.

Since most of our group had left the crater rim before us and we were all going to regroup at the 8th station, I decided to zoom down the trail as fast as I could. I had learned the technique on Aconcagua. Soon I was passing almost everyone on the trail who was not "skiing" down. Miles stayed with Don and Ann, who were walking at a good clip, but who had not climbed down on scree before. I looked back up at the end of some of the downward switchbacks and could still see them above me. But after a while I got far enough ahead that they were no longer in sight.

I reached the 8th station in less than forty-five minutes and was surprised to learn that some of our group had not yet gotten there. Victor was sitting on the wooden bench across from the snacks and drinks window, still looking sick. The girls and younger American guy were inside the dining room, having arrived a few minutes before. Apparently, the entire New Jersey contingent was still coming down, though I had not noticed passing them coming down the trail.

Don and Ann arrived a few minutes later and said that Miles was helping with the older teenage boy and the New Jersey mother, who had "altitude sickness" and were not even able to climb the steep steps up to the 8th station hut to rest and recover.

Not good.

But several minutes later, Miles stuck his head into the dining room, assuring us the New Jersey crew would be alright. He instructed us to pack up all our things and get ready to go down the mountain. He would be shuttling back and forth between us and the New Jersey family to make sure everyone got down okay.

MT. FUJI

When we reached the spot below the hut where the scree trail came down from the top, the mother and older son were lying on the side of the trail with their heads in the father's lap. They did not look good at all, but Miles motioned us away.

"Take the trail past the huts, turn right down the Subashiri trail at the red sign just beyond the huts, and wait for me at the 7th station below. Don't go straight down the main trail, or you will end up at the wrong trailhead. There is a red sign at the junction and go right."

The red sign was just as he described. We took the right fork, and from that point on, we were back on the much less-crowded trail headed for the Subashiri trailhead. Once again, the trail was almost all deep, soft scree with ropes on both sides, so there was no danger of anyone getting lost without a guide leading the way.

At this point, the twins, the girls, the American guy, Don, Ann, and I were on our own. Miles was back with Victor, the New Jersey parents, and their older son.

I was anxious to get off the mountain and wanted to zoom down. But without a guide in the picture, I stayed within sight distance of the group, stopping for water breaks and waiting for them to catch up. Periodically, some big caterpillar machines came up the trail, spewing dust all over us as they smoothed the wide pathway. We just had to turn our faces away and cover up as they went by. The best thing about that was that the machines left excellent tread marks on the path that were uniform and solid, making our footing very secure on those sections.

It took about thirty minutes to reach the 7th station. Don, Ann, and I had moved ahead by a few minutes and sat at some tables and chairs on a little patio area and watched the others come down. The sun was out and the warmth felt good on our faces and back. However, soon I realized I was getting too hot. Though I knew we were cruising down scree slopes, I unzipped the bottom sections of my trekking pants, leaving me with just shorts on.

While baring my legs made the heat more comfortable, in hindsight, it was not the best decision, as I did not have any gaiters. Consequently, rocks and sand got into my boots as I skied down the next scree slopes.

After a while, Victor arrived at the 7th station hut on his own, feeling a bit better as he dropped down in altitude. Miles and the older members of the New Jersey family were still nowhere in sight.

After resting for about fifteen minutes, we saw Miles walking briskly down the trail above us. Upon arrival, he explained that the New Jersey mother and older son were struggling and that Miles and the father would be staying with them.

He then pointed us in the right direction. "The scree trail will bypass the 6th station completely. Do not try to find it. And make sure you have enough water because it will be hot and dry the rest of the way."

"Just go at your own pace," he said. "The trail goes down to the right, then turns sharply to the left and goes straight down until you get into the trees. Turn right at the junction with the trail we came up. It will take you straight down to the trailhead. I will meet you there."

I was reminded of the old comment, "You can't miss it." Ironically, that comment always seemed to precede one getting hopelessly lost.

Miles then turned and headed back up the trail.

"Hot and dry" was an understatement. I would describe the trail down from the 7th station as more like "parched and arid." It was all scree, mixed in with some loose rocks the size of bowling balls. Our challenge was to avoid the rocks and just keep our balance as we boot-skied down.

Don and Ann were picking up the technique, so we moved ahead of the others after the first ten minutes. Soon they were completely out of sight behind and above us. When we reached the left turn and the straight-down-the-mountain section, I decided to push myself. After all, I was in training for a Grand Canyon rim-to-rim-to-rim in October and knew that going downhill was a big part of that trek.

A couple of guys and a very fast Japanese girl "skied" past me near the top of the straightaway. I fell in behind them and tried to keep up. I was not able to, but in the process, I got considerably ahead of Don and Ann. I was tempted just to go on by myself, but I did not want to desert them. So, I zoomed down the section as fast as I could, then waited at a couple slight turns in the trail for them to arrive. They were doing a great job, but I sensed that they were more comfortable going up the mountain than coming down, especially at above-normal speeds.

MT. FUJI

The scree straightaway seemed to last forever, but finally disappeared into a grove of trees where I waited in the shade until Don and Ann joined me. I removed my baseball hat, thinking that I would not need it the rest of the way. I mistakenly thought we were getting really near the trailhead. However, the grove of trees was just a small oasis. After a few minutes of shade, we were back on the wide-open scree downhill course in the hot, dry sun.

This time, I really picked up the pace. At the same time, Don and Ann were slowing down. I literally left them in the dust and just kept going, pushing myself to the limit. We had been coming down from the 8th station for almost three hours and I was ready to get to the trailhead.

After another ten or fifteen minutes, I looked down and saw several climbers resting near another grove of trees. There the trail turned to the right again with a sign pointing that way. I quickly sped down, looked to my right, and saw a nice little makeshift café with a drink stand and plenty of shaded benches. Twenty or thirty climbers had stopped and were enjoying drinks and snacks.

I again thought we must be very close to the trailhead—maybe ten minutes down through the trees. But the red sign for the Subashiri trail pointing to the right said it was still forty minutes to the 5th station.

Dejected, I decided to relax in the shade with a fresh Coke from the drink stand, and I pulled a Snickers bar from my pack. The Coke was lukewarm, but still tasted good. The Snickers was halfway melted, but went down quickly. I figured as long it was going to be another forty minutes, I may as well wait for Don and Ann, so we could finish the mountain together. Meanwhile, I pulled my boots off and emptied them of all the scree and sediment that had filtered into them on the scree slopes.

Next time I'll take gaiters.

Ann and Don arrived after about ten minutes. I invited them to sit and cool off a bit, telling them the sign said it was another forty minutes to the trailhead.

They groaned, but chose just to keep going without a rest stop. Soon we were in the shaded forest for good. We reached the junction with the "up" trail, took a right as instructed, and began working our way down the knobby volcanic rock and black dirt trail we had come up the day before.

It was more difficult coming down that section, as there were a lot of deep downward steps, putting a lot of pressure on the knees and thighs. Don and Ann took it very carefully and I found myself waiting for them again, even though I had slowed my pace considerably.

At one point, three guys and a little girl, maybe six years old, passed us, cheerfully chattering away. The little girl looked like a pro coming down through the rocks.

"That girl is going to be a helluva climber someday," I said to Ann.

"I think she already is. I wish I had young legs like that," she responded.

At two minutes past 11 A.M., we finally passed under the entrance gate to the trail and headed down the paved path to the little alleyway of shops, cafés, and restrooms marking the 5th station trailhead.

Miles's café friend motioned us to the tables under the bamboo shoots. I set my pack down, made a beeline to the bathroom, purchased a nice cold Coke from the vending machine across from our table, and then relaxed on the wooden benches. Sweat was still pouring from my pores, but I didn't care. I had climbed Mt. Fuji and returned to the bottom safely and on time.

Life is good.

We had no idea how long it would take the rest of our group to arrive. After about thirty minutes and still with no one in sight, we ordered some food. I opted for a mushroom pizza and Don and Ann got some rice dish shaped like Mt. Fuji, complete with little red peppers symbolizing erupting lava on top. My pizza was surprisingly good, though just about anything edible would have been welcome, as I was starving again.

About an hour after we reached the end of the trail, Victor and the twins arrived, followed shortly thereafter by the girls and the American guy in their souvenir headbands with the red circle and Japanese letters.

The three ninjas!

Victor was back to normal, the altitude sickness completely gone after he descended seven thousand vertical feet. The twins were happy, talkative, and excited about having finished the climb. But their faces told me they were a bit worried about their mother and brother. They all ordered food and soon we had a happy group, replenishing our energy levels.

Miles appeared around 1 P.M. I was surprised to see him alone, but he quickly explained that the rest of the family was just behind and feeling tired but much better. They showed up about ten minutes later.

Bottom line: Twelve hikers and a guide made it up to the top of Mt. Fuji and all thirteen returned to the trailhead safe and sound. A successful climb!

Fuji was not a difficult climb compared to others I have done, but it was a true pilgrimage, a community experience, a wonderful trek to the top of Japan with thousands of folks of all ages to share the experience at the summit.

And climbing Fuji was a nice start to a great trip to see Japan with my daughter, wife, and son. On Fuji, communication in English was not a problem. For the rest of the trip, it was very nice to have a daughter who could speak Japanese to everyone in Kyoto, Hiroshima, Kyushu, and Okinawa.

But that is another story involving eating raw horsemeat, bathing naked in public baths, and experiencing, through somber museums and building remnants, the horrors of the nuclear bomb that helped end World War II, among other highs and lows of Japanese culture.

4

Inca Trail/Machu Picchu

A Rocky Road

Machu Picchu has long held a mystical, magnetic pull on my adventuresome spirit. Something about National Geographic photos of the Incan ruins high on a mountain in the middle of Peru, surrounded by jungles and jagged mountains, always intrigued me. Stories about the famous Inca Trail trek to the Sun Gate above Machu Picchu have always been compelling—and for me have promised an adventure on their own.

"One day, I am going to hike the Inca Trail to Machu Picchu and see it for myself," I kept telling my wife for years, indeed decades. But I never got around to planning it. One problem is that my wife, Kim, wanted to see Machu Picchu also, but she had no desire to step foot on the Inca Trail. One cold night with me in a small pup tent in the Smokies with Vienna sausages for breakfast a long time ago ended any further overnight camping trips for Kim. So, I never could figure out how to plan a trip so that she could see Machu Picchu while not doing the Inca Trail with me.

Some friends told me about special treks connected with Machu Picchu that involved hiking, but staying at luxurious lodges each night. That had great appeal. Upon investigation, I learned that the cushy, luxury lodge trek followed the Salkantay route, named after a majestic, snowcapped mountain in the area. But Kim did not want to do that either. Her decision was probably a good one, since that route involves an ascent to a pass at over 15,500 feet in altitude and five or six days of hiking—even more challenging than the Inca Trail.

Unfortunately, no itinerary I saw quite fit our needs—with one spouse wanting to do the Inca Trail and the other spouse just wanting to ride the train and bus to the entrance and see the Machu Picchu ruins. So, I kept putting the trip off.

But a plan finally came together in 2015. My oldest brother, Brent, told me that Machu Picchu was one of the last places on his bucket list. His wife wanted to go see it as well, but she did not want to hike the Inca Trail. So, Brent and I could hike the trail, our wives could hang out in Cusco or the Sacred Valley for a couple of days, and we could all meet up at Machu Picchu on the fourth day. The perfect formula!

Brent worked with a company called SA International to streamline the itinerary. We settled on doing the standard Inca Trail with initial nights in Lima and Cusco, and a few nights in Aguas Calientes and Cusco on the back end with our wives. Our wives would spend an extra day in Lima and several days in the little town of Ollantaytambo in the Sacred Valley while we hiked. They would then ride the train to Aguas Calientes on the third day, spend a night there, then ride the bus up to Machu Picchu and meet us at the visitors' gate on our fourth and final morning on the trail. We would all be together for the tour of Machu Picchu and for three days in Cusco and its surroundings.

We booked the trip six months ahead of time, aiming for July 2015, but after dawdling to get our deposit in, the trip was moved to August. Apparently, the permits to hike the Inca Trail get snapped up fast. By the time we finally pulled the trigger, all the July permits had been issued. Fortunately, we were still able to schedule the hike at the end of August before the dry season in Peru expired.

The flight to Lima on August 22 was direct from Atlanta—on Delta—six hours. We watched a couple movies and landed at about midnight at Callao Airport just north of Lima. Outside passport control, Inti, a native Peruvian with an English accent, met us with sign in hand and quickly escorted us to a van parked in an outside lot near the terminal.

My initial impression of Peru and Lima was that it is a well-organized, well-maintained, and civilized place. Inti told us Peru had about thirty million citizens, eleven million in the Lima metropolitan area. So, over a third of the country's population was housed within about a fifteen-mile radius from the center of Lima.

Traffic was light at midnight. We exited the airport and soon we were zooming along an expressway with the Pacific Ocean to our right. The expressway ran along the shore, which was rocky with occasional narrow "beaches" of dark sand. To our left was a vertical wall of dirt, perhaps three hundred feet high, sometimes encased in wire to prevent rock slides coming onto the highway. All the developed areas were up on the cliff and in the flat areas inland from there. Lima will have no problem if global warming causes the oceans to rise a few feet. Several miles ahead at the other end of the shoreline was a mountain with a lighted cross on it. Our speed was controlled not by speed-limit signs, but by sporadic washboard-like cuts in the road, which automatically caused the driver to slow down every mile or two.

After about thirty minutes, I saw a huge Marriott Hotel up on the cliff above us, indicating that we had reached the Miraflores suburb of Lima. Just past the Marriott, we made a U-turn and then took a sharp right turn off the highway and onto a steep cobblestone avenue working its way up a canyon that split the cliff. Why the road was paved with cobblestone was not clear, but it certainly kept us awake as we went up the hill. Minutes later the van pulled up in front of the Radisson Hotel, our initial home away from home. Since it was already after 1 A.M., we went directly to bed.

For some reason, I awoke at 7 A.M. the next morning, ready for action. I felt like going for a run and managed to get dressed and exited the room without waking Kim. I had no idea where anything was, but upon leaving the hotel, I could see far enough around the corner to realize that with one left turn at the nearest corner, I would be heading directly towards the ocean. Soon I was jogging along a road that ran parallel to the cobblestone stone hill we had ascended from the beachside expressway. Amazingly, clay tennis courts, workout facilities, and a small soccer court were built into the side of the canyon. They were all already being used on that Sunday morning. Everywhere I looked, people were walking their dogs, riding bikes, or just exercising.

Does no one sleep in on Sunday mornings in Peru?

I ran three or four blocks until I reached a road running parallel to the ocean on the top of the cliff. A large yellow bridge with plastic glass skylights curving above its sidewalks spanned the wide canyon with the cobblestone avenue below. I ran across the bridge on the narrow sidewalk and immediately came to the Park D'Amor, a small terraced park with mosaic tiles everywhere and a rather pornographic statue in the middle with carved lovers in a carnal embrace.

Okay, that leaves nothing to the imagination at seven-fifteen in the morning!

Going north, I ran through a series of nicely appointed parks, some with grass, some with flowers, all with some exercise stations, and the final one with a large lighthouse with multiple flagpoles and the Peruvian flag flying proudly in the wind. At one park, which we later realized was a jumping-off point for hang-gliders and parasailers, a group of Asians were exercising with sticks and some sort of ju-jitsu.

All in all, it was an interesting scene, full of active participants, running, exercising, walking their dogs, or just watching the proceedings early on a Sunday morning!

After I returned to the hotel and asked for a local map from the concierge, I realized that without knowing it, I had found one of the primary tourist areas for Miraflores: the clifftop parks, full of lovers, pedestrians, dogs, and bicycles.

Kim was awake when I returned, so shortly thereafter we joined Brent and Mpopo, his wife, on the second floor for breakfast. They had been there for a while already, having ordered hot plates from the waitress to supplement the sumptuous fruit, cheese, sliced meats, and cereal buffet. The hot-plate menu was impressive and the presentation of the dish I selected was even more so. I quickly learned that Peru has a reputation for fine cuisine.

Once my appetite was satisfied, I told them about the parks. We all agreed to stroll down through them after breakfast, then head into the center of Miraflores, where there were some churches and marketplaces. A friend of Brent's who worked at the USAID office in Lima planned to meet us at 1 P.M. at our hotel to take us to lunch, so we had about three hours to sightsee on our own.

The second trip through the ocean-view parks was a bit anticlimactic for me, but I enjoyed playing the tour guide as much as the others would let me. We strolled through all the same areas, but took our time, enjoying the details and watching the people…and the dogs racing around some of the grassy areas. Mpopo tried out some of the exercise stations. Brent and I watched as the surfers tried to catch some waves.

At one point, we noticed thousands of birds flying across the water perhaps a hundred yards off shore. The black cloud of birds stretched as far to the south and the north as we could see. It was a massive migration that seemed never to end. Strange, but incredible.

On the way back, we took a left before the canyon and headed inland towards the Miraflores city center. We passed a hospital and a series of apartment buildings before reaching several shops and restaurants, culminating at a roundabout with a two-story McDonald's on the left and a posh Burger King on the right. American fast-food restaurants—they are everywhere around the globe! Despite my pleas, Kim refused to go into either establishment.

Mambo music filled our ears as we passed the McDonald's. There, the next block in the road had been closed and several hundred Peruvians were dancing in the streets, trying to follow the moves of some long-haired Yanni lookalike dude up on a stage. It was not long before Mpopo joined in the dancing, showing some good moves and rhythm, something I clearly lack. I did not join in, as I was already sweating like a pig in the humidity and heat of the morning.

Once past the dancers, we crossed over to our right and found a series of "artisan" markets, intermingled with what I commonly refer to as "ticky-tacky" souvenir shops. Purses, scarves, blankets, sweaters, silver items, and leather belts and hats dominated that scene. Everything was supposedly alpaca or, even better, baby alpaca. I tried on a couple of sweaters and quickly realized that an XL in Peru is more like a medium in the U.S. Most of the places did not have XXLs, so I was out of luck. I saw one beautiful silver and dark-wood Christmas nativity scene with five nice pieces, but Kim talked me out of buying it. She also talked me out of buying some neat "alpaca" scarves with built-in beanies after the poor young lady had dropped her price by thirty percent to get me interested. Of course, it's generally a mistake to buy gifts and souvenirs on the first day of the trip because then you must carry them around in your luggage for a couple of weeks.

After a few hours of "shopping" we headed back to the hotel, but not before checking out the local cathedral and traipsing through a popular park that was home for hundreds of kittens. The rumor was that the park had been infested with rats and a few cats had been brought in to take care of the problem. Now the park is completely overrun with cats of all varieties. The people feed them, and the park is now famous not for the Kennedy after whom it is named, but for its feline inhabitants.

The upscale, popular lunch place selected by Sam, Brent's USAID friend, was packed by the time we arrived there. It was located just a few blocks further inland from the markets where we had been shopping that morning. Sam's girlfriend, a young lady from Quito, Ecuador, who also works at the USAID office in Lima, had reserved a table for us and was already there.

The treat for the meal was the guinea-pig platter, which Sam ordered as an appetizer. Guinea pig is a specialty in Peru and I planned to try it in Cusco, but there was no use waiting. And frankly, it was nothing worth waiting for. The guinea pig was sliced into squares, consisting of a heavy layer of greasy skin, tasting much like pork rind. Below that was about an eighth of an inch of meat over small bones. It was like eating an extremely thin chicken breast with a pork rind on one side and bones on the other. Tasty, but hardly worth the effort or the expense.

The rest of the meal was outstanding, filling, and extremely slow. By 4 P.M., I just wanted to get out and walk it off.

We said thanks and goodbye to Sam and his girlfriend, and headed to the central historic district in a taxi. Sam warned us about cab drivers potentially high-jacking tourists. He advised us to get into cabs only with certain markings and to take a photo of the driver as we got into the cab. I thought he was being a bit paranoid, but I held my breath until we were let off at the main plaza in the center of Lima.

The main square was surrounded by a huge cathedral, a palace that reminded me slightly of Buckingham Palace, with its metal fences, gates, and guards (complete with changes of the guard at designated times), and several other nicely appointed buildings. The cathedral had statues of bishops on its roof, one with an enormous eagle-like bird perched on it. Since the ladies had a "city tour" scheduled with a guide the next day, we did not go in anywhere. Instead, we enjoyed strolling around the historical district for a few hours, watching people and pigeons, window shopping, and generally getting a feel for the city.

Behind the main plaza was an area filled with young people listening to live music, sipping on ices, and doing robotic dancing in circles built for an intimate audience of about a hundred people. Other sections were filled with blocks or round boulders, simply to provide seating of some sort. There were thousands of locals enjoying the evening, milling around or just sitting there. As dusk approached, we realized that we were almost the only tourists left, so we headed back to the main plaza and grabbed a properly marked taxi for the trip back to Miraflores. I don't think any of us took a photo of the driver!

The next day, after a quick breakfast at the Radisson, Brent and I were picked up by Inti and a driver and fought the traffic back to Callao and the Lima Airport. Check-in was quick and soon we were at our gate. The flight to Cusco was spectacular. The skies were clear and the snowcapped Andes mountains were plentiful beneath us. We had many "ahhh" moments during the one-and-a-half-hour flight.

On this flight, we were treated to our first corn "nuts," a poor imitation of peanuts made from dried corn kernels. Dry and tasteless except for a bit of salt. Brent also tried Inca Cola, a sickeningly sugary cola reminiscent of cream soda—but sweeter! I declined a sip after a simple sniff gave me a sugar high.

The descent into Cusco was interesting, to say the least. Cusco sits in a three-sided bowl of mountains. We entered the bowl on the open end, flying low above endless orange-tiled roofs towards the closed end of the bowl. The airport runway was clearly visible in front and to the left of us. But we were not lined up to land and soon the runway was to our left. We passed it and flew dangerously close to a hill on the closed end of the bowl before making a sharp U-turn to our left. Looking out the windows, Brent and I could see the tops of roofs a few hundred feet below us. After making a hundred-and-eighty-degree turn, the plane quickly descended the rest of the way and landed in the opposite direction from which we had come. I guess they make that same harrowing landing a dozen or more times a day, but to us, it was hardly routine.

Once on the ground, we waited for about ten minutes before they waved the plane in for unloading. The Cusco Airport has only five gates, so waiting ten minutes for a spot to park is typical. Someone told me that they are building a new airport to handle all the tourist needs for Machu Picchu, but we did not see any signs of construction.

This time, a young lady named Julia met us at baggage claim and led us to a van for the ride to the Maytaq Hotel near the main plaza in Cusco. It was a twenty-five-minute ride from the airport, primarily up a long boulevard flanked with shops and businesses. At the top of the avenue, we turned right, passing the main plaza on our left before making another right and a quick left. The hotel was not well-marked. Inside, it was equally unimpressive, and our room on the third floor was tiny. But the hotel was clean and well-situated, only a block from the main square. It also had a nice garden patio on the third floor with great views of at least three sets of church steeples, domes, and towers.

Cusco is at approximately 11,000 feet in elevation, but neither Brent nor I had any issues with the altitude. We wasted no time before checking out the main plaza, snapping photos of the cathedral, the Jesuit church, the statue of the Incan king in the middle of the square with the fountain. I declined to photo the KFC, the McDonald's, and the Starbucks. Kudos to the city for prohibiting any golden arches, red or yellow lettering, or any other advertising that did not blend in with the historical feel of the plaza. In fact, the McDonald's was not noticeable at all until we walked right in front of it and peered into the windows below a covered-arch walkway on the northeast end of the square.

Brent and I were famished, so we stopped for lunch at the corner pizza joint at the main intersection just south of the plaza, grabbing a table next to the window so that we could watch the pedestrians strolling by. There appeared to be a lot of Europeans there on vacation, many of them in hiking or athletic gear. Cusco is the stepping-off point for a lot of treks and adventures, not the least of which are Machu Picchu and the Inca Trail.

The pizza was great—the beer not so much. But at that point anything would have tasted good. Somewhere I read that drinking beer/alcohol is not good for preventing altitude sickness, but I did not have so much as a slight headache, so I did not worry about the dietary recommendations.

INCA TRAIL/MACHU PICCHU

After lunch, we walked down the main avenue to the Sun Temple, an old Incan complex on which a church and monastery had later been built. Apparently, it was one of the holiest places in the ancient Incan world. It was on the itinerary for a tour on the back end of our trip, so we walked past it and explored some of the narrow streets beyond it. There we found a beautiful shop with unique items that I immediately knew Kim would like. I carefully marked in my mind where the shop was located so that we could find it when we returned to Cusco with our wives. We also found a restaurant located on an inner courtyard on the second floor that looked fantastic, but decided to save it for later as well.

Instead, after about three hours of exploring the streets, we headed back to the plaza and finally settled on a local, low-class restaurant/pub on the far end of the plaza with tables overlooking the square on the second floor. They practically begged us to come in. Despite a rather pedestrian menu, we succumbed to the pressure. At least we had a good viewpoint of the whole square as we ate.

The table behind us was filled with young people who were also going to start the Inca Trail the next day. Small world. Surprisingly, we never saw them again for the next four days.

By 6:30 P.M., the sun had set and the square was filled with the golden glow of streetlights. With our stomachs full, we headed back to the Maytaq for our 7 P.M. Inca Trail "orientation session." At that point, we did not know how many people would be in our group or who our guide would be (other than that his name was Alejandro), and we expected that six to eight other people would be waiting in the lobby with us for the meeting.

But no one was there. No guide. No other hikers. Nobody.

We asked the guy at the front desk if he knew anything about a meeting or about Alejandro, and he just gave us a blank stare.

We waited at the appointed spot in the lobby until 7:15 P.M., and still no one showed up. Just as we were about to go back to our room, a short, athletic guy with a backpack hustled into the lobby, looking flustered. He profusely apologized for being late.

"We got lost trying to find the hotel," he quickly explained. "Are you William and David Scha…Schaeffer?"

"Close enough," Brent said. "But I go by 'Brent.' William is my first name."

"Okay, Brent…Brent," Alejandro said, trying to remember it.

"Are there others joining us?" I asked. "We haven't seen anyone else."

"No," he explained. "The rest of the group is out in the country. We'll pick them up on our way to the trail tomorrow morning. I am sorry I am late. Let's sit over here."

After catching his breath, Alejandro gave us a rundown of the Inca Trail and what we could expect each day. He would be guiding us and a couple from England—just four in our group. But another guide from the same Wayki Trek tour operator would be leading a group of six, and we would share porters and cooks. So, the whole group would be ten hikers and fifteen or sixteen guides, porters, and cooks. It sounded a lot like the Kilimanjaro expedition, fully porter supported. All we would have to do is carry raingear, a dry change of clothes, snacks, and water. He quickly rattled off a list of Incan ruins we would see, showing where they were located on a small, colorful map. He explained how Brent could rent a sleeping bag and hiking poles. He gave us some warnings about the altitude and suggested that we could try some cocoa leaves to help with the altitude if we needed it.

He then gave us some relatively small green canvas duffel bags into which we were to stuff our permitted fifteen pounds of gear for the porters to carry. I had brought my favorite yellow North Face waterproof duffel bag for that purpose, but he said the green bags were mandatory. I looked at it and wondered if I could fit anything in it besides my sleeping bag. Now I had to reconsider completely what I was bringing on the trail with me. Oh, well, adjusting to the local customs and trekking regulations is always part of the game… We could leave extra baggage at the hotel in Cusco, but would have to make do with whatever we could carry in our daypacks or stuff into the green canvas bags for the next five days.

With the meeting over by 8 P.M., there was nothing to do but organize and pack our gear and go to sleep. We had to be in the lobby at 5:30 A.M. for the ride to the Sacred Valley and the trailhead, so we needed to get plenty of shuteye. Who knows what sleep we would get once on the trail?

INCA TRAIL/MACHU PICCHU

THE INCA TRAIL DAY 1: GETTING STARTED

The hotel's complimentary breakfast opened at 5:30 A.M., so Brent and I grabbed some fruit and wolfed it down just before Alejandro arrived with our driver. Minutes later, we were heading out of town in a large van with seats for about twelve people. But for now, Brent and I were the only passengers.

Up and out of town is more accurate. The first fifteen minutes of the drive was all uphill, through a maze of narrow streets flanked by steep stairs and wall-to-wall abodes of various sizes and shapes. We finally merged onto a main street, four unmarked lanes wide, with dirt and rubbish for sidewalks. Wherever garbage had been dumped in plastic bags by the side of the road, scavenger dogs had ripped open the sacks and were rummaging through them for food and anything else edible.

Nasty.

But the scenery changed quickly. Once we got a few miles past the hill that surrounded the historical district and main city center, the road returned to two lanes and the buildings disappeared. Dry-looking farmland was all around with some rolling hills in the distance. Beyond them, I could see snowcapped mountains.

We saw a narrow-gauge railroad track on our way out of Cusco and followed it through the countryside most of the morning. It was the main track for the train to Machu Picchu, at least for the tourists with the money to pay for it. However, at 6:15 A.M., we did not see any trains moving along the tracks.

Somewhere along the way, the van pulled off the paved road and began climbing some hills on gravel and dirt roadways with dozens of switchbacks. Brent and I wondered whether there was a better way to get where we were going. Alejandro finally told us that we were making a detour into the countryside to pick up the other hikers at a remote farm where they were immersed, learning the ways of the Peruvian subsistence farmers.

It was pretty country, but the fields looked dry and barren. Of course, though we were near the equator, we were in the Southern hemisphere, so it was late winter there. This explains why the crops were not much to look at. Most of the fields had been plowed, and seeding was just beginning.

After several hours of driving, we stopped in front of a couple of mudbrick shelters, which turned out to be the farm where the other hikers had stayed the night. Alejandro waved us up to the first adobe-like shelter, a rectangular structure about ten by fifteen feet, with an open door and a few small windows in the front. At least a half dozen pigs and a couple of chickens were running around outside. Inside, the shelter had a dirt floor with a cooking area in the back right. To the left was a roughhewn table with the other hikers "enjoying" a local breakfast on a makeshift bench behind it. The cooking area had a hole above it for smoke to escape, but not all the smoke left the building. Some of the farmer's family members sat on the floor with their backs to the windowless back wall. They were drinking something green and remained silent.

The other climbers introduced themselves, almost all at once. In the confusion, I did not catch their names. They invited us to sit down with them and handed us a bowl of what looked like peanuts. Unfortunately, once again, they were dried corn nuts. I stuck a few in my mouth and bit down. Suddenly my mouth was filled with the driest grit I have ever tasted. Luckily, I had some bottled water with me to wash most of it down or else I might have choked. I declined some of the green mystery juice that was offered in a large plastic pitcher and thanked my lucky stars that I had taken a Cipro tablet that morning as a precaution.

It was very interesting to see how this farming family managed its water and its cooking. The food was nothing that I wanted to eat, but they seemed to be enjoying it. I noticed the one small window above the table on our end of the room was a four-pane, open window with partial blue glass, pretty fancy compared to the rest of the place. It helped provide a soothing blue haze as the sunlight streamed through it. All in all, despite the rudimentary surroundings, it provided a pleasant place to rest and eat. I just was not going to eat anything else after barely managing to ingest the arid corn nuts.

Goodbyes were said and soon we were back in our van. The other guide and climbers had their own identical van, with a lot of gear loaded up on its roof. Apparently, most of the kitchen gear and tents for the trek were already loaded on the other van. A young British couple, John and

INCA TRAIL/MACHU PICCHU

Naomi, joined Brent and me in our van. They would be the other two hikers in our four-person team with Alejandro.

The rest of the detour back to a main road was just as bumpy and winding as the way in. At one place, we cut directly across a field on two dirt tire paths, turning right on another gravel road at the other end. To our right was a large natural lake glistening in the morning sunlight. There did not appear to be any streams feeding it or any dam holding the water back. Alejandro confirmed that it was a lake formed only from rainwater collected in a bowl-like area surrounded by higher ground.

Eventually we found a paved road with the railroad track alongside. We were approaching Urubamba, another small town on the way to the trailhead. But first we had to stop in the quaint Sacred Valley town of Ollantaytambo. That, Alejandro said, was the last stop and last chance to go to the bathroom, get water, and buy any final snacks for that day's hike.

After a quick stop at the snack shop, Brent and I spotted some Incan ruins spread across a nearby ridge a few blocks from the main square. We had only twenty minutes to explore, but hustled down to get a closer look. At the base of the ruins were dozens of souvenir stores in a small market area. Beyond the entry walls, the Incan ruins looked impressive. Ever-rising walls with steep stone steps led up the mountain ridge to what looked like a fortress at the top. Unfortunately, we did not have time to go in, but we knew we would be back later with our wives, so we quickly returned to the bus.

For the next few miles we were on a nice paved road running alongside the railroad track. Then, with no warning, we turned left between a few small buildings. I saw no signs pointing toward the Inca Trail trailhead or anything like that, but the driver surely knew where he was going. Soon we were on a very narrow gravel road meandering through little villages and occasionally crossing the railroad track, back and forth. We still had seen no train. The sizeable Urubamba River was to our left, sometimes filled with rushing rapids and sometimes wider and slower, with calm water. At one point a large tourist bus came from the opposite direction and its driver and our driver engaged in a short standoff, trying to figure out if the vehicles could pass without crashing into each other.

Eventually, our driver backed up about a hundred yards to a slightly wider area so the other monster bus could get by.

I wondered if we were ever going to get to our destination, the "82 Km Marker." I did not know what the "82 Km" signified, but finally after seeing a few signs along the railroad track, I realized that it was the distance on the railroad track from Cusco. We were at the 77 Km marker, so we still had five kilometers to go on the tiny gravel road before getting there.

Once we arrived, everything on the buses was dumped out onto tarps spread out on a small grassy area. Alejandro explained that the porters would then pack their bags and go through a weighing and permit process that would take a few minutes. He told us to get our daypacks together, use the toilet if we needed it to make sure we had lots of water, and apply sunblock. I also quickly determined that spraying on some insect repellent with Deet bug repellent was in order, as the air was filled with some sort of tiny black insects that were already nibbling at my calves.

The "few" minutes for the porters to be approved to move along the trail took forty-five minutes or more. Meanwhile, we posed for photos at the sign showing the route for the next four days of our journey and then again at the "82 Km Marker," which signified the beginning of the trail. Alejandro spent about fifteen minutes telling us the history of the Incas and the trail, then we waited and waited and waited some more down at the final permit line as other groups' porters and hikers worked their way through the process. Everyone had to have a permit stamped before they could cross the narrow pedestrian suspension bridge across the river.

Apparently, each porter is allowed to carry only sixty pounds of gear. Our group was slightly overweight. So, an extra porter had to be hired to hike with us the first day. After the first meal and fuel were consumed, he would return to the trailhead since the weight surplus would be eliminated. Because of this delay, we were one of the last groups, if not *the* last group, to finally have our permits stamped and head across the bridge.

After the first short, steep hill on the other side of the bridge, which got me breathing hard, the trail flattened out. For the first two hours, the wide dirt path was slightly downhill. We were hiking along the river with the water flowing in the same direction. It was very pleasant with tem-

INCA TRAIL/MACHU PICCHU

peratures in the low 70s and the sound of the water rushing by on our right. Above us on both sides were high mountain ridges, some on the right with snow at the top.

Nice.

At one point, on the other side of the river, we saw the ruins of an old Incan village with terraced rock walls and the foundations of rock structures. Just as we were trying to focus our cameras on it, a train came along the railroad track on the other side of the river, its blue passenger cars filled with tourists taking the easy way to Machu Picchu. It was the start of more than a dozen such trains we saw before we took a left and headed into the mountains and away from the river. After that we would see no more railroad track for the next three days. Lots of people were taking the fast train to Machu Picchu.

We were taking the long, slow, and arduous footpath.

Once we turned left, the going got tougher. Everything was uphill now. At first, we went up a very steep section. Then mercifully, the path leveled off. Not long thereafter we were treated to our first major Incan ruins. Down in a valley, perhaps three hundred vertical feet below us, was an entire Incan village surrounded by wide, sweeping terraces and a stream. As Alejandro gave us some history about the village, known as Llaqtapata, we took turns gaping at the view. It was an impressive site, so well-defined and organized in its design. It filled the greater part of the valley below us and demonstrated the agricultural terracing that enabled the Incas to farm the land in such mountainous terrain.

Above the village was a watchtower close to the trail, so we had our first opportunity to explore some Incan walls and rock ruins up close and personal. It was filled with a maze of walls and sections, some of which had been partially restored. Other sections just had piles of Incan rocks, which presumably had at one time been in walls. Alejandro told us to explore the watchtower on our own and to get a little rest, as the rest of the hike that afternoon would be uphill.

For the next two hours, we steadily climbed a stone-filled path surrounded by jungle on all sides. I began consuming water much more rapidly to make up for the moisture lost through sweat. Fortunately, we kept a slow and steady pace…just my speed.

After another four miles of climbing, we began seeing tents already set up on adjacent clearings for earlier arriving groups. Alejandro reminded us that we were one of the last groups to leave, so we would have to keep climbing beyond the usual spots before reaching our resting place for the night.

"The more we climb today, the less we climb to Dead Woman's Pass tomorrow morning," he told me on one break during which I rested my head on one of my hiking poles.

"Excellent. Tomorrow is the toughest day—looking forward to it," I lied. But I appreciated the opportunity to cut several hundred vertical feet off tomorrow morning's ascent, which would take us to the highest altitude of the trek.

We passed through an area that looked like the center of the camps for the first night and Alejandro told us we had only about thirty minutes more of hiking before we would reach our camp. It turned out to be only about twenty minutes. But it was the steepest section we had encountered so far, leading me to believe that tomorrow indeed was going to be a challenge. We were only at slightly over 10,000 feet in elevation and the next morning we had to ascend to almost 14,000 feet to go through the high pass. And there would be no long, gradual switchbacks to make it easy. Towards the end of the day, we were just going straight up steep inclines or series of rock steps.

Finally, behind a vine-covered wire fence, we saw our group's tents set up on a two-tiered pasture on our right. Alejandro confirmed that this was our camp for the night and advised us to arrange our sleeping bags inside the tents, organize our gear, and then relax until dinner.

Brent and I had the last tent in the row on the upper tier. The porters had already lined the bottom with two thin Thermarest air pads, and our duffel bags were laid out on a canvas near the tent. But I was not getting inside the tent yet. The weather was magnificent. The area in front of the tent was nice, thick grass. I grabbed a dry shirt out of my duffel bag, stripped off my hiking shirt, which had become soaked with sweat on the last few hours of the climb, kicked off my hiking boots, and soon was lounging in the grass barefooted enjoying the afternoon and massaging my sore thighs and calves. After a short rest, I felt great. Today's hike had not been too bad. I began to worry about tomorrow morning.

Mt. Rainier from Paradise trailhead

Starting up Mt. Rainier (author in yellow boots)

Mt. Rainier summit/crater rim (author and Bert Reeves)

Mt. Everest and Mt. Lhotse

Mt. Everest from Pangboche bakery shop

Mt. Everest base camp (author and Sherpa Lakpa Rita)

Author with Mt. Everest in background from above Namche Bazaar

Mt. Fuji from scree trail

Mt. Fuji Summit

Beginning of Inca Trail at marker KM82

Author with Sayamarca Ruins on Inca Trail

Author with Alejandro and team at Machu Picchu

Author with his wife Kim at Machu Picchu

Cho Oyu from Chinese base camp (16,100 feet)

Cho Oyu and Puja Ceremony at advanced base camp (18,750 feet)

Author at 21,000 feet camp, with Summer Law Intern Program card

One nice surprise was that the porters had set up a mobile port-a-potty, in its own little tent. Apparently, the head porter carried it all the way on his back and would do so the rest of the trip.

Better him than me!

It seemed like forever before we had dinner. But the meal, in a small tent with Brent, the English couple, John and Naomi, and Alejandro, was quite good. Soup, followed by three large plates of rice, noodles, and potatoes, with a bit of chicken and a nice platter of cucumbers and tomatoes, were brought by our porter/server. It was much more than we could eat, but anything left would be eaten by the porters. The meal was completed with a special dessert custard with caramel sauce.

Delicious.

The other group of six climbers and their guide ate in a separate tent but enjoyed the same meal prepared by the same cook and "kitchen-tent" staff.

After dinner, all of us gathered to watch the stars, with one member of the other group named Dave pulling out his phone and using an app to tell us the name of each star. His app was not exactly accurate, but he certainly had fun trying to make it work. We stayed outside until the temperature dropped into the low 40s, then nestled in for the night. With a 5:30 A.M. wakeup call, we were not about to stay up too late.

THE INCA TRAIL DAY 2: THE CLIMB TO DEAD WOMAN'S PASS

Brent was up at 5 A.M., making noise in the tent and getting ready early. I had experienced a fitful night, sleeping a few hours, but mostly waking up and going outside to pee. Without contacts in, I could not see the stars clearly, but I could tell there were a lot of them up there as there was plenty of light to see what I was doing. I groaned, but quickly joined Brent in getting ready for what I knew was going to be a painful morning of climbing the steepest section of the Inca Trail.

After a hearty breakfast, we headed up the mountain. Alejandro told Naomi and John they could go ahead and that he would stay with the slower climbers (looking straight at me). He told them to wait for us at the first "snack stop." With permission granted, Naomi and John took off, followed by Brent.

I started at my usual slow and steady pace and soon Alejandro and I were alone, the others nowhere to be seen.

Alejandro had told us the night before that there would be three sections to climb to get to Dead Woman's Pass, also known as Warmiwanusca. The first would take about an hour, to a rest stop at approximately 11,000 feet, where there would be snacks and water available for purchase. The second would be up to another rest stop where we would have the last water and drinks available. He also said that would take about an hour and bring us to just under 12,000 feet. The last section would be the longest and steepest and would take us two-and-a-half to three hours, culminating in the pass at 13,870 feet. So, I was not about to burn myself out in the first hour.

I concentrated on breathing and just putting one foot in front of the other. I tried to avoid the rock steps wherever possible, knowing that if there was a smoother path in the dirt to the side, it would take less of a toll on my legs. However, most of the time, the steep rock-step sections were impossible to avoid. Sometimes the steps were six inches high, sometimes eighteen inches or more. Sometimes they were wide steps and gradual ascents, other times they were narrow and very steep, almost to the point that it was easier to go up them using both hands and feet.

Surprisingly, after about forty-five minutes, Alejandro said the first stop is "just up here." I looked up and saw, beyond the next set of ten rock steps, a table with two ladies selling sodas, waters, and candy bars on the left. There were at least eight to ten climbers crowded around the table. But Naomi, John, and Brent were nowhere to be seen.

I took a quick pit stop at the "squat" toilet building below the trail to the right, grabbed some more water, then told Alejandro I was ready to go. He asked if I wanted more time, but I said I was ready.

"The first section was not so bad—I think we're ahead of schedule. Besides, the other guys obviously did not stop long, so we should try to stay close," I added. "Slow and steady with short stops is my plan."

"A good plan," he replied as we headed up the next section.

At this point, the Inca Trail is not a dirt hiking trail, but almost entirely an ever-ascending cobblestone corridor, interrupted continuously by long, steep sets of rock stairs. In this section, for the first time, I watched even the porters slowing down and taking more rest stops at the bottom or top of the steepest sets of stairs.

I worked hard to keep a steady pace, but found myself gasping for air at the top of many of these sections, blowing out carbon dioxide with strong exhales through my lips, using the technique taught me by the guides on Elbrus and Aconcagua. Alejandro did not know what I was doing and thought I was having serious problems with my breathing until I explained the technique to him.

"Interesting," he said, not sure if I was telling the truth.

But we kept going. Every time I looked up, there was an even worse set of rock steps ahead.

However, once again, after about forty-five minutes of pain, we emerged onto a flat, open lookout with an amazing view down to our right. This time there were two tables with ladies selling snacks and water. Waiting for us on the right were Brent, Naomi, and John, who quickly explained that they thought this was the first stop.

"Fast but oblivious," I thought to myself as I tried to catch my breath. They had already been there for "ten to fifteen minutes" but did not mind waiting a bit longer for group photos and for Alejandro and me to take a good rest. Okay, for *me* to rest. Alejandro looked like he could run up the mountain. I dropped one more load in the nearby toilets and, after being at the level area for less than ten minutes, said I was ready to go.

Once again, Naomi and John took off as if they had rockets on their shoes. I guess I did the same thing when I was thirty years old. Brent also moved a bit ahead, but I noticed that he was holding back, this time keeping me in sight and waiting for me to stay close for the first hour or so. I could easily pick him out, as he was wearing a floppy Kilimanjaro hat and carrying a brightly colored small knapsack on his back that he had bought in Ollantaytambo. Not exactly stylish, but quite in keeping with the local culture. He certainly stood out from a distance.

We were now above the tree line, so the trail had many, many great viewpoints. Behind us was a snowcapped mountain called Veronica, magnificently filling the end of the valley. Brent stopped to take quite a few photos in this section, allowing me to stay in contact with him as we ascended the steepest and highest part of the trail.

I could see other climbers working their way up a long traverse to a corner viewpoint, which looked like it was only about a half hour's climb below the pass. I began to have some hope that I would be able to handle this climb without too much difficulty. It did not look like we had that much more to go.

Looks can be deceiving.

Somewhere before I reached that corner lookout, Brent picked up the pace and disappeared from view. I assumed he felt we were nearing the finish line and was making a push to get to the top. I was seriously out of breath when I reached the corner lookout, so I plopped down on a rock for a short rest. Then I looked up towards the pass and instantly thought, "You've got to be kidding me!"

But "Shit!" is what came out of my mouth.

The pass was further up and a lot further away than I thought it would be at that point. I looked at my watch and saw that it was not yet 10:30 A.M. We had been climbing only a little over three hours so far and Alejandro had predicted at least four and a half hours to get to the top—"maybe five." Alejandro had stopped to talk to some friends and had fallen back, so I had no one to verify how much time it would still take to get to the top.

It is hard to explain all the factors that come into play when one is exceeding 13,000 feet in altitude without a lot of acclimatization, especially when encountering never-ending flights of steps for hours at a time. Breathing is the biggest problem. The oxygen is reduced by about twenty percent, so sucking in air effectively is critical. Tiredness of the legs is the next problem—particularly after limited sleep and three hours of tough stair climbing. Not to be outdone, one's mental state and attitude can be problematic if one allows oneself to let up.

Getting to the top of a mountain ridge or pass takes persistence and a calm approach. I try to block out what everyone else is doing. I remind myself it is not a race. It is just a destination to be reached, regardless of the time taken.

Slow and steady. Take a break when needed. Get water whenever possible. But keep going and make the stops short.

That is exactly what I did on the last section up to Dead Woman's Pass. Until I got a few hundred vertical feet below the pass, I concentrated on nothing but my steps, my breathing, and, every five minutes or so, my water bottle. Alejandro was still nowhere to be seen. So, I was totally alone, except for some younger folks passing me.

Just keep going, David.

Every time I looked up, the pass appeared slightly closer, but it still looked like a long way away.

But then, just when I had completely internalized my thoughts and was working up the steps mindlessly without noticing the pain, one of the other group members yelled down from the pass.

"Woo-hoo, go, David, go! You're almost there!"

I looked up and saw most of our group up on the ledge looking down. But this took me out of my trance. Instantly, I felt an impulse to pick up the speed and hustle to the top. Luckily, my experience and perhaps my high blood-pressure medicine nipped that impulse in the bud. The worst thing I could have done was to try to blow up the last twenty sets of steep sections of rocky stairs and collapse at the top. We still had several miles to hike on the other side of the pass with an over-two-thousand-foot vertical drop on equally or even steeper steps. I had to conserve energy and stick to my plan.

So, I slogged up, one set of stairs at a time, calmly taking a sip of water at the top of each and resting my legs for just a few seconds before taking on the next set. It took a while to work my way through them as the group above urged me on.

"You're almost there, David…keep going strong!"

Just shut up and let me climb in peace!

Alejandro suddenly appeared, encouraging me as he quickly zoomed past and practically ran to the top. Before I knew it, I had just two sets of rocky stairs to go. The gang above were still shouting encouragement. This time I did not stop at the end of the first steps and pushed on to the top.

"Made it," I said weakly to Brent as I found a place to sit next to Naomi and John.

"Well done, David." "Great job!" "Way to go." "Knew you would make it."

Everyone was supportive. It is always nice to get to the highest point of the trek and have new friends pat you on the back. But I just wanted to rest, drink more water, wolf down a Snickers bar, and get going down the other side. I had made it to the top in just over four hours, so I did not feel too bad about slowing anyone down. Still, I did not want to hold them up any longer.

I looked around and everyone in our larger group was there except an Italian couple who were probably in their late forties. The wife had been having some difficulties adjusting to the altitude the prior day, so it was not surprising that she struggled on the much harder second day. An assistant guide had been assigned to stay with them as they ascended. Not very long after I arrived, Alejandro advised us to lengthen our rubber-tipped trekking poles for the trip down and to get moving again. A steady, brisk wind was blowing across the pass and some of the folks who had been there for twenty or thirty minutes were already getting cold.

So, we headed down the other side.

Talk about steep. I am glad that we did not come up that way.

At the bottom of the first lengthy set of very steep steps, we stopped at a conveniently located toilet hut. The line was long, but I had to go.

By the time I got back to the path, Brent had gotten impatient and had headed down the trail. Alejandro, Naomi, and John were still there, as Naomi had waited just as long in the women's line. So, we started out together. I stayed with the group for about twenty minutes, slowly working our way down a seemingly endless series of steep rock steps. By then I realized that Naomi and John were much more comfortable going up steep sections than coming down them. After growing impatient when getting to the bottom sets of stairs and having to wait for them to catch up, I picked up the pace and left them behind. With about a two-thousand-foot descent over the next hour and a half, I figured that I would catch up with Brent and we could find the camp together.

Descending on scree slopes or rocky steps has always been a fun part of climbing for me. At several times that day, I even fell in behind some of the porters and literally ran down some very steep sections, making sure that every step was solid. Of course, I was not hauling a sixty-pound load on my back. The porters handled the steps like mountain goats, smoothly skimming down them as if they had nothing on their backs. I was much less smooth, but could keep up for a couple of sets of stairs at a time. Then I had to stop to catch my breath.

The very steepest part of the descent was in the first hour. After that, the trail turned slightly less steep and into more of a steadily dropping cobblestone highway five or six feet wide with larger stones on the outsides and smaller stones crunched in the middle. I found it much easier to travel on the right edge where the bigger stones were placed, but by hugging that side, I realized I was sometimes on the edge of a large drop-off. After about an hour, the pathway consisted of about seventy-five percent gradually descending stones and only about twenty-five percent steep rocky stair steps. I could keep up a nice pace on the flatter sections, then rapidly scoot down the shorter sections of steps.

However, I never did catch up with Brent. At sixty-six, Brent was the oldest one in our group, and, from all appearances, he was the oldest one anywhere on the Inca Trail. At fifty-nine, I might have been the second oldest. Brent mentioned he had a sore knee and was worried about going downhill with it. But he clearly handled the first downhill challenge like a champ.

A porter was stationed at the point in the trail where a path forked off to the second camp area. Our porters had green t-shirts with the name of the Wayki Trek guide group so they were easy to pick out. I recognized the porter from introductions that had been made with the other part of our group early that morning. He motioned me to take the right fork and I followed him down through the trees, alongside a grey stream, past several sets of tents, and down to a terrace on which our group's tents had been set up.

Brent was lounging on the grass, rubbing his legs, having just taken off his shoes. He had made it into camp a few minutes before me and was still recovering from the day's exertion. I quickly joined him, pulling my boots off, with some serious groans.

We had been hiking up and down very steep trails for about seven hours without any meal break. But it was only about 2:30 P.M. Alejandro had warned us about the long break between meals and told us to bring plenty of snacks to eat on the way that day, probably so that the porters did not have to unpack and set up lunch on the steepest part of the trail. Frankly, I would have been too tired to eat much up at Dead Woman's

Pass anyway. Certainly, not a full hot lunch. Instead, I had consumed several Snickers bars and a few meat sticks on the trail that day to keep going.

While we rested, the cooks and porters were scurrying around, preparing lunch. They all looked very happy—their toughest day was also over. I was also pleased to get the highest pass behind us, but knew that the third and longest day of hiking was still ahead of us.

To numb my aching feet, I walked over to the nearby stream and stepped in barefooted. The water was very cold, as we were still at almost 12,000 feet in altitude. It felt great. For a moment, I thought about stripping naked and lying down for a full-body, freezing massage, but decided against it. The water looked a bit murky and there were too many people around. Instead, I retreated to our tent.

Alejandro, Naomi, and John arrived about twenty minutes later, looking no worse for the wear. Naomi commented on how I had "taken off like a bolt of lightning" and I said that I like going downhill. She replied that she prefers going uphill. I believed her. I had been almost thirty minutes behind her and John on the way up to Dead Woman's Pass earlier in the day. Downhill was entirely different. But now everyone in our smaller group was into camp safe.

All but two of the other hikers in our larger group had also arrived at camp by 3 P.M. However, the Italian couple finally dragged in at about 4:30 P.M. long after the rest of us had lunch. While the guy looked fine, clearly his wife looked whipped. But the claps and cheers of the porters and her fellow climbers helped revive her spirits, at least momentarily. The couple retreated into a tent, and she came out only for dinner that evening. I hoped that she was alright.

Dinner that night was excellent—chicken legs with rice, a noodle dish, fried potatoes, a platter of avocados, tomatoes, and cucumbers, topped off with a cake with red and white icing. The only problem was that the campsite seemed to be infested with tiny black mites that were relentless in their efforts to nibble on our legs and necks or any other exposed area. Before the meal was halfway through, I had to go back to the tent and get a jacket and a woolen beanie just to avoid having them infest my hair, face, and neck. I also brought out my spray bottle of Deet repellant. Soon everyone, including the porters, were spraying and rubbing Deet onto their hands and necks.

That night, with the campsite at around 12,000 feet in altitude, it got a bit chilly, but it was still very warm inside the tents. When I went to the bathroom, the problem was not the cold, but the continued presence of the tiny insects, still looking for victims and exposed skin.

THE INCA TRAIL DAY 3: LOTS OF RUINS

Amazingly, after the tough second day, I did not feel stiff or sore the next morning. Everyone was wearing plenty of layers as we ate our breakfast. It was still quite cold at 6 A.M. Naomi and John looked no worse for the wear. Brent mentioned that one of his knees was sore from the descent the afternoon before, but he did not show any signs of it as we hiked the third day.

Before we knew it, we were back on the trail, once again heading uphill. That day's journey would take us past several Incan ruins and over another pass at about 12,500 feet, but we would have a lot of stops on the way.

The first stop was after less than an hour of climbing. To the right of the trail was a well-defined set of ruins, a semi-circular structure known as Runkurakay. Its center section overlooked the valley from which we had come, surrounded by two sections of rooms divided by an entrance hallway. Alejandro explained that it was a guard post protecting the Inca Trail from unwanted travelers, carefully positioned to allow the guards to see anyone approaching from below. We took photos, then rested for about ten minutes before resuming a quite steep section of the trail.

The next two hours involved more gradual, but steady ascents through the forest. The path was now all rocks but most of the rises were ramp-like hills rather than steep sets of stairs. I found the going to be a lot easier than the day before. Brent, Naomi, and John stayed fifty to a hundred yards ahead of me, allowing me to catch up at several viewpoints. Alejandro trailed behind me by varying lengths, but always kept me in sight. On several occasions, we walked together and talked about our backgrounds. To be able to talk as we hiked means that the trail was not as tough.

Eventually we reached the second big pass, called the Runku Raqay Pass, at just under 12,500 feet. Sixty or seventy climbers were gathered there, resting from the morning's exertion, getting some water and snacks, and waiting for stragglers.

After giving us a few minutes to catch our breaths, Alejandro motioned us up a steep, grassy bank to the left of the pass. Brent, Naomi, John, and I struggled up the same steep embankment that Alejandro practically ran up. We followed him to a viewpoint at the top of the hill. There Alejandro explained one of his religion's rituals, which involved praying to the three most prominent mountains in the area, plus Machu Picchu, while holding three cocoa leaves and blowing on them. We watched him demonstrate. Then he invited us to join in the ritual. Being respectful, we obliged, each praying towards Mt. Veronica, then Mt. Salkantay, then another mountain I could not pronounce, and finally Machu Picchu, blowing the cocoa leaves just before naming the mountains. At the end of the ritual, we placed the cocoa leaves under a flat rock and built a small stack of rocks on top of it, signifying our permanent oneness with the surrounding environment...or something ecumenically ecological like that.

Freshly full of mountain spirits and blessing, we zipped back down to the pass and headed out to our next destination with renewed energy and a sense of well-being.

Or maybe we were getting high on the cocoa leaves!

After another hour and a half of mostly downhill trekking, we came around a corner and could see a huge fortress up on the hill to our left and another guard post down in the valley below us. The stairs up to the fortress, also known as Sayacmarca, were quite narrow and steep, allowing only one climber to go up or down at a time. Alejandro advised us to ditch our daypacks and just take a water bottle up to the fortress with us. I was feeling good, so I went up the steep steps at a fast pace, reaching the top without much problem, but I found myself quickly gasping for breath at the top.

This fortress was known for its aqueducts and baths. It was amazing how they had devised a way for water to flow all around the buildings, filling small bathing areas hidden behind rock walls. Brent and I scurried around the structures, finding one bath after another on different levels.

The place was a maze, with walls, terraces, hallways, and stone steps leading towards multiple sections of the ruins. The structure followed the contours of the hillside. So, there were many viewpoints of the surrounding valleys and hills, including the ruined guard post below. Across the way, at the top of the hill on the next ridge, sat another stone building, which also served as a snack-break point and restroom stop.

About twenty minutes later we pulled into that rest stop after working our way down into the valley and then up the hill on the other side. Alejandro suggested that we just take a short break, indicating that we had less than another hour of trail before stopping for lunch. I wolfed down an apple, used the facilities, and hurried to catch up with the others as they started back down the trail.

The next section of the trail was one of the most moderate of the whole trip. Most of the time we were walking on relatively flat stone paths, only occasionally reaching gradual uphill sections. I kept Brent, Naomi, and John within sight distance without too much trouble, and Alejandro and I chatted along the way. After about thirty minutes, we ascended briefly to an open, dusty ridge on which the porters had set up the cook and dining tents for a special midday meal. Other groups had their tents up as well, using every bit of open space on the ridge. Even our port-a-potty was set up beyond the tent.

This time when they brought us our lunch, we were surprised to see beautifully carved birds adorning the cucumber and tomato tray and the rice dish. One bird was carved from a rather large carrot and the other from an enormous cucumber. Both had carefully sculptured heads and carved tails. Instantly, we grabbed our cameras to document the gastronomic artwork. I realized later that the head cook was raising our appreciation at the critical time for maximum effect, as that evening would be the time to tip the help.

The only problem with lunch that day was the weather. When we sat down in the dining tent to start with, the sun was out. The inside of the tent was so hot that the porters opened the flaps just to give us a little breeze. But within minutes, the sun went behind the clouds and the wind picked up. We added layers and asked them to close the flaps again. Just as we were finishing our meals, it started to rain, first little drops and then increasingly larger drops.

Instantly, the porters kicked into high gear, scrambling to get things covered or packed up. Everyone almost instantly finished their meals and began to cover up. I reached into my daypack and for the first time on the trip, pulled on my rain jacket, thinking that it would be needed all afternoon.

Because the porters were starting to dismantle the dining tent, we had no option but to grab our daypacks and head down the trail in what looked like increasingly treacherous weather conditions.

However, within five minutes, the rain stopped, the sun came back out, and we stripped down to a single nylon layer once again. The rain jacket went back into the bottom of my pack, never to be pulled out again.

Such is the unpredictability of the Inca Trail. The terrain is so jagged and the valleys and hills so steep that within minutes and a turn of the corner, a completely different weather pattern can appear. Luckily, we were hiking in the dry season, so any lengthy period of rain was unlikely. Except for that one downpour, we had beautiful weather.

At one point on the trail, we looked ahead and down a few thousand feet at a less-jagged mountain in the center of a valley, still several ridges away. The mountain rose from right to left and at the very top of the peak on the left there was a flag flying.

This was Mt. Machu Picchu. On the other side of it was our destination—Machu Picchu itself. I instantly assumed that Machu Picchu would be near the top of Mt. Machu Picchu. But, as usual, I would find out later that I was wrong.

But first we had to get there. We had two more Incan ruin sites to see that afternoon on the way. The first was Phuyuptamarca, a large structure with diamond-shaped terraces flowing down the hill on which it sits. It was impressive for its angular design, but otherwise I do not remember much about it. After seeing about a thousand Incan rock walls and terraces, they tend to blend together!

The second, Intipata, was more memorable. It consisted of dozens and dozens of walled terraces on a very steep hill on a side trail forking off to the left. Across the valley from Intipata was our third night camp. Apparently, most of the Inca Trail hikers skip this site and take the shorter trail on the right side of the valley directly to the camp, especially if it is getting late in the day. However, by the time we reached the fork in the trail it was only 3:30 P.M., and Alejandro said that we could see Intipata and still make it to the camp on time. So, we took the longer side path to the left of the valley. Even though I was getting tired, I am glad we did.

Intipata was amazing. From the path at the bottom, the rock walls of the terraces kept going up beyond where the eyes could see. I imagined a very difficult jigsaw puzzle being made from a photo of it, as each wall looked identical, one above the other. In the middle of the whole thing, a single set of steps went straight up the steep hill as far as we could see. There did not appear to be any abodes on these terraces, so they were used solely for growing crops on the side of a steep mountain where otherwise nothing edible could grow.

We worked our way up the right side of the terraces part of the way up and then hiked down a steep path to the right of the terraces, stopping to try to fit the whole ruins in a single photo—unsuccessfully. To me, this was the most impressive Incan ruin on the trail up to that point. I felt sorry for those who missed it just to save a few minutes of hiking.

We arrived at Camp Three around 4:30 P.M. This camp was situated on the side of a steep forested hill, with tents and restrooms set up on its own set of terraces. One of the porters led us down and down and down some more on some narrow switchback trails until we saw our tents set up on a narrow ledge beyond a concrete bathroom and shower structure. In between the bathrooms and our tents was a wider terrace with the cook and dining tents set up on it. We apparently had one of the best spots, as some of the other groups' porters griped about our porters claiming their spot.

But it is "first come, first served" on the Inca Trail!

At first, I did not think it was such a great spot, as our tents were scrunched together in a very small space and we had only about two feet of clearance in front of them, with a rather steep drop-off beyond that narrow ledge. But we had an awesome view of Mt. Machu Picchu, now almost level with our eyes. Plus, having an actual shower was a real bonus after three days of sweaty climbing.

Of course, the shower was only a little booth between the two toilets. The showerhead was just the end of a pipe with freezing-cold water coming out whenever a valve was turned. We were still at about 9,000 feet in elevation, so hoping for warm water was a pipedream. I turned on the water, took a deep breath, and jumped in with gusto, getting myself frozen from head to toe in a matter of seconds. I cut the water off, grabbed the soap, thoroughly applied it everywhere in another fifteen seconds, then rinsed off with another dose of freezing H2O. I ended the shower with a head-dunking swoon in the cold water and a "Shit, that was cold," which probably could have been heard down by the tents.

However, the numbness and tingling after drying off (with a less-than-clean towel) were worth every minute of the brutal coldness of the shower. After putting on a clean shirt and a fleece for the evening, I felt like a new man.

That night, after dinner, Alejandro had each of the porters and cooks introduce themselves one by one. None of them spoke English, so Alejandro had to interpret. Some were so shy that Alejandro had to coerce answers out of them. The veterans were much more comfortable, having done the introductions week after week for different hikers for several years. It was so meaningful to hear about their families, how long they had been working as porters, and where they were from. Most were from villages near Cusco and some had been porters for dozens of years. A couple were in their fifties and sixties and yet were still lugging sixty-pound bags up and down the steep sections of the Inca Trail, making meager wages for doing so.

Of course, the introductions were the precursor to the tipping of the porters and cook...and Alejandro. At dinner, Alejandro finally shared with us what level tips each of the categories of our helpers would be happy with. The rank and file porters were at the lowest level. The lead porter who had carried and cleaned the port-a-potty for the whole trip was given double the tip of the others. The cook and his assistant also received extra-generous tips. Brent, being the senior member of our group, led us in thanking each of them for their excellent service, with Alejandro translating for him. Each of the other three of us added our thanks at the end. Finally, we thanked Alejandro with a well-deserved tip at a level higher than recommended in the travel group's materials. He really did a great job and was one of the most sincere guides I have had the pleasure to encounter on my many travels.

We hit the sack almost immediately after dinner that night, as we had to be up early for our last day on the trail.

THE INCA TRAIL DAY 4: THE SUN GATE AND MACHU PICCHU

Early is an understatement. Three-thirty in the morning, to be exact. Apparently, most of the porters had to pack up all the gear, including the tents, and hike down to Aguas Calientes to catch the first train back to Ollantaytambo or Cusco. So we had to be up by 3:30 A.M. and out of the tents by 4 A.M. Breakfast snacks in brown paper bags had been prepared so that the cooks and porters could make their early departure without cooking. And Alejandro told us that we needed to be at the registration checkpoint just down the hill by 4:15 A.M. to be able to sit on comfortable benches while waiting for the gateway to the final section of the trail to the Sun Gate to be opened at 5:30 A.M.

Alejandro miscalculated. We left the camp at just before 4 A.M. and hustled down the dark path, illuminated by our headlamps, and arrived at the checkpoint at about 4:12 A.M., three minutes early. But obviously, a lot of groups got up even earlier. All the benches were already filled. We had no option but to sit on the muddy, damp ground or on our daypacks in the dark while attempting to eat the contents from the brown paper bags and waiting in the cold for over an hour until they finally let us through the gate to the last part of the trail.

All the while, other members of our group kept talking about how important it was to cover the final few miles of trail quickly to get to the Sun Gate by dawn. By then, from talking to Alejandro, I had learned that the Machu Picchu ruins were down on the lower right side of Mt. Machu Picchu and that the Sun Gate was about halfway up the right-to-left slope that we could see from our camp. Surrounding Mt. Machu Picchu on all sides are mountain ridges three to four thousand feet higher. So, there would be no horizon to see the sun rise above early that morning.

I mentioned this to several people in our group, but they persisted in their intentions to rush to the Sun Gate by dawn.

As soon as we cleared the checkpoint, Naomi, John, and about half of the other group took off at a rapid pace, almost race-walking. Brent and I kept a slightly faster pace than usual. The trail was almost flat as we went around one outcropping and worked our way over to the side of Mt. Machu Picchu. However, I did not feel any need to kill myself since there would be no sunrise to see.

The final part of the trail took less than an hour and a half to complete and was mostly downhill at first. We still needed our headlamps for the first forty-five minutes, but then it was light enough to see without extra illumination. The second forty-five minutes were decidedly uphill, traversing the side of Mt. Machu Picchu up to the Sun Gate.

Close to the top of the ridge, we encountered two particularly steep sets of rock steps. The first was not too bad, but the second one was so steep with such narrow steps that Alejandro told me to give him my hiking poles and just climb up with my hands and feet. It was the final challenge of the four-day hike, followed by a more gradual and long set of steps up to the fortified walls of the Sun Gate, also known as Inti Punku.

When I reached the top of the steps and crossed through the stone gateway, I saw for the first time the ruins at Machu Picchu, instantly recognizable some eight hundred vertical feet below the Sun Gate. There were approximately one hundred hikers perched on walls and terraces at the Sun Gate, most of whom were taking group photos with the ruins below them. There was no sun in sight and it quickly became chilly, as a cold wind whisked up and across the lookout area. We, of course, joined in the group photos and I tried to zoom in on the ruins, which were still a twenty- to thirty-minute hike away. The photos from that distance really did not do justice to the ruins.

After about fifteen to twenty minutes, we finally started down the trail on the other side of the Sun Gate, stopping every five minutes to take more photos. I found myself mesmerized by the sight, which kept coming more in focus. I could see tourists entering the ruins from the lower-right corner and starting to work their way into this most amazing Incan complex. Huayna Picchu, the small but steep peak just beyond the ruins, made an impressive backdrop to the view. Before long, I got pictures much like those I had seen for years in National Geographic magazines and tourist literature.

Brent and I reached the top end of the ruins together, working our way down a narrow descending ramp until we arrived at two terraces overlooking the main section of Machu Picchu. To our right was a switchback path down to the visitors' gate where the normal tourists arrived on buses from Aguas Calientes. Down there Kim and Mpopo would be arriving momentarily. Meanwhile, Brent and I took dozens of photos of the ruins below, culminated by group photos with Naomi, John, and Alejandro.

I was anxious to get down to the visitors' gate to reunite with Kim, but even more so to wash up, change into a clean set of clothes, and use the facilities. Luckily, I had some coins to get into the restroom changing area.

Kim and Mpopo had arrived by the time I emerged from the bathroom. I don't think Kim has looked any better to me than she did on that occasion, waving at me from at the top of some stairs. She looked ready for the tour in her new multicolored top, black pants, and an awesome sunhat purchased just for the trip. I hurried up the stairs to give her a long hug and kiss.

Normally my mountain climbs or treks end in some faraway city while Kim is back at home in Atlanta and we don't reunite until I land at Hartsfield-Jackson Airport. This is about the only time Kim has been there at the end of a trek ready to join me at the climax of the trip.

And what a climax! Machu Picchu was so carefully designed to make maximum use of the mountaintop space on which it is situated. Walls and terraces work their way up from the right lower side until the ridge is flat. There the living quarters were built for workers and visitors in a series of structures and chambers, several of them three-section rooms with multiple entrances. All of them were at one time capped with roofs. Now only the stone walls and doorways are left, with the triangular stonework that supported the roofs still well-preserved. Beyond the living quarters is a large flat field, which reminded me of jousting fields in England.

In the center of the massive complex just above the large field is the most sacred section of Machu Picchu, with its very finely sculpted rock walls topped by a temple vault of sorts and three sacred windows overlooking the large field. The windows are strategically placed in an astrologically significant direction—at least, that is the theory. Beyond and above that temple is a high, rocky section on which sits the famous sundial rock and a ceremonial sacrifice place.

Finally, up closer to where Brent and I came down from the Sun Gate is a series of steps and structures leading up to what looks like a cottage at the top of the ruins. Kim and I worked our way up to that cottage after our formal tour of the place ended, to get the penultimate photos of Machu Picchu.

The photos show what Machu Picchu looks like. But walking through it, up and down the steep steps, through roofless rooms and chambers, touching the smooth, enormous stones of the sacred temple structure, and wondering how they managed to fit all the pieces together so tightly with no mortar between the huge rocks is an experience that cannot be duplicated by just looking at photos or describing them in a book.

To truly experience Machu Picchu, you must feel the place. And to really experience what it took to get to the place, you must hike the Inca Trail. Up and down, over and through, past the guard posts and Incan villages, farms, and fortresses, and over the Sun Gate. It is amazing that people so long ago actually traveled that trail with provisions and supplies, not just hiking it with small daypacks. Machu Picchu remained hidden for many centuries, because there are so many steep mountains, passes, curves, and valleys all around it. Without the Inca Trail, no one could hope to find it.

We found it and we liked it!

But I don't care if I never see another Incan rock!!!

The lines for the return buses at the visitors' gate were long, but they moved quickly. Soon we were zooming down a harrowing series of very sharp switchbacks down to the little town of Aguas Calientes. Interestingly, some signs indicated that Aguas Calientes had been recently renamed "Machu Picchu Town."

Kim and Mpopo had already spent one night at the hotel there, so they had scouted the place out. To me, it looked like a ski village, complete with a railroad track running right through it. Streets were filled with cafés with tables out on the sidewalks and souvenir shops were everywhere, right and left. Every fifteen minutes or so, a train would come through, bringing more tourists or taking them away back to Cusco.

We would be taking the train the next morning, but we had all afternoon and evening to enjoy the quaint little mountain town. After settling into a very nice, modern hotel up a steep street from the railroad track, we spent most of the afternoon drinking beers at a café alongside the railroad track where the porters had dropped our green canvas bags of gear. Other members of our Inca Trail group joined us sporadically and we introduced them to our wives. All our fellow climbers were catching the late train to Cusco that evening, so they had no chance to shower and clean up. Brent and I felt great having already had that luxury.

After saying goodbye to our hiking friends, we strolled around the town a bit, then met for drinks and dinner at our hotel, where the dinner was part of the price. The hotel was a bit too modern for my taste, but the food was quite good. Unfortunately, by that time I was so tired, all I wanted to do was go to bed.

We did not expect much from the day after seeing Machu Picchu, but we were pleasantly surprised. The train ride from Aguas Calientes back to Ollantaytambo was spectacular. The narrow-gauge train track meandered along the Urubamba River, with its rapids and small waterfalls cascading to our right and multiple views of snowcapped peaks visible through the sky windows on the top of the train car. Brent and I struggled to determine exactly where we had left the river on the Inca Trail four days earlier, but recognized some of the smaller ruins we had seen along the way.

We pointed out where we had started the trail at the "Km 82 Marker" to Kim and Mpopo (who were dutifully unimpressed), and soon we chugged into the train station at Ollantaytambo. There we retrieved extra bags left by our wives at a hotel adjacent to the tracks and loaded everything into a small van waiting in a nearby parking lot. The driver cut a corner a bit too sharp on the way out of the parking space, dragging a small boulder under the back-right tire and creating quite a ruckus. But once the boulder was removed, we quickly sped to the center of town and back to the ruins visible from the town square that Brent and I had briefly explored on the morning of the first day to the Inca Trail.

This time, however, Brent and I had time to explore the whole complex. While Kim and Mpopo strolled the gardens at the bottom of the ruins with Marco, their guide, Brent and I worked our way up some steep steps to a landing area of sorts on the top left side of the ruins where a wall of huge stones was erected. From there we could see the whole town and much of the valley leading to it. At the top of the ruins was a fortress-like set of walls and rooms with a door at the back, which led out onto a steep mountainside. We could see more Incan walls higher up, but they were so dilapidated that it did not seem worthwhile to try to climb up to them.

Instead, we retraced our steps and worked our way across to the right side of the complex along a narrow path around a rock outcropping. The path was maybe two feet wide and the wall between the path and a long drop-off was only knee high, so I stayed very close to the inside rock wall as we worked our way towards the right side of the complex. It did not help that a large group of tourists were coming around the corner from the other side, requiring us to slide by them on the more exposed side.

The right side of the ruins was capped by a small barnlike structure above multiple terraced areas and walls. Brent and I worked our way up to it and noticed even more walls in the very steep section of mountain above us. But again, we decided not to explore further. After four days of climbing, it was not worth it. I raced down the steps back to the bottom at a good clip to show off for Kim. But it turned out that she was not watching, so my efforts went unnoticed. She was too busy strolling the garden areas and taking pictures of the llamas grazing in the grass near the entrance.

We grabbed some sandwiches "to go" from a small café at the corner of the town square and hit the road again in the small van. After about ten minutes on the main road, we took a right across the train tracks and the river and began a tortuous ascent up a series of gradual switchbacks up to the "central plateau" as Marco described it. The views of some of the surrounding mountains were spectacular, but I wondered why we had taken such a detour just to see a bunch of plowed fields on a high plain.

I soon found out. We passed a square building with a big sign—"Toilets"—on our left, then passed a row of souvenir stalls on our right before pulling into a gravel parking lot next to a red chalet-like hut. On the other side of the street were some view stands overlooking one of the most amazing Incan ruins in Peru. The Moray ruins are circular-terraced walls forming a huge amphitheater of sorts, which filled the bowl-like depression in the mountains in front of and below us. The view was almost like a modern art painting with its concentric circles and sweeping curves. We stood there staring at the beauty of it for about ten minutes before Brent and I spied a trail going down and around it and decided to take yet another hike.

It was easy going down and all the way around to the far end of the ruins, but I found myself huffing and puffing on the way back up the far side. I almost forgot that we were at almost 13,000 feet again at that point. To think that the Incas built this amazing set of walls at that altitude is a bit mind-blowing, but after this trip nothing was too surprising about the Incas' ingenuity.

From there, we crossed the rest of the central plateau and hit another series of very sharp switchbacks and S-curves on our way down the mountain. This time, however, there was another surprise awaiting us. The "salt flats." Down in a narrow valley beneath that series of switchbacks was a place where saltwater flowed out of the mountainside and into thousands of little terraces built into the side of the hill below, creating pools of pure-white salt crystals across the hillside. We first saw it from almost straight above at a viewpoint between the switchbacks, but then the driver negotiated a narrow dirt road down to a series of small buildings right next to the salt ponds.

Marco showed us how the stream fed each of the ponds. The salty water flowed right out of the mountain and into ever-splicing aqueduct systems, which diverted the water into different ponds, with each pond having a plug to stop the water flow when it got to the desired four to five inches in depth. The heat and sun then crystalized the salt on the top of the ponds. The crystals were then scraped off the top and placed in hills to dry before being bagged and hauled back up to the storage shed above. The next layer of the pond would then dry and be scraped for a second batch of salt crystals, but those would be of second-tier quality. Eventually, the pool would be drained and refilled to start the process again. There must have been a thousand ponds or pools on the hillside and each of them was tended by a different individual in the cooperative.

Before we left, Kim took way too much time in a very "ticky-tacky" souvenir shop up near the salt storage area. Not to be outdone, I quickly purchased a nice little purse for my daughter, which Kim insisted was too small to be of any use.

Au contraire.

The rest of the drive back to Cusco was not too memorable except for the traffic and a side trip to Marco's neighborhood to find a mandolin-like guitar(ish) instrument that Kim wanted to buy for our son. We looked at three tiny and dusty musical-instrument shops on an unpaved street before settling on the chosen instrument, which was quickly wrapped in a colorful case. The vendor looked very happy to sell the instrument, which was not at all cheap. The price was probably a half year of earnings for her. Our son was thrilled with the gift, and we were happy to help the Cusco economy. A win-win.

We arrived at the Maytaq late that afternoon and settled into two slightly nicer rooms. We were on our own and the girls had not yet seen Cusco, except for the Cusco airport on their way to Ollantaytambo. So, we strolled the town square to give them a feel for the place, then hustled over to a restaurant named Uchu, which was recommended to Kim by one of younger members of the Inca Trail hiking group over beers in Aguas Calientes.

Luckily, we got there early, as we got the last unreserved table. Uchu is famous for its heated rock platters. I ordered a three-meat combo of chicken, shrimp, and alpaca steak, which came sizzling on a hot stone embedded in a wooden tray, with sauces and a salad alongside. The others ordered similar platters, some with regular steaks and seafood and some with more exotic lamb and alpaca. Soon the whole table was sizzling, as we were tasked with completing the cooking of the meat to our own choice of rare, medium, or well-done. It was delicious, and the atmosphere was, as they say, divine!

Next to us was a young couple from the United States who had just flown in and were heading out on a trail the next day. However, they booked too late to hike the Inca Trail and were doing a trek somewhere else in the vicinity and then would take the train and bus to Machu Picchu.

Brent and Mpopo went directly back to the hotel that evening, but Kim insisted that we take a walk down to the main square to get some time alone together. It was getting cold, so we bundled up a bit and headed out.

As we entered the square, we noticed a lot of festivities going on. It was Saturday night and a lot of local couples were getting married. A bride dressed in white (and clearly freezing) was posing for pictures at the top of the stairs in front of the cathedral. Another bride was over at the fountain with a professional photographer snapping photos right and left. A crowd gathered around one of the benches where a third bride was posing in a reclining position as photos were taken by several friends or photographers. Apparently, posing for photos at the main square is a popular wedding tradition in Cusco. I noticed that none of the grooms were posing or freezing alongside their goose-pimpled brides!

Kim and I sat at a bench near the fountain for about fifteen minutes before deciding to call it a night. It was just too cold to enjoy the festivities, and our romantic evening was constantly interrupted by women persistently approaching us to buy various trinkets.

Our final day in Cusco started with a trip to Saksaywamam, a mammoth archeological site at the top of the hill beyond the main square. Marco, our guide, fondly referred to the site as "Sexy Woman." Kim and Mpopo instantly posed as our "sexy women" in front of an archway sign at the visitors' center. Then we listened as Marco gave us a history of the various Incan kings in front of a sign listing each of them with their years of reign.

A short hike led us to an amazing set of ruins with enormous black stones forming long castle-like walls. The huge stones made the granite rocks at Stonehenge look like small Lego pieces. Much like those stones at Machu Picchu, these stones were smooth and stacked so tightly together that no mortar was needed. How they were put in place without cranes is a mystery, as they must have weighed ten to twelve tons apiece. At one point, after coming through a gateway formed by these huge rocks, we stood on a large field adjacent to several hundred yards of fortress walls formed from the dark-black rocks. Presumably this was a well-protected fort or castle at some time in the distant past.

Over on another hill near "Sexy Woman" was a large, white, sculpted Jesus figure shining in the sunlight, overlooking the city. Apparently, this figure was a gift to Cusco by a group of Palestinians who had lived there as refugees. When they left to return to their homeland, they gave the sculpture to their Christian friends in Cusco who had welcomed them at their time of need. At night, the white Jesus figure is lit up and looks over the main square of Cusco, much like its counterpart in Rio de Janeiro (though not on the same magnitude). We drove over to the figure to get some close-up photos, working our way through a multitude of picnickers and soccer players in the surrounding park.

The next stop on our tour was the Sun Temple, which Brent and I had skirted on our first day in Cusco. This time we went into the multiphased structure. Once inside, it was hard to tell what was original and what had been added in later years. In the center was a more modern Spanish-style courtyard with numerous columns and porticos. To our left was an original section of smooth black rocks forming the walls for several rooms. The interior walls had a small opening in them so that if a person stood on a raised stone in one room, that individual could see all the way into the room at the other end. Above that section were modern glass windows leading up to a high roof, which had been built to protect the original walls from the elements. Around to our right was a hallway, consisting partly of original walls on one side and of a small chapel that had been built on the other side. Marco took us around the chapel to the outside where we turned right into a narrow passage with original black stone wall on the left and the outside chapel wall on our right. At the very end of the passage was the most sacred spot in the building, where, back in the heydays of the Incas, some golden objects were kept in nooks in the wall. The nooks were still there, but no gold was seen. Marco explained that before the chapel was built, that sacred area was much larger. But, for me, it was hard to imagine how it might have looked in its original form.

I found the Sun Temple to be fascinating but confusing...a mishmash of cultures, architecture, and religions, almost as strange as the famous church built inside the mosque in Cordoba, Spain. Things just didn't fit.

In the Sun Temple, they even had a mock oil painting of the Last Supper, but with a guinea pig on the platter instead of lamb and Pizarro's face instead of Judas's.

What were they thinking?

With the formal tour completed, we headed down the main avenue about a half mile to a huge collection of over a hundred souvenir shops under a single roof. Kim was in heaven as we walked through long corridors of never-ending little shops, all offering almost the same wares. Fortunately, there was a little café in the back of the facility with passable sandwiches and drinks. I was still taking Cipro every morning…

We found another excellent place for dinner that night, once again arriving just in time to get the last unreserved table before the place became totally packed. All I remember from the meal at Cicciolina was the best onion soup I have ever tasted. With a sherry-based broth and large crouton with amazing bleu cheese in the center, it simply was mouthwatering. Whatever I had for my entrée was also excellent, and the desserts were equally incredible. But the onion soup was so good, I will never forget it.

Who knew Peru would have such great cuisine?

It was a wonderful way to spend our final night on a magnificent trip to see Machu Picchu, to explore the Sacred Valley, and to experience the challenges and beauty of the Inca Trail.

5

Cho Oyu at 60

The Final Chapter

Why would any sane person attempt to climb a mountain almost 27,000 feet in altitude at age 60? That is the question I was most likely to be asked when people learned about my plans to climb Cho Oyu two months after my sixtieth birthday.

Dave, my doctor friend who advised me regarding medications for the trip, went a bit further. He e-mailed me the following message: "Personally, I think you are absolutely crazy and an absolute 'nut job' for your continued pursuit of 'dying of unnatural causes.'"

I quickly forgave him for being so concerned, since he deals with death every day as a critical-care physician. It makes sense that he would hate to see someone die from an elective recreational activity when he sees so many deaths from unsolicited diseases and natural causes.

Next, everyone wanted to know where Cho Oyu is located. This is because almost no one has ever heard of it. They know Everest, K-2, Kilimanjaro, McKinley (most of them do not know that McKinley has now been formally renamed "Denali"), and perhaps Rainier, Mont Blanc, and Mt. Fuji. But Cho Oyu, the sixth-highest mountain in the world, with a summit at 26,906 feet in elevation, is unknown to just about anyone other than "crazy" people who dare to climb one of the fourteen peaks higher than 8,000 meters in elevation.

"Twenty kilometers west of Everest...and almost as high," I almost always responded to that second question. "At the summit, if you take photos from the west, looking east, Everest is right at shoulder level...not way up in the sky, but almost level."

"Are you demented?" they said with their eyes, if not aloud. Their faces revealed immediate concern for my well-being and mental status. So, my doctor friend was not alone in believing that I must have been insane or psychologically unstable to attempt such a climb.

The conversations usually moved into questions about how long the trip would be, how many days it takes to climb a mountain that high, how high is it again, who are you going with, and inevitably, what does your wife think about this adventure?

"Just another *stupid* mountain, is what she thinks," I would reply. "She doesn't think I'm crazy...just dumb!"

But the toughest question of all that people always returned to was: "Why would you risk your life to climb a 27,000-foot-high mountain at your age?"

The adage "because it is there" does not satisfy folks anymore. And that existential and somewhat evasive response by a famous mountaineer long before me was not a very good reason in the first place. Rather, the reason I have chosen to climb a lot of high mountains is basic. I like to challenge myself, physically and mentally. As I go through life, I need a goal in mind to keep in shape, to focus my energy, and to drive my motivations. If I don't have a project or a challenge in front of me, I get bored. I drift, apathetically. A planned mountain climb is something to train for and to set the course for my non-business pursuits for a year or more. The high mountains beckon and raise my adventurous spirit and my yearning for a tangible physical accomplishment in the twilight of my life. Once in training, I constantly imagine reaching the summit of each mountain. It drives me forward with enthusiasm and purpose.

And, if I am going to climb, why settle for training hikes on nearby Kennesaw Mountain or Brasstown Bald on Saturday mornings? Those are great training hikes with my regular hiking buddies, Lee, Jim, and Rick. But they are just warmups. To get me motivated, I say to myself, "Go for the gusto—go big!"

Besides, who would not want to train and endure substantial misery for almost a year just to have twenty minutes or less of glory at the top of a "stupid" mountain?

Sarcasm aside, that is what climbing high-altitude mountains is all about for me: the training, the beauty, and the challenge of the climb itself. And, of course, the summit experience. But unless you have done it, it is very hard to explain the sense of pride and accomplishment when, after all that work and effort, you stand atop a prominent peak with the whole world below you. You feel exhilarated and exhausted at the same time. You cry uncontrollably and without shame. You experience sheer unfiltered happiness. But usually the euphoria lasts only for fifteen to twenty minutes, just long enough to take in the view, snap some photos, and then head carefully back down to civilized safety and a routine existence.

While the immediate thrill is fleeting, the total experience lasts a lifetime.

What motivated me to climb Cho Oyu in 2016, though, was even simpler. I had become fat.

Having thoroughly enjoyed my trip to hike the Inca Trail to Machu Picchu in August 2015, I was not expecting to cringe when I saw the photos from the trip taken by my brother Brent.

"David, you're a fat shit," I said to myself, looking at my protruding gut in every picture.

Deep down, I knew I had gotten lazy in the last few years. After getting prostate cancer three years prior and dealing with three surgeries and thirty-four radiation treatments, a combination of apathy and lack of exercise, compounded by an unhealthy dose of binge-eating junk food, had finally taken their toll. I was over 240 pounds and had lost only four or five pounds training for the Inca Trail. My legs were still relatively trim and strong, but my belly was soft and rotund. The photos showed the result of a lot of skipped sit-ups and the consumption of a lot of Cokes and crap food for too many years.

As a young adult, I had always been able to keep off the pounds. I was playing competitive soccer, practicing twice a week and playing another two times a week, plus running 10Ks and constantly sweating off any excess pounds doing one thing or another. In my twenties and thirties, my playing weight was between 185 and190 pounds and I could eat anything I wanted. After I retired from soccer at age forty and merely started coaching the kids a few days a week, my weight slowly, but constantly, rose until I was carrying between 205 and 210 pounds. At 6 feet, 1 inch, that was a respectable weight, but I did not want to go much higher.

After four years of relative inactivity and in part to deal with the threat of weight gain, I started my mountain-climbing career at age forty-four. I trained to climb Mt. Whitney with my brothers. After that, I trained to climb Pico de Orizaba in Mexico, losing ten pounds before the climb and another seven pounds on the climb. As soon as one mountain was over, I started planning another. But in each case, there was always at least a short interim period of enjoying candy and cookies and chips and cake—the bad C's! My weight kept going down during training and the climb itself and then back up within six weeks of getting back.

I managed to keep below 215 pounds through two climbs of Mt. Elbrus in Southern Russia and Kilimanjaro in Africa. Then, with ten months of training for Aconcagua and the climb itself, I was in top condition at a firm 205 pounds by the time I returned from that month-long climb.

Then I turned fifty and returned to my bad habits.

Shortly thereafter, while training for Mt. Vinson in Antarctica in 2007, someone told me I would lose at least ten pounds on that climb just from the freezing temperatures. So, I figured a little padding wouldn't hurt. Plus, Vinson is only 16,100 feet, so I did not bust it to lose the weight before heading to our most southern continent. But with six days of drinking and dining in Punta Arenas, Chile, while waiting to fly over to the "ice," and AAI guide Vern Tejas feeding us so well once on the climb, when I returned from that trip I had gained almost ten pounds and was approaching 225 pounds.

After Vinson, I had no other high-altitude mountains on the radar. My wife had vetoed Denali and Everest. I picked up my fifth continental summit, the Australian hill, Koscuiszko, in 2009 on a family trip to New Zealand and Australia. My kids and wife bagged their first continental peak on that one. I climbed a couple of Colorado peaks and did three climbs of Mt. Rainier in Washington over the next few years. But I seriously trained only for Rainier, successfully dropping my weight to 215 again momentarily until I returned from my first two unsuccessful attempts to climb Mt. Rainier.

Then came a surprise PSA reading of 115 and prostate cancer. I never would have known, except I applied for a new life insurance policy at work and it required a routine blood test. At first, I thought that reading must be a mistake, as a normal PSA level is between two and four. But a second blood test at the urologist's office was 112.5. I was tentatively diagnosed with the big "C" a week before finally making it to the top of Rainier on my third attempt in late July 2011. I felt fine, so my urologist did not object to my completing the climb before moving forward with the definitive biopsy.

My radical prostatectomy was in September 2011. Unfortunately, the pathology report from the surgery showed positive margins in four directions, indicating that the cancer had spread beyond the outer confines of the prostate itself. So, I had to choose among several options for dealing with the residual cancer, eventually choosing to have radiation treatments—thirty-four of them. However, the toughest part was that the prostatectomy involved a major vertical cut below my naval, rendering any type of serious abdominal workouts and sit-ups impossible for many months.

More devastating to my mid-section was my changed mental attitude.

To put it bluntly, cancer sucks! As much psychologically as physically.

No matter how hard I tried to brush off the cancer and move on, I kept feeling sorry for myself. I wondered whether it was even worth trying to keep myself in good shape for future climbing. I compounded the mental and psychological effects of the cancer by deciding not to tell anyone about it and forbidding my wife and family from disclosing it to even our closest friends. I did not want every conversation I had with friends for the rest of my life to begin with a sad look and a question about how I was feeling. I did not want a cancer diagnosis to define me. Nor did I want my attorney colleagues to think I was dying and stop referring cases to me.

The more I internalized my feelings, however, the more apathetic I got. I had no one except my wife to talk to about the cancer or my misgivings about the future. I slowly drifted into a funk like I'd never experienced before. I stopped exercising and started becoming the couch potato I never wanted to be. By the time the surgical area had healed and a plan had been put together for radiation treatments to zap the rest of the leftover cancer cells, I was almost 245 pounds (at least, on the doctor's scales with shoes and clothes on). My blood pressure had shot up well beyond any normal levels and seemed to be rising even further every time I went to the doctor's office. I was getting splitting headaches in the afternoon and just feeling crummy.

Something had to be done. My apathy needed to be dealt with. I needed to move on with life.

High blood-pressure medications were the first step. But that did nothing for me psychologically. I needed a goal to reach, a project to complete, a destination to aim for. I needed something to push myself out of the doldrums.

So, almost out of desperation, I sent in my deposit for an Everest base camp trek that was to start four and a half months after my seven weeks of radiation treatment were to end. That would give me from just before Memorial Day 2012 until early October to get back in shape enough to climb up to 18,000 feet in altitude over ten days in Nepal. I immediately started walking two miles after each radiation treatment before going to the office.

Then, as soon as the radiation was done, I intensified my workouts and scheduled a trip to Colorado to climb four 14,000ers in two days in August with my son. I did not have time for apathy. I had time only to get in shape and sweat some flab off my midsection. My son and I successfully climbed Mt. Democrat one day and Mts. Cameron, Lincoln, and Bross the next day without too much difficulty. It helped that the trailhead for these four mountains is at 12,000 feet and these climbs are among the easiest in Colorado. Nevertheless, I felt confident that I would be able to handle the Nepal trek to Everest base camp. Somehow, I managed to drop my weight to about 227 by the time I left for Kathmandu. Not great, but a lot better than 245.

Luckily, the Everest base camp trek was not particularly strenuous compared to many of the climbs I had done, so I survived it without significant medical or physical problems. However, on that trek, for the first time in my mountaineering career, I found myself lagging the leaders and almost pulling up the rear by the end of each segment of the climb. The year of medical treatment and inactivity had taken its toll on my endurance, leg strength, and speed. The high blood-pressure medications, which included beta-blockers, had, in effect, placed a governor on my heartrate. I could feel it telling me to slow down when I pushed too hard to keep up with the others.

More concerning, while returning from the afternoon hike to Everest base camp from Gorak Shep at just under 18,000 feet, I felt slightly disoriented and clumsy, tripping on some rocks and nearly going down three or four times, my trekking poles keeping me up. I shrugged it off, but decided not to risk climbing Kala Pattar, the small peak above the final outpost below Everest base camp, the following morning. Fortunately, I had no problem during the five days coming back down the Khumbu Valley.

Still, I was fifty-six years old, a cancer survivor, and now a would-be climber with an uncertain future.

Was I too old to climb? Should I hang up my crampons and climbing boots and call it a day?

My wife said yes. My children would have probably erred on the side of caution as well, had I asked them. My mother-in-law clearly would prefer me to stay at home and never climb again.

But climbing is still in my now well-medicated blood. But for the minor disorientation near Everest base camp and temporary headache on Kilimanjaro years before, I had never had any problems with high altitude, due in large part to the excellent acclimatization protocols of my guide groups. I knew I could do it, and I pledged to myself that I would not let this cancer business scare me off from continuing to climb. So, continue to climb, I did!

In 2013, for the first time, I climbed in the Alps, including reaching the top of the Aguille du Tour, a spire of boulders atop a glacier bordering France and Switzerland near Chamonix. I was supposed to climb Mont Blanc on that trip, but an incoming snowstorm and a young guide who refused to move up the climbing schedule led me to decline to start out on the climb, which I felt was not safe under the predicted conditions. Four others made the attempt, only to be turned around 1,500 feet from the top when the snowstorm hit as scheduled. They retreated to an upper hut above the Grand Coulier under horrendous weather conditions and appeared totally shell-shocked when they finally returned to Chamonix. I made the right, smart decision not to make the attempt in those conditions.

ANOTHER FIVE BIG MOUNTAINS AND TREKS

A year later, on a trip to visit my daughter in Japan and while my wife and children were sightseeing in Tokyo, I climbed Mt. Fuji to the top, along with thousands of Japanese. I had trained for a few months for that climb and performed adequately on the way up, but I was nowhere near peak condition. However, I was getting my strength back, my attitude was shifting, and my confidence was building.

In October 2014, I joined two friends, Jim and Richard, on a Grand Canyon rim-to-rim-to-rim trip, hiking from the South Rim to the North Rim in one day, resting a day, then hiking back to the South Rim on the third day. It is about twenty-four miles across, and the elevation gain from the bottom of the canyon at the Colorado River up to the North Rim is over six thousand feet. So it takes a lot of endurance and persistence to make it through the twelve- to thirteen-hour trek and then do it all over again on the way back two days later. Jim and I completed the arduous trek, but Richard, who had led the way up to the North Rim, suffered a foot injury and a flu bug, which knocked him out of the return hike back to the South Rim. Richard has since successfully climbed with me to the top of a 14,000er in Colorado, just for fun.

Still, I was having a hard time dropping weight in preparation for these climbs. I was essentially carrying an extra backpack of weight everywhere I went. After another few months of heavy food intake over the holidays, I was back up at 240 pounds.

My only trip in 2015 was to Machu Picchu and the Inca Trail in late August. I had planned to climb two more 14,000ers in Colorado in early August, but my hiking buddy, Jim, started having heart problems and was unable to go. So, I never got the type of training or weight loss I should have had before hitting the Inca Trail. But I did not think it would be that much of a challenge. The highest point on the trail is only 13,840 feet, several hundred feet lower than a dozen or more mountains I had climbed in Colorado in prior years with little or no training.

As it turned out, the Inca Trail was very doable, but the almost four-thousand-foot ascent to the highest point at Dead Woman's Pass on the second day of the trek was quite exhausting. We covered that ascent in just less than four hours, and I was sucking wind during the last hour or so. Still I felt I was in relatively good shape. The photos told a different story. The guy in the mirror who has always been tall and thin since eleventh grade looked pudgy and bloated. His midsection was, to say the least, thick, if not sagging. Embarrassingly so. Even his face looked fat. Once again, something had to be done.

Time to get serious again—one last time. Well, maybe *the* last time. A true climber never says "never."

The answer was Cho Oyu. I had been criticized by one commentator on Amazon that the mountains depicted in my book, *Five Big Mountains*, were not truly serious mountains. Well, no one can say that Cho Oyu is not a serious mountain. Cho Oyu is the sixth-highest mountain in the world and almost two miles higher than Kilimanjaro. At 26,906 feet, it is only a little more than two thousand feet lower than the summit of Everest. Even though Cho Oyu may be the easiest and safest of the fourteen peaks over 8,000 meters, it is clearly a huge challenge for almost any climber, let alone a sixty-year-old cancer survivor.

I knew there could be no laziness in my training if I really wanted to successfully climb it to the top.

No apathy—no excuses, David.

I decided to go for it. I set a goal not only to climb higher than I had ever climbed before, but to turn back time, to regain my physical condition equal to when I climbed Aconcagua at age fifty. I would be sixty when I climbed Cho Oyu, but my body would feel like it was fifty again. First, I had to lose the weight and get down to between 210 and 215 pounds. Second, I had to intensify my training and regain speed and leg strength. Third, I had to work out my upper body because there would be an ice cliff to climb and a lot of fixed rope to pull myself up on ascenders when tackling the steeper snow slopes of Cho Oyu. Fourth, I had to get healthy and hopefully lower my blood pressure significantly enough to wean off the high blood-pressure pills.

It was a tall order, but one I embraced wholeheartedly.

Surprisingly, my wife did not try to persuade me to change my mind or threaten to divorce me if I went through with this climb. Cho Oyu may be safer than Denali (which she has vetoed), but it is over a mile higher and can be just as cold. But I promised it would be the culmination of my climbing career and my last high-altitude climb.

The final chapter.

And I hoped to use it to return to a healthy lifestyle and weight to carry with me as I approach retirement on the golf course!

Six months into my ten-month training schedule, I felt great. I was down to 222 pounds, my legs were strong, and my training runs and hikes were down to pre-Aconcagua times. I still needed to lose another eight to twelve pounds, but I was busting it up the steeper climbs in the North Georgia mountains. I handled my twenty-two-miler on the Bartram Trail to the top of Rabun's Bald in record time. I then pushed myself up the Arkaquah Trail section of the Appalachian Trail to the top of Brasstown Bald, the highest point in Georgia, in another record time for me, with another hiking friend, Rick.

Then came the Cold Mountain hike in Western North Carolina. It was a cold, foggy, and misty day, with intermittent winds, and no views from the tops of any ridges. Hiking with my brother Brent and hiking buddy, Lee, we were getting soaked as we squeezed through narrow gaps in the bushes on the Art Loeb Trail after reaching the top of Black Balsam Mountain and working our way over to Tennant Mountain. Both are just over 6,000 feet in elevation. We trucked along at a good pace and reached Shining Rock ahead of schedule after a slight detour on a side trail. Then the going got tough. Not far beyond Shining Rock, the trail started descending and ascending through a series of rocky stretches, which tested the knees and balance, especially for a trio of climbers averaging sixty-four years in age.

Shortly after reaching the top of one of the rocky ascents, I relaxed as we resumed a wider, smoother path down the side of a hill through a wooded area. I relaxed just long enough to turn my left ankle outwards on a root. A sharp jolt shot up my leg. If I were not wearing my high ankle leather hiking boots, I probably would have broken my ankle, or sprained it badly enough not to be able to walk. But I put some pressure on my foot and it seemed okay. I tightened my laces just a bit to give my ankle a little more support and then kept going. I noticed a slight amount of pain the rest of the day, especially on the way down from Cold Mountain, but I figured the pain would go away by the next day.

Back in Atlanta, I kept training regularly, assuming the pain was temporary. However, three or four weeks later, that pain was still there, midway up the outer edge of my left foot. I decided to give my training a rest for a week. The pain seemed to subside, so I resumed my training runs. But the pain in my left foot returned, and, to make it worse, my left knee started hurting.

My guess is that I suffered a slight stress fracture of a bone in my foot that just would not fully heal due to constant pounding as I trained and ran up and down stadium stairs and hills. I was in a quandary. I did not want to hinder the healing process, but I did not want to neglect my training. So, May 2016 was a bad month. Just when I wanted to intensify my training and get my weight down to my goal of between 210 and 215 pounds, I had to stay off my aching left knee and the painful left foot for two to three weeks. At the same time, I also had a lot of social functions with too many drinking and eating temptations. Before I knew it, I had reversed my progress and added another five pounds instead of losing weight.

But by June, my foot and ankle were pain-free and I resumed full workouts.

My last training climbs before leaving for Cho Oyu were two 14,000ers in Colorado on a four-day weekend early in August 2016. The itinerary involved two travel days from Atlanta to Denver and back, with back-to-back climbs of Quandary Peak near Breckenridge and Mt. Antero near Salida on successive days in between. My son, Daniel, and a sixty-five-year-old lawyer colleague named Watson, joined me for the climbs. Another lawyer named Nick, who had read my first book, *Five Big Mountains*, and contacted me through Linked In, joined us for Mt. Antero as a warmup for his planned climb up Mt. Rainier the next weekend. Nick was an in-house counsel for a major satellite TV dish company headquartered in Colorado, so he regularly climbed 14,000ers.

On the flight to Denver from Atlanta, my son and I checked the weather forecasts for the weekend. Both days looked like disasters—60 to 100 percent rain and lots of thunderstorms. Indeed, when we landed in Denver, the entire Rocky Mountain range was shrouded in clouds. As we drove up I-70 into the mountains, it began to rain.

"Good we brought our rain gear," I said, looking at the increasingly darkening sky ahead of us.

The rain got especially hard as we came out of the long I-70 tunnel a few miles before our turn-off for Breckenridge.

"This could really suck," I said matter-of-factly.

"No pain, no gain," Watson said, laughing out loud.

We exited the highway and turned left towards Breckenridge. The heavy rain subsided, but we still had enough of a drizzle to keep the windshield wipers going full speed.

Rather than go directly to our hotel, I decided that we would check out the trailhead for Quandary Peak. But first, we stopped by the house of a climber on the Cho Oyu roster whose name and e-mail I had just gotten from my guide group, Alpine Ascents. John was his name. He had mentioned in an e-mail that he lived less than five minutes from the Quandary trailhead and had climbed it at least twenty-five times for training. So, we plugged his address into the GPS and headed that way. About nine miles south of Breckenridge, we turned left onto a dirt road and after a few lefts and curves up the mountain we pulled into his driveway.

To say that John lives in a nice mountain cabin is an understatement. The house, all glass and wood, was situated on a hill looking directly out at a long range of mountains above the Breckenridge ski slopes. Expenses clearly had not been spared on the inside of the house. Wood beams, expensive kitchen appliances, high-grade counters and cabinets, a beautiful stone fireplace, and classy furnishings led me to believe John had put some serious dough into the place. He confirmed it by telling us that he had sold a credit card processing company six years ago, built the house, and retired. He now enjoyed skiing and doing volunteer trail repair while pursuing his mountaineering hobby. His plans included climbing Everest after a successful "training climb" on Cho Oyu!

It was nice to know that there would be at least one person in my general age group on Cho Oyu. John was fifty-six, only four years younger than me. And he looked very fit. Living at 10,000 feet elevation also gave him a decided advantage. Let's just say he was very used to thin air, regularly working and climbing at altitudes over 14,000 feet.

After a very enjoyable chat with John, we headed over to the trailhead for Quandary Peak. It was only three miles beyond the turn-off to his house. We pulled in next to a sign indicating it was the trailhead parking area. At the far end on the right were two port-a-potties and on the left a metal trail sign. As it was still raining, we did not get out, but I was sure we had found the right place.

About ten minutes later we pulled up to the Marriott Mountain Valley Resort at the south end of Breckenridge, unloaded our stuff in the pouring rain, and checked in. Fortunately, after a few hours of rest and relaxation, the sun appeared and we headed into down for dinner. Luigi's Pizza place was almost empty when we walked in and ordered an 18-inch pizza for the three of us. The restaurant was full and becoming quite loud by the time we left at about 7 P.M. Since we planned on being on the trail by 6 A.M. the next morning, we hit the sack early.

The next morning, we quickly found the same trailhead parking area. This time it was about half full of vehicles. It did not take us very long to figure out that this was the overflow parking lot. We hiked across a private property lot to another road heading up the mountain and immediately saw a line of cars parked on the right side of the road ahead of us. About a quarter mile up was another small parking area, completely full of cars, but there was a nice open spot just beyond it where we could have parked.

"Geez, we could have already saved ourselves a quarter mile up and another quarter mile at the end of the day," I said sheepishly. "I wonder why John didn't tell us about the parking up here!"

No matter. With our legs already stretched and warmed up, we located the main trail beyond a metal post on the left side of the road and headed up the first incline. Despite the rain the previous day, the trail was well-drained with no discernable mud or puddles.

This trail did not start slowly. The rise through the pines was steep from the outset. I deliberately kept a slow pace, but after I inadvertently followed a shortcut off the main trail, Daniel jumped ahead and led us up some switchbacks at a slightly faster pace. Soon I was breathing hard and sweating into my Duke baseball cap. It was no steeper than the trails in the North Georgia mountains, but at almost 11,000 feet elevation and very limited acclimatization, it sure felt steeper. Still, we moved steadily upwards, clearing the tree line at about 12,000 feet in less than an hour.

The second hour involved a much rockier path with intermittent series of stone steps, ever ascending between 12,000 and 13,000 feet in elevation. The best part of this section were the views of the surrounding mountains. We could see clouds rolling in around the summit in front of us, but the sky was clear to the left. We could see miles across to a mountain range and down to the valley below. We rested briefly after a few of the lengthier stone step sections, but kept on going until we reached a level spot on the shoulder of the mountain just before it started going up the summit ridge.

After a snack break, we attacked the final ridge. The path was easy at first, almost level. But then it turned upwards, becoming more and more steep with each step. The clouds came in, making visibility of the mountain ridge above us impossible. Eventually, the trail disappeared and we found ourselves picking random paths up through the talus, taking fifty steps up, resting to catch our breaths, and then pushing up another fifty steps.

About halfway up, a young lady in gray spandex and a bright smile passed us as if we were standing still.

"Damn, what I would give to have young legs like that again," I thought to myself.

She soon disappeared into the thick mist above us. About fifteen minutes later, the same girl passed us again—this time on her way down.

"It's not much further," she said. "Listen for the whoops!"

Not much later, I heard Daniel and Watson hollering just above me. I had been keeping my head down and, in the clouds, I did not realize that I was only about thirty feet below the summit. I pressed ahead and joined them at the top. I looked at my watch—just over three hours to the top—not bad for about an elevation gain of 3,600 feet from the lower parking lot.

I looked around. There were perhaps twenty people on the small summit. I found the round summit marker, tapped it with my trekking pole, and took a seat on a rock. But there was nothing to see. The entire view, 360 degrees in all directions, was just a grey cloud. With nothing to look at, I grabbed a Snickers and some celery and carrots to replenish my energy for the descent.

After a short rest, a couple handed Daniel a cardboard sign with "Quandary 14,265" on it, and we posed for photos. With no view behind us, we could have been standing next to a rock in a rainstorm anywhere in the world. But the sign provided some sense of legitimacy for the photos! Fifteen minutes later we were on our way down, making it back to the car in a little over two and a half hours. A good warmup for Mt. Antero the next day. But I was starving!

Alma, Colorado, is the home of the "highest bar in the world," at least that's what the sign outside the place proclaims. Daniel and I had sampled beers and sandwiches there after our climbs of Mts. Lincoln, Cameron, and Bross a few years back, so the three of us stopped in again for lunch on our way down to Salida. A slight warning: It may claim to be the highest bar in the world and the food is passable, but the service is certainly not the fastest in the world.

The drive from Alma to Salida was beautiful. To our right was the incredible Sawatch Range of mountains with the collegiate peaks of Mts. Harvard, Columbia, Yale, and Princeton dominating the western skies. Further down, Mts. Antero, Shavano, and Tebegauche form a major triumvirate. We took a short cut over to Salida on a small road through some farmland, skirted downtown Salida, and found the Silver Ridge Lodge on Paradise Boulevard. Paradise it was not, but a clean and comfortable, old-style motel, complete with actual metal keys for the doors and push-button A/C units it was. Amazingly, my legs were not the slightest bit stiff after the almost six-hour climb and two hours in the car.

Maybe I was getting in good enough shape to climb Cho Oyu.

We met Nick at a restaurant called the River's Edge, quite an appropriate name given that it features a patio right above the Colorado River in downtown Salida. The House Pub Burger and fries hit the spot, along with a local porter ale to wash it down. I highly recommend the place, not only for the food, but for the outdoorsy atmosphere.

Nick filled us in on his company and his boss's annual mandatory climb of a 14,000er for all his company's interns. This apparently was his company's favorite way of testing character.

"It's hard to bullshit your way up a 14,000er!" he said.

He told us that most of the young interns made it to the top each year. That is, all except for the engineers, who struggled just to get above tree line before turning back.

Unlike his young interns, I guessed Nick was in his mid-forties. He clearly was into mountains. Antero was his last training climb before he planned to climb Mt. Rainier in Washington State the next weekend. Over the phone, he had mentioned a desire to do Rainier at some point, and I had sent him a draft of a book chapter on my trials and tribulations in my three attempts to climb Rainier, but I did not realize that his climb was imminent. I did know he was thinking about climbing Aconcagua in the winter, which is why he bought my book in the first place. Obviously, his job allowed him to take time off from work for some mountain adventures.

In any case, it was fun to share Colorado climbing stories with him over a relaxing dinner, with the calming sounds of a rushing river in the background.

Mt. Antero is 14,264 feet high, just one foot lower than Quandary Peak. But it is much harder to climb—at least on the trail we selected, which involved an elevation gain of 5,350 feet. The more popular "main" route is a hike up a 4x4 dirt road from a much higher trailhead at over 11,000 feet. However, we decided to take the "hiker's" trail from a trailhead at just above 8,900 feet elevation. It entailed at least a fourteen-mile round trip from the bottom to the top and back down. As it turns out, the round trip ended up being closer to 17.5 miles and we took over 43,000 steps to get up and back, if you believe our Fitbits.

The hike started out easy. We covered a quick 1.5 miles along a gradually rising trail to a junction with the Colorado Trail, which apparently runs down the middle of Colorado for over four hundred miles. But we stayed on the Colorado Trail for only .3 mile before turning left onto the Little Brown's Creek Trail, which runs alongside an ever-narrowing creek almost four-fifths of the way to the summit. I signed in for our group at a box on the right side of the trail. I'm not sure why, but it seemed like the proper thing to do.

After more than two hours of hiking through thickly forested sections with the summit of White Mountain soaring above us to the left, we emerged onto a long, steadily rising valley with grassy fields and small flowers to our left and right. The valley seemed never to end as we trudged upwards, the path sandy under our feet. I felt like we were hiking in dunes at the beach. I kept targeting rocks in the distance to gauge our progress, but every time I reached the next rock, the end of the valley looked just as far away. We just kept marching upwards.

After a while, we noticed what looked like a path stretching diagonally across a yellowish mountain ridge up to our right. Daniel spied a red Jeep going up that path and pointed in that direction. The path did not look wide enough for a vehicle from where we were. But we were still too far away to gauge it.

"That must be where the 4x4 track comes in from the other side of the mountain," I said. "I didn't think the road went up that far."

Soon after that, we noticed another road just a hundred yards or so up the hill to our left. We were coming close to joining the other "main" trail. We stopped for a snack break and watched as a dozen or more climbers crossed over a pass just above us and headed up the diagonal road across the yellow ridge. Another SUV joined them and, at the end of the diagonal stretch, turned up a switchback in the road and worked its way up the other direction.

Obviously, that was the way to the top. With no other choice, we cut the corner over to the bottom of the visible diagonal road. Sure enough, it was a wide track with enough large rocks to make it impassable for most passenger cars, but still doable for SUVs with four-wheel drives. I hate hiking on roads, but that seemed the only way to our destination. It was a slow trudge up the muddy switchbacks.

Towards the top, three guys had an ATV and were offering rides to some of the hikers who looked tired. We refused, but watched several hikers hop on and cheat their way up to the top of the pass. The ATV guys told us to make sure we took a good rest up at the pass before tackling the top of the mountain. When we reached that point, we saw why. The summit peak was situated beyond a narrow ridge, which looked like a huge dinosaur's back with vertical fins on the top of it. They called the trail through that section the "knife's edge." At first sight, I hesitated, thinking that we might be breaking off more than we could chew. But after watching a few other climbers work their way over the dinosaur's back, I knew we could do it as well.

As we approached the rocky section, I realized that I would be better off climbing with free hands rather than with trekking poles, so I took the time to pack them up carefully in my daypack. The next thirty minutes or so were a bit tricky with some exposed areas where a fall could be calamitous, but it turned out not to be as bad as it looked. Nick took a direct path across the top of the dinosaur back, drawing some criticism from the ATV guys who were following behind us on foot. Daniel, Watson, and I followed the worn path as well as we could, climbing up between large boulders and grabbing on with our hands when necessary. Eventually we all four reached the bottom of the summit peak, which simply soared upwards at a very steep angle. Now there was no path, just hands and feet, crawling up, then standing up and moving sideways around boulders, and then crawling up again. After about twenty minutes of hard labor, we reached the tiny summit, which was no more than fifteen by twenty-five feet. It was a challenging end to a long climb. I looked at my watch. It was just after noon—we had left the trailhead about six hours earlier.

This time the views were magnificent. When we first reached the top, the skies and surrounding mountains were clear in all directions. After about ten minutes, however, several lightning bolts lit up the sky, creating quite a contrast with the dark clouds in that direction, followed by a booming thunderclap coming from a low dark cloud hovering over a ridge just beyond the valley we had hiked up.

"Shit," I said, "we're gonna get nailed on the way down."

"Not a problem," one of the ATV guys said. "That cloud will just hang there for hours. It was just like that yesterday."

"Well, just in case, I think we need to be heading down, boys," I said to our group. So, after a hurried flurry of photos, we headed down within twenty minutes of our arrival on the summit.

No rest for the weary.

Daniel and I moved down the rocky ridge and over the dinosaur back "knife's edge" at a fast pace, waiting at the bottom for Watson and Nick to arrive. They both were more comfortable going up than down, with Watson's knees making him take it slowly. Once over the pass and back on the 4x4 road, we picked up the pace. About a third of the way down the final switchback on the road, we veered left through the side of the valley, cutting off at least a quarter of a mile to intersect with the trail at the top of Little Brown's Creek. There it started to rain, hard enough that we immediately dropped our bags and donned outer shells to stay dry. But the rain lasted only about five minutes. Within ten minutes, we stripped our raingear back off as the sun started beating on our backs and warming us up.

The valley seemed to fly under our feet. Soon we were back in the pines, meandering down through the forest. This is where the sheer length of the climb caught up with us. It seemed like we would never get back down to the Colorado Trail. I kept looking for the sign-in box, anticipating the end of the trail. But we still had several miles to go. It was hard to imagine that we had come up through this forest and all the steep areas without really noticing how long it was on the way up. And we had not seen another soul from the moment we left the trailhead until we got up to the end of the valley on the way up and from the moment we started down the valley on the way down. The guidebook said that the "hiker's trail" was less crowded—a trail of "blissful solitude." And it was right. And long!

Finally, after almost four hours, we reached the damned sign-in box and I signed us all out. Then it was only 1.8 miles back to the car on a trail with quite a few hikers, including a group of young, healthy ones spending a few weeks on the Colorado Trail with full backpacks and tanned legs and arms, making it look easy. I used to be that young—a long time ago…

My left big toenail took a bit of a beating on the way down. But otherwise, I felt fine once back at the car. Surprisingly, I had no soreness that evening or the next day. But don't even ask about our plane trip back from Denver when all of Delta's computers shut down completely for six hours, stranding everyone across the country!

Doha, Qatar, is a dry, hot, dusty place—at least it looked that way from inside its incredibly modern and fancy Hamad International Airport. The place is full of people twenty-four hours a day. In the middle of the main terminal was a huge, yellow, inflated bear, presumably the mascot for the World Cup, which, at the time of this writing, is scheduled to take place in Qatar in 2022. Dozens of very high-end jewelry and clothing shops surrounded the main terminal, interrupted only by some classy-looking restaurants. Christian Dior, Tag Heuer, Bulgavi, Gucci,

Salvatore, Chanel, Coach, Victoria's Secret, Swarovski, a Bentley for sale—the list of fancy shops in the main terminal goes on and on. This airport made Hartsfield-Jackson Airport in Atlanta look like a strip mall in comparison.

After a thirteen-hour flight from Atlanta on Qatar Airlines, I just wanted a place to lie down and sleep. I had an eight-hour layover, with my flight to Kathmandu leaving Doha at around 2 A.M. However, for the next eight hours, it was almost impossible to get any shuteye. The main terminal was too full of lights, shops, noise, and people. Plus, the seats on the concourses all had hard arm supports, making it impossible to spread out comfortably across several seats. I ended up finding the one Burger King in the airport and camping out in front of the TV with CNN anchors and pundits discussing the upcoming presidential election. Just what I was trying to get away from!

About three hours before my flight, the departure board finally listed the flight to Kathmandu. Only then could I find my gate, hopefully in a more relaxing area. I traveled over what seemed to be a half mile of endless moving sidewalks before seeing a sign to my gate, with an arrow pointing down a set of escalators to my left. Below the main level, there were six gates with rows and rows of seats as far as the eye could see—that is, if you could see through all the people, most of whom were wearing burkas or long white robes with red and white checkered headwear.

I'm in the Middle East now!

The departure board listed multiple flights to destinations in Saudi Arabia, Syria, Yemen, Ethiopia, Egypt, Jordan, India, and Pakistan. I appeared to be one of a handful of Westerners in the entire room and felt considerably out of place. I am embarrassed to say that my initial reaction was to visually check everyone I saw for hidden bomb vests, a bad thought prompted I am sure by so many news reports regarding suicide bombers in crowded airports. But everyone there was just traveling to a destination just like me. Kids were running around, women and men were laughing or watching their kids scurry up and down the aisle of chairs, some men were watching soccer games on the overhead TV screens.

Regular folks—just like us.

I soon relaxed and tried to sleep.

About an hour before my flight to Kathmandu was to leave, another Westerner arrived and sat down in a row close to mine. He was wearing trekking pants and boots and had an unmistakable climber's look about him. He looked to be in his mid-forties.

"Are you headed to Kathmandu?" I asked as I approached him.

"Yeah," he responded.

"I thought so," I said. "Are you by chance part of the Alpine Ascents team for Cho Oyu?"

"Nah. But I'm headed for Cho-yu. Sort of with a group," he replied, shortening the name of the mountain into two syllables.

"Sort of?" I asked.

"Well, I'm traveling with them until we get to advanced base camp, but then I've got my own guide to take me up from there. After that, I have the option of moving up the mountain at my own pace."

"Nice deal."

We spent the next two hours talking about climbs we had both done, until they finally called our flight for boarding, almost an hour later than scheduled.

Working my way through the Kathmandu Airport was "old hat" since I had flown in and out of it on my Everest base camp trek four years before. This time I got a cheap, fifteen-day visa instead of the normal thirty-day one, since we would be flying out to Tibet in two days. Like four years before, once I got through customs, I waited forever for my bags to appear on one of two conveyor belts in baggage claim. I had checked three bags from Atlanta—two large North Face duffel bags and a mid-sized expedition pack, the same one I used on Rainier. To my relief, all three bags eventually showed up.

Jiban, the Kathmandu liaison for Alpine Ascents, waved at me as I exited the airport. I recognized Jiban from my prior trip to Kathmandu. He had set up a golf outing for me following the trek to Everest base camp. Jiban is an operator extraordinaire and seems to know everyone in Kathmandu. He can arrange for anything, from golf to restaurant reservations, from spa treatments to massages, and even other more questionable activities.

This time, having been there before, the dense traffic, filled with motorcyclists weaving in and out, and the constant horns beeping in all directions did not bother me.

Been there, done that!

As we worked our way towards the Yak & Yeti Hotel, I scanned the buildings to see if the recent earthquake damage, which had been widely reported in the press, was visible. Not seeing any, I asked Jiban whether everything had already been repaired.

"This part of town was not hit badly," he said. "Some of the older, historical buildings suffered some damage. But most of the damage was in another part of town."

As we passed a few older walls and buildings, he pointed to some cracks and a few places where parts of walls had collapsed. However, the damage was a lot less than I would have thought from the media reports…at least on the route between the airport and our hotel.

It was nice to see Sherpa Lakpa Rita waiting for us to arrive in the lobby of the Yak & Yeti around noon. I had climbed twice with him before. He greeted me warmly and introduced me to Ben Jones, our other lead guide. I could tell Ben was immediately sizing me up with his eyes. I wondered immediately whether my weight loss and conditioning were sufficiently visible to give him some assurance I was a legitimate climber. He seemed satisfied—at least, he did not say anything to make me think otherwise.

Lakpa and Ben then explained that two or three of the other climbers in our group of seven had already arrived and the rest would be arriving later in the day. We would have a gear check first thing in the morning after breakfast. I was on my own until then.

Jiban joined us after arranging my room number and having the bags taken up by the hotel porters. He asked if I wanted a short tour of the area, but I declined, indicating that I was tired and just wanted to "chill." I went up to the room, which had a nice view of the back gardens of the hotel. I quickly got a shower and a shave and intended to take a short power nap.

Two hours later I woke up, starving. With no information about the other guys' room numbers, I had no way of communicating with them to make any plans for lunch or dinner. So, I went down to the lobby area to see if anyone looking like a climber was hanging around. I found a short, sturdy guy at the lobby bar who had the look of a climber. Sure enough, he was also planning to climb Cho Oyu, but he was not with our group. I ordered a sandwich and an Everest beer, which comes in about a 22-ounce bottle, and we chatted for about an hour. The guy had climbed many of the same mountains I had climbed, but, in addition, had scaled several other peaks in Nepal and Tibet, had made one unsuccessful attempt to climb Everest, and planned another in spring 2017. He explained that he had put mountain climbing ahead of his marriage. Now that he was divorced, he was free to climb whenever he wanted. He seemed gleeful about jettisoning his wife, so at the first opportunity, I jettisoned him.

In the lobby, I ran into another guy in trekking pants and a Patagonia long-sleeved hiking shirt. He looked very fit, almost too thin, but his features were all muscle and sinew, not an ounce of fat. He looked to be in his mid-fifties, not too much younger than me.

"Hi, are you by any chance here to climb Cho Oyu?" I asked.

"Yes, but it's pronounced 'Cho-yu,'" he replied in an Australian accent. "I'm Malcolm."

This time, I recognized the name Malcolm from the Alpine Ascents roster I had gotten by e-mail a few weeks earlier.

"I'm Dave Schaeffer and I think you are climbing with Alpine Ascents, yes?"

"Yes, nice to meet you."

"Cho-yu? What happened to the second 'o'?" I asked.

"Who the fuck knows? It's just how they pronounce it over here."

"Damn. I have been pronouncing it as 'Cho Oyu' with both o's for ten months!"

"I can't help it if you are a dumb shit, but you better start saying it right or everyone here will think you are a moron," he warned.

"Yeah, okay. Cho-yu? Just slide it all together?"

"Exactly."

I liked Malcolm from the start. He obviously had his act together and had a good sense of humor—the same type of sarcasm I enjoy.

He told me that he had met the other two guys who had already arrived and that they were all planning to go out for dinner at six-thirty.

He didn't know where they were going. I mentioned that there was a good American-style pizza place down in the Thamel tourist district at which we had eaten a few years back, and he said that sounded great. I told him I would meet them at the lobby at six-thirty and headed back up to my room.

At six-thirty, Malcolm and I stood next to the concierge desk waiting for the other two guys to arrive.

"You said half past six, right?"

"Precisely."

"Whatta they look like?"

"Well, one looks like a complete dirt bag...there he is now."

I looked over toward the entrance of the hotel and a guy with multiple tattoos, a bandanna, and dreadlocks was approaching us. He had that Johnny Depp pirate look about him. He also had a big smile on his face and quickly held his hand out.

"I'm Jason," he said, looking at me.

"Dave Schaeffer," I said, shaking his hand. "Malcolm, I thought you said he looks like a dirt bag."

I smiled at Jason to let him know I was teasing.

"I take that as a compliment," Jason said, with an even bigger smile. "I am a dirt bag, but sometime on this trip I'm gonna talk to you about first impressions not always being accurate."

"I was just screwin' with you," I responded, slapping him on the shoulder.

"I know," he said. "But I want you to know I'm a complicated guy. And we'll have plenty of time to talk about that later. Where's Steve?"

"I don't know," Malcolm said. "But if he doesn't show up soon, we'll go without him."

About fifteen minutes later, Steve finally showed up, as if he was on time. He was about six feet, five inches, dark-haired, and was dressed in gym shorts, a short-sleeved nylon shirt, and some loose-looking high-top hiking sneakers of sorts. He had iPod earphones hanging out of each ear and was fiddling with his cell phone as he approached us. I wanted to tell him to ditch the electronics and enjoy the sights and smells of Kathmandu, but I kept silent.

We made more introductions and then decided to head down to the Thamel district and try to find the Fire & Ice pizza joint that I had remembered from my prior trip.

It was just about dusk when we started down the sidewalk towards Thamel, passing by beggars and malformed children with their hands out. Mothers sat on mats or towels near the wall and let their children do all the begging. I had not changed any money yet, so I had nothing to give them on this trip down the lane, but I knew I would be able to give them something on the way back.

Since I was the only one who had been there before, the others followed me. We crossed over to the right side of the street to look at the Mountain Hardware and North Face stores, not realizing that Fire & Ice was down an alley on the left side almost directly across from the mountain-gear shops. I had a vague visual memory of the pizza place, but did not figure out that we had missed it.

We ended up going several blocks into the narrow alleys and multitude of colorful shops and signs of the Thamel district before I confessed that I had no idea where the pizza place was. So, we opted for a second-story local café overlooking a busy intersection of narrow lanes and shops.

We huddled around a small table and waited for our food while Jason embarked on his life history. He was a construction foreman from Chicago and had many rough times in his past, with romantic and work-related breakups, followed by alcohol and drug abuse, and a "cleansing" period several years before this trip. He had stayed sober ever since, and was the only one at the table who did not order a beer. Though he had some rough edges, Jason was a cool guy with a very good heart. I could tell this from the start. He also looked like he could be one hell of a climber. He had climbed Mt. Elbrus in southern Russia about a month before meeting us in Kathmandu and had taken a train through Russia and done some more hiking in Bhutan in the interim. He had lots of stories to tell.

Malcolm was a businessman from Australia, but had lived all over the world and had settled down in Seattle. He also had lots of stories to tell, but it was only later that we learned he had worked in the steel industry, had been an intelligence officer in the Middle East, and had made his fortune from being the inventor and distributor of Bobblehead dolls. He was, without a doubt, one of the most interesting people I have ever met.

Steve was a cardiologist from Washington State, but had immigrated to the U.S. from Iran as a child. He already had a thick dark beard after a few days of not shaving and was a fount of knowledge about almost any subject. He confessed that he had not done much training for this climb and had just signed up for it at the last minute. From the outset, I wondered if he was fit and focused enough to climb the sixth-highest mountain in the world.

The food was surprisingly good and unbelievably cheap. Even with beers, our bills averaged about three dollars. There was no cash register or receipt, just cash in the hand. With some Nepali coins for change, I had some money to give the children on the way back to the hotel.

The next morning, John from Colorado arrived, hobbling into the hotel with a bad back. He had somehow wrenched it on the way over to Kathmandu and looked to be in some serious pain. Phil, a urologist from Boston, and Keith, an engineer from Mississippi, filled out our team. We all met on the lawn in the back of the hotel for an orientation meeting.

After everyone introduced themselves, Ben and Lakpa laid out the plan for the next two weeks. We would have a gear check the next morning, packing all the high-mountain gear in one duffel bag and the gear we needed for the acclimatization part of the trip in another bag. Street clothes could be left at the Yak & Yeti as we would not be needing them over in Tibet. The high-mountain gear would be taken by our supporting Sherpas by truck across the border into Tibet. We would fly to Lhasa, stay there two nights, and then drive by van back towards Cho Oyu, stopping at several towns along the way, with acclimatization hikes in between the two nights at each stop. We would link up with the Sherpas at the Chinese base camp at 16,100 feet in about a week. After that we would be on foot the rest of the way.

Ben spread out a map that showed the entire region. Only then did I realize how much further away Lhasa was from Everest and Cho Oyu than was Kathmandu. Although we were avoiding a very bumpy and precarious drive across the border from Kathmandu by flying to Lhasa, we were flying much further away from Cho Oyu, leaving us with essentially three days of driving to get back to the mountain. Ben later told us that it was not so much the rough roads that prevented us from traveling by truck over the border to Tibet. Rather, the Chinese government, as part of its clampdown on Tibetan independence, did not want any sympathetic Westerners traveling across the border without the security and tracking available with air travel.

In ignorance, I had thought that Lhasa was right at the base of the Himalayas, as I had seen photos of Lhasa with snowcapped mountains directly behind it. But I learned on this trip that Lhasa is considerably north of the main Himalayan range and it was a three-day drive from Lhasa before we could see Everest.

After the orientation session, Ben and Lakpa told us that there was a nice pizza place on the way down to the Thamel district where we would go for lunch…precisely the same one I missed the prior evening. Jason and Malcolm looked at me with knowing glances, as if to say they were glad we did not find it last night.

This time we turned down the alley across from the mountain-gear shops and quickly found Fire & Ice. The pizzas were good and the beers and sodas were cold. That night, we ate at a restaurant on the roof of a four-story shopping center near the Yak & Yeti. We enjoyed steaks and pasta with shrimp, among other nice entrées. I didn't know then, but it would be the last good meal for quite some time.

The next morning, we were up early for breakfast at seven and a van ride to the airport at seven-thirty. The rest of the day was "hurry up and wait." The Kathmandu airport is always crowded. Just waiting for ticketing and bag check in the international terminal was a marathon. Then there was the low-ceiling lounge surrounded by little gift and snack shops on the second floor, where we waited so long that people were charging cell phones at charging stations before we finally moved through the security screening to yet another waiting room. Of course, they then changed our gate assignment, requiring us to move down a brighter, but narrow building with windows on both sides, our final stop before boarding.

At the other end of the flight at the Lhasa airport, things were even more complicated as we worked our way through the Chinese security and customs, being lined up in exact order to match the sequence of names on two group visas arranged by Alpine Ascents. Keith, Steve, and I were on one visa, and the rest of the group was on the other. There never was any complete explanation for why the group visas were separate, but we strictly followed the directions of the Chinese security agents who were brandishing firearms and were not to be messed with.

Lhasa, at 12,000 feet in elevation, was well worth the visit. Lhasa, in what used to be known as Tibet, is the home of the Dalai Lama, though he is now in exile. Now Lhasa is merely denominated as the largest city in Western China, with no official mention of Tibet or the Dalai Lama. China is cracking down on any sense of independence among the Tibetan people and had a strong military presence in Lhasa, complete with numerous armed guards and multiple convoys of military vehicles, some pulling long-barreled artillery. Our guides warned us not to express any sympathy for Tibet or to mention or refer to the Dalai Lama under any circumstances.

No need to make any waves in China!

Surprisingly, the Lhasa Airport is over an hour from downtown Lhasa, primarily because the area is surrounded by fourteen- and fifteen-thousand-foot peaks and ridges and is riddled with highly-braided river basins. There simply is nowhere to locate an airport close to the city.

After going through at least five tunnels and traveling along a very nice four-lane expressway, we entered Lhasa proper, being greeted by streets lined with red China flags and other colorful adornments. But first we had to make it through another major checkpoint as we entered the city.

Once inside the city limits, I could easily see that Lhasa was a well-organized city with an assortment of modern and older buildings and shops. Unlike Kathmandu, it was spotless. Clean sidewalks. Nicely painted buildings. Modern signs. Long avenues. Colorful lights. Thousands of Chinese flags everywhere. Quite civilized, but I wondered whether the people enjoyed many freedoms.

We drove to the other side of town and pulled into a parking lot in front of two massive, museum-like structures, the gray stone one on the right side being our hotel, the Brahma Petra Grand. Inside, the hotel was partially a museum, with artifacts and artwork displayed in the lobby and mezzanine level, with very expensive shops to the right and left of the concierge desk. The rooms upstairs were spacious and surprisingly plush. However, finding any Western station on the TV was not in the cards. Nor was making any call or getting any internet service on my Google-based cell phone.

Anxious to start acclimatizing, Lakpa led us on a walk through the center part of town. We seemed to be the only Westerners on the streets, so many locals gawked at us as we passed by. What started out as a short walk turned into quite a jaunt. We could see the Potala Palace on a hill in the distance on the other side of the city and headed in that direction. Like a magnet, it drew us to it.

But before we got there, Lakpa led us into some narrow streets to our left, through a metal-detector guarded checkpoint, and into the oldest part of town surrounding the ancient Meru monastery. There we began a pilgrimage walk clockwise around the monastery with hundreds of locals doing the exact same thing. Except, every few yards, local women or men would drop to the ground prostrating themselves before various objects connected with the monastery. They wore padded aprons of sorts to avoid bruising themselves as they hit the ground or pushed themselves along the well-worn paving stones surrounding the monastery.

On the outside of this wide circle were shops and souvenir stores galore. But for the most part, we passed them by, making sure to go to the left of the tall columns of prayer flags situated every hundred yards or so. This was a similar custom as always going to the left of the muni stones on the way up to Everest base camp. We strictly followed Lakpa's lead and followed the local custom to a tee.

When in Rome...

It took us at least an hour to make our way around the monastery before working our way out through another checkpoint and resuming our march towards the Potala Palace on one of the main streets.

We passed narrow shop after narrow shop. Just before reaching the palace, we veered to our left down a wide pedestrian-friendly street lined with expensive jewelry stores, with rings, bracelets, and baubles arranged meticulously, shining at us through the windows. Not one of them had any customers. We turned right at the end of the street onto a tree-lined avenue leading up to the Potala Palace, which is situated on a hill overlooking the city. Just then the sky let loose and we found ourselves scurrying down an underpass to avoid the pouring rain. The other end of the underpass led directly to a walkway with flowers and gardens in front of the palace, so whenever the rain let up for a few seconds, we ran up some stairs to the walkway and snapped a few photos. The air felt thin, and I huffed a bit as I came back into the underpass, but at 12,000 feet, I really did not have any problem adjusting to the altitude.

The next morning, we took a formal tour of the Potala Palace. This time the weather was good—no rain in sight. This was our first acclimatization hike of sorts, as we had to work our way up a series of steep ramps to reach the entrances to the palace behind the white walls that spanned the entire hill from end to end. I decided, rashly, to run up the first few ramps. I tried to get Malcolm and Jason to join me, but they declined, so I darted up on my own. The slanted cobblestone rocks underfoot made a graceful ascent impossible at top speed. I made it to the top of the first ramp clumsily, but without too much difficulty, and quickly realized that running uphill at over 12,000 feet was rather tough on the lungs. After about thirty seconds, I stopped gasping for air. Then, with the rest of the group applauding or laughing, I dashed up the second ramp just to show them I was okay. This time I made it only two-thirds of the way up before running out of steam. Sucking in oxygen, I walked the rest of the way up the second ramp. By the time the group reached that level, I had recovered sufficiently to jog up the two short sets of steps up to the entrance to the palace. I realized that I had ascended about 500 vertical feet in less than ten minutes, but my calves and my lungs were paying the price for the effort. Fortunately, I had plenty of time to rest before the group entered the home of the many Dalai Lamas who had lived there since the seventh century.

Apparently, the upper, dark-red section of the Potala Palace was built in the seventh century by one of the early Dalai Lamas. The larger white section below it was added in the seventeenth century. Inside the palace is a series of small rooms, most with metal Buddhist gods or other figures filling one side of the room. Three female statues in different forms seemed to be in every room. As we climbed higher and higher into the palace, we began to see rooms with thrones that the Dalai Lamas used when greeting guests, and further up, we worked our way through a series of rooms with huge caskets made of tons of gold and adorned by expensive jewels in which many of the Dalia Lamas were buried. A sign in front of one indicated that 3.4 tons of gold were used in making that casket. After about an hour and a half of touring the palace, we exited down some cobblestoned ramps on the rear side of the hill on which it sat.

But we were not done with our walking or acclimatization for the day. Jason, who had spent several days researching the region, repeatedly told us there was a local festival in Lhasa that he wanted to go to and showed us the book that referenced the festival. The guides finally caved in and told us that going to the festival was not on the itinerary, so participation was voluntary. However, everyone in the group joined Jason on his quest. The name of the festival escapes me, but it was loosely translated as the "sour milk" festival...or something like that. It was never clear what the festival celebrated, but it involved a long walk up a steadily rising hill behind the Sera Monastery, an even larger one, above which a huge tapestry was unfurled from a rocky outcropping on which a grey stone wall had been built.

We got as close to the event as possible in our van, but the sheer number of vehicles and people heading in the direction of the festival forced us to get out and walk long before we even reached the large monastery. From that point on, we just followed the people steadily upwards, not knowing where we were going or how far it was to the blessed tapestry. We hiked up a steep block, then turned right on a level street for a quarter of a mile, then turned left up a steep alley, and turned right again on another level street. This pattern was repeated several more times before we found ourselves in roped-off chutes, like cattle being herded to the slaughterhouse. Eventually, we passed by the outer walls of the monastery and kept going up the hill, following the people and staying inside the ropes. To our right, we had a nice view of the city below us, so I realized that we had gained quite a bit of elevation over the several miles of zigzagging pathways.

The final climb up to the tapestry was steeper. I found myself huffing and puffing as the air got thinner. I could feel the altitude. I checked my altimeter on my cell phone and realized that we were now at over 13,000 feet. I was very glad when we finally caught a glimpse of the colorful tapestry, worked our way up the final steep trail, and joined hundreds, maybe thousands, of people staring at it and taking pictures beneath it. Some locals were prostrating themselves or rigorously waving prayer shawls in front of the tapestry.

We watched the scene for fifteen or twenty minutes, but then got the word that the festival was about to end. Several young men climbed up the nearby rocks to the top of the tapestry, apparently in preparation for dismantling it. Others began directing the mass of people down the hill to our right. We gathered our group and followed them down.

Of course, this took us down the other side of the monastery and required our guides to contact the van driver to work his way over to the "exit" avenue, which was just as blocked off as the avenue where we started walking. It seemed like we would never stop walking. Then, when we got to the intersection where the van could get to us, no van was in sight. So, we waited and waited and waited some more…all the while getting more acclimatized.

That night we had the first of many Chinese "Lazy Susan" dinners, mostly meatless noodle, rice, vegetable, and seaweed dishes shared among the nine of us. The dishes were placed on a large rotating surface in the middle of the table and turned until everyone got a spoonful of the tasteless fare. I would have preferred a single dish a la carte, but that was not in the offering. Fortunately, I found a small store with apples, nuts, and a Coke in front of the hotel parking lot to supplement my diet.

Our van was packed solid the next morning: Everyone was on time…except Steve, who showed up ten minutes late, mumbling something about his cell phone. I found a seat in the far back of the van, my favorite place for group travel, with everyone in front of me. After leaving town we headed west on a two-lane road that apparently runs thousands of kilometers from Beijing through Western China. It was slow going due to speed limits and a ridiculous system requiring a minimum travel time between checkpoints. If you show up at the next checkpoint in less than the designated time, they charge you for speeding. This essentially enforces the speed limits, as there is no advantage in getting there early. More accurately, the drivers still speed, but then there is always a restaurant, ice cream, souvenir, or extended piss stop for twenty minutes or more just before reaching the next checkpoint.

By the way, ice cream bars in Western China are horrible. They all taste like they have been in the freezer for years and melted and re-frozen three or four times.

Our destination that day was Shigatse, the second largest city in Western China. Even though it was probably less than two hundred miles from Lhasa, it took all day to get there. There was not much to see on the way…just some foothills and rivers…and a lot of checkpoints, along with an even worse "Lazy Susan" meal at a small "café" in a strip town just before one of the checkpoints. The restroom in the back of the café was a section of mud and grass behind a wall in the backyard. Jason, Malcolm, and I watched in amusement as Steve kept asking the café staff where the toilets were before he finally realized that he had to pee *al fresco*.

Shigatse is a very nice town. At 12,500 feet, it was only slightly higher in elevation than Lhasa and it had a lot less "pomp and circumstance" and less of a military presence than Lhasa. The hotel at which we stayed was nicely situated in a courtyard off the main street and the beds were comfortable. The little restaurant, plainly called the "Breakfast Restaurant," on the right side of the courtyard stayed open an extra hour for us the first night. Phil and I had been paired as roommates in Lhasa and again in Shigatse. After stowing our gear, we took a walk on the nearby streets, finding mostly furniture and auto-related shops and a few vegetable stands. We quickly realized that the hotel was nowhere close to the tourist district and there were no souvenir or tourist-friendly stores anywhere to be seen.

On our "rest" day in Shigatse, Lakpa led us to yet another monastery situated on a hill on the outskirts of the town. We had hiking boots and poles with us, but all of us were a bit surprised when Lakpa jumped a short wall on the rear of the monastery and headed up the steep mountain behind it. It appeared that God's only creatures regularly traveling up this mountain were goats. But we followed barely discernible goat paths upward, trying to avoid losing our footing on the loose, tiny gravel. I hiked immediately behind Lakpa and felt a certain amount of peer pressure to stay close to him, no matter how hard the climbing was on my legs and lungs.

This, of course, was a test of our conditioning. After a few minutes, we were high above the monastery. I wondered how far up we were going. I could see a rocky outcropping with a bunch of prayer flags about two-thirds of the way up the mountain and figured that this was our destination, especially when Lakpa veered in that direction. Indeed, that was our destination, but only our first stop. We rested briefly upon reaching it, but then we headed upward to our left, where I could see another small peak adorned with many more flying prayer flags. The climb up to that peak was even more steep and strenuous. But by then my legs and lungs were warmed up, I had gotten into a good breathing rhythm, and I had no problem keeping up with Lakpa (who was taking it slow).

At that peak, there were so many prayer flags that it was impossible to walk without stepping on or over some of them. We took a longer snack and water break and my altimeter indicated that we were closing in on 14,000 feet. But we were not done climbing. Further to our left was yet another higher peak with more prayer flags. Beyond it was another similar peak.

This could go on forever!

To my pleasant surprise, once we reached the third peak, Lakpa announced this was as far as we were going today and confirmed that we were "a bit" above 14,000 feet. We sat in the sun, enjoying the view for ten to fifteen minutes. Everyone seemed to be doing well and we were all in good spirits. We were already as high as some of the highest mountains in Colorado, it was a beautiful Tibetan sun-filled day, and we had just gotten started. Of course, over in Tibet, none of these small foothill peaks had any names. We could only designate them by describing them as the third peak with prayer flags on the ridge to the left above the monastery.

The trip down from that spot was more treacherous than the hike up. Lakpa decided to take a circuitous route down, completing a counterclockwise circle back to the monastery walls. The only problem was that there was no trail, and the steep downhill surface was littered with tiny bits of sand and small pieces of gravel, making each step a possible downhill slide. Luckily, I had rubber tips on my hiking poles that day, which gave me some traction to balance as my boots moved under me. I almost wiped out fifty times on the way down, trying to keep up with Lakpa and Jason, both of whom seemed to glide down the hill without any problem.

After working our way through several gullies that seemed impassable from above, we finally reached a relatively flat pasture and waited for the others to catch up. I was not the only one having difficulty with the terrain, but all of us made it down unscathed. The whole hike had taken almost five hours and once again we had gained almost another thousand feet of acclimatization.

I slept very well that night.

Tingri was our next stop. To get there, we drove over two passes at just over 15,000 feet and 17,250 feet, according to my altimeter app. At the first pass, Phil and I climbed steps up to a radio tower surrounded by prayer flags a few hundred feet above the parking area. Ben Jones warned me before I headed up the steps not to run and just take it easy, apparently remembering my stunt at the Potala Palace. So, I worked my way up slowly, taking deep breaths along the way. I could feel the thinness of the air and did some "pressure" breathing towards the top, a method involving almost violent exhaling of the lungs to expel all carbon monoxide and allowing for more oxygen to enter the lungs on the inhale. Phil appeared winded by the time he reached the radio towers, but we both had no problem zipping back down the steps when the van was ready to move on.

At the 17,250-foot pass, the horizon was filled with snowcapped peaks, but still we could not see Everest or Cho Oyu. However, we certainly could feel and experience the strong winds and colder, thinner air. Just walking a few hundred yards to pee behind some buildings had me huffing and puffing.

Somewhere on the way to Tingri, we pulled over to a parking area on the right side of the road, with souvenir tables spread to the right and left of a large white sign. The sign marked the five-thousand-kilometer mark on "The Most Beautiful Landscape Road in China," which apparently started in Beijing. We were a long way from civilization, and getting further and further away by the kilometer.

I had heard Tingri described as "a dusty town straight out of the wild, wild west." And frankly, that was a good description. At 14,000 feet, Tingri has one long street with a few cruddy shops and cafés on both sides of the street in the middle of what otherwise is a flat plateau in between mountain ridges. The street itself is paved, but the surrounding twenty feet on both sides of the road is dust, which the wind blows all over the place. Add to that dozens of stray cattle and packs of dogs roaming willy-nilly down the streets, and you have quite an "Old West" rustic scene. The atmosphere was only made worse by the seemingly endless lines of construction trucks rolling through the town, honking at the cows, and spreading more dust and fumes along the way.

Interestingly, the town was building a huge monastery up on a hill to the north, which glowed a golden color as the sun set. If we had not been distracted by the monastery on the way into town, we might have noticed Cho Oyu and Everest on the southwest horizon amid the clouds.

We stayed at the "best hotel" in town, the Haltoo Hotel, with accommodations that would make a Motel 6 seem like a Ritz-Carlton. In front of the hotel was a small café called the Base Camp Restaurant, filled completely with Cho Oyu climbers heading to the Chinese base camp, now only a few hours' drive away. We patiently waited our turn to eat, as all the tables were taken. By the time our turn came, nothing but rice, some soupy vegetables, and cold French fries were left to eat, on cold metal "prison slop" trays. Fortunately, I had a meat stick to fill in the diet once back in the room.

The next day was one of the best of the whole trip. We hiked down the road towards a ridge of mountains we had passed on the way in, crossing a small river on the way out of town. As we crossed the bridge, Lakpa pointed out Cho Oyu on the horizon to our right. Visibility was clear and the snowy summit ridge of Cho Oyu was very noticeable among scattered clouds in the distance.

"When we get to the top of that peak up ahead, we may be able to see Everest," he said, pointing to a mountain ridge in front of us.

We walked about a half mile down the road, passing the cutoff to the road to the Everest base camp (on the Chinese side), then turning to our right at the base of the steep scree-filled mountain ridge Lakpa had pointed to a few minutes earlier.

Here we go, David…try to stay up!

The first hundred yards of the climb were tough as we moved slowly up the scree slope. Lakpa set a modest pace as Ben encouraged us to use rest steps and pressure breathing to make the climb manageable. Once again, I had fallen in right behind Lakpa, so I worked hard not to slow down the progress of the whole group. But I found myself getting stronger and stronger the higher we got. Fortunately, after climbing about five hundred vertical feet, the mountain leveled off a bit, making the next section a much more gradual and comfortable ascent. Soon we were high enough to see Tingri and its monastery-in-progress way down below us.

It looked like an airport runway with a control tower in the middle of a desert.

After about an hour and a half of climbing, we reached the top of the mountain. There was another peak to our left that was another thousand feet up, and I fully expected Lakpa to tell us that was our destination. However, we stopped at the first peak this time and he told us to get some water and snacks before we headed down.

"And in case you haven't noticed, that's Everest over there in the clouds to the left of Cho Oyu," he said, again pointing to the horizon.

Sure enough, the highest mountain in the world was visible on the horizon, framed perfectly by clouds. It looked so different from the China/Tibet side, as compared to the view from the Nepal side I had experienced on my Everest base camp trek four years earlier. Instead of a gray monolith standing out above everything around it, this time it looked like a snow-clad pyramid stacked on white blocks.

For the next half hour, we stared at Everest and Cho Oyu, stopping to take pictures whenever the clouds cleared and the peaks shone on the horizon. Ben had carried his tripod up with him and took some great photos of the mountains and the group for the cybercasts back home. It was a warm, sunny day, fifteen hundred feet above Tingri, and we enjoyed the mesmerizing view of the highest and sixth-highest mountains on the planet off in the distance. We were in no hurry to get anywhere.

We had already done the tough climbing for the day. Life was good! I could have stayed up there at 15,500 feet for hours.

However, after about forty-five minutes, Lakpa and Ben advised us to head back down to avoid getting too much sun.

"You will burn up at this altitude if you are not careful," Ben told us. "It doesn't take much to get a sunburn on days like this. Make sure you cover your ears, neck, and nose with your buffs on the way down."

In another hour, we were back in the dusty environs of Tingri, with nothing to do but check out all the little shops lining both sides of the street. Amazingly, there were some "finds" in between a lot of junk. I bought some yak-wool yarn for my niece who manages a yarn shop in Baltimore. Jason found several pieces of jewelry he swore were worth ten times what he paid for them. Steve bought a leather cowboy hat that did not quite fit his large head, but he liked it and wore it continuously for several days. And in one "grocery" shop, I bought a bunch of grapes, three apples, and some of the largest carrots I have ever seen. Given the miserable fare at the hotel restaurant, I needed some good fruit and vegetables.

Next stop was the Chinese base camp. To get there the next day, we traveled on a partly paved and partly gravel road across a long, gradually rising plain. The road was under construction of a rudimentary sort. Concrete borders had been laid about eight inches high and maybe sixteen inches wide on both sides of the hard-packed gravel road, which rose about five feet above the surrounding plain. Stones were lined up to mark where the workers would set the wooden molds for the concrete borders. Presumably, the gravel road between the borders would later be filled with asphalt or concrete, but for most of the way, we traveled on gravel, the dust pouring out and up behind us. On a couple of occasions, we had to leave the road and travel along ruts in the surrounding desert running parallel to the road. Fortunately, the trip only took about an hour and a half.

Chinese base camp, a relatively flat area on the right side of the road just below a Chinese military camp atop the hill to the right, was the end of the road for the van. We were now at 16,100 feet in elevation and had a great review of Cho Oyu in the distance beyond a half-dozen foothills.

From this base camp, we would hike and climb all the way to the summit of Cho Oyu—at least, that was the plan. Immediately to our left as we turned in was a row of shabby-looking stone huts, which we later learned contained a small bar, with beers for purchase. Clearly this was a higher bar than the one in Alma, Colorado! However, at this altitude, our guides advised us not to drink alcoholic beverages.

To our right was a series of large green group tents and dozens of individual three-man tents that Ben described as "the Chinese camp," meaning that the climbers were all local Chinese and not Westerners. The Westerners with Nepali or American guides were situated on the left side of the compound in smaller yellow tents.

Obviously, several groups had beaten us there, as our Sherpas had to set up our tents in the back of the camp, beyond a gully and almost on the upslope towards the military camp. Ben warned us not to take any photos in the direction of the military camp or of any soldiers in the area. In the middle-rear section of the camp, somewhat up the slope above us was the six-hole outhouse, the left side for the guys and the right side for females. I, of course, did not realize the gender division and used the right side the first time before being advised I had just used the ladies' room. I can confirm, however, that both sides had the same three squat slots and it was strictly BYOTP—"Bring your own toilet paper."

I shared a tent there with Phil, the be-speckled urologist from Boston. He and I got along well, and he let me use his satellite phone a few times on the trip, allowing me to give my wife a few updates personally. Phil is a great father, regularly checking in with his children and wife, always telling them he would be home soon, and always listening to everything that was going on back in Boston.

Once we settled in, we had the opportunity to meet our cook, Gopal, and the assisting Sherpas, all of whom had driven over from Kathmandu with our provisions and high-mountain gear. Gopal had been our cook on my Everest base camp trek four years earlier, so I recognized him immediately. He greeted me warmly. Lakpa uses him as a cook on most of his Nepalese and Tibetan climbs.

Four assisting Sherpas were also there, one of whom, named Nima, had been a junior guide on the Everest base camp trek. I also met Lakpa's younger brother, Cammie Rita, a very accomplished climber in his own right with nineteen successful summits of Everest at the time (now twenty-one summits), and two other Sherpas. Between Ben, Lakpa, his brother, and the other three Sherpas, they had fifty-one summits of Everest on their résumés! Even young Nima had successfully made it to the top of the world one time since he had helped guide us on the Everest base camp trek.

I think I am in good hands.

The rest-day hikes from the Chinese base camp were now getting serious. With three nights at that camp we had two days climbing the surrounding ridges and peaks. Some of the surrounding peaks were snowcapped, but Lakpa led us on a barely discernible trail up a series of steep sections with switchbacks and then up a gradually rising landscape of rocks and talus until we reached an elevation of 17,500 feet. Once again, I stayed directly behind Lakpa and followed each of his steps as closely as I could. As he climbed so efficiently, I wanted to mimic him in every way. I, of course, could not mimic his condition or ability to climb effortlessly at over 17,000 feet. I stayed up with some very helpful encouragement from Jason, who typically fell in right behind me and Lakpa. I was breathing hard, but my heartrate was staying at reasonable levels with full beta-blocker support, and my legs felt strong.

I did begin to notice that my mucus was getting a bit red, with tinges of blood, indicating that my lungs were working hard to gather in the oxygen needed to support the exertion level we were maintaining. I figured that was normal, so I did not worry so long as it was not openly bleeding.

We took a nice rest at 17,500 feet. The guys gave me grief for always reporting the elevation per my altimeter on my cell phone every time we stopped, but I explained that I had to keep track for my charity, given that people in the Atlanta legal community were pledging one cent per foot of elevation that I reached, all for a summer internship program of the Atlanta Bar Association. All the climbers and Lakpa made it to the 17,500-foot rest stop that day except Steve, who seemed to be sucking wind. He stopped with Ben a few hundred vertical feet below us after he fell behind the group on the way up. He rejoined us on the way down and seemed to be okay. But he began complaining of a cough later that night.

The next day's hike was even higher. We took an almost identical route up to where we stopped the prior day, but continued up the mountain over three ridges and false summits to a large flat peak at 18,100 feet in elevation. Now we were even with some of the surrounding snowcapped ridges, higher than Everest base camp on the Nepal side, and only about thirteen hundred feet lower than Kilimanjaro's peak. I must admit that I struggled up the last few rises, cursing each time we reached a false summit. But I kept going, and we all reached the top together, including Steve, who seemed to have gotten a second wind from the prior day.

The weather that day was glorious until about ten minutes after we reached the flat summit, when a cold wind swept across the top of the mountain. We scrambled to add warm layers and our outer windproof shells. After snacks, drinks, and more photos by Ben, who again carried his tripod all the way to the top, we headed down to the warmer environment of Chinese base camp. I felt tired, but not exhausted, when we arrived back at camp. After some stretching, I felt good as new. Amazingly, despite numerous steep climbs at altitudes between 13,500 and 18,100 feet, I had not suffered as much as a sore muscle. No need for even a single Advil. My leg-strength training had really paid off.

Later that afternoon an enormous flock of sheep, with literally thousands of sheep, crossed the hill above the camp. The entire hill was a dull white, creating an illusion that the hill itself was moving. It also was a subtle reminder that we were now walking and sleeping on areas covered with animal poop and whatever bacteria accompanies it.

So far no one had gotten sick. Unfortunately, I had no wood to knock on!

My only concern at all was that when I blew my nose that evening, the Kleenex was covered with bloody mucus. When I woke up the next morning, I had to pick out dark, red, crusty clots of blood from my nostrils to clear them for breathing. Again, I kept this to myself as there was no continuous bleeding. I passed it off as a normal symptom of pressure breathing at this altitude. There is simply no training one can do at lower levels to prepare the lungs for this type of strain.

Three days after arriving at Chinese base camp, much of the Westerners' side of the camp had been dismantled and many of the climbers had left for higher ground. We spent a couple of hours taking down our tents and helping the Sherpas pack up everything from the large dining and cook tents, to the pads for our tents, heavy propane gas tanks, and our own gear, and lining it up for a truck to transport it all up to the intermediate camp at 17,700 feet. The Sherpas and all the gear and supplies would travel there on the back of a construction truck while Lakpa, Ben, and the seven climbers would hike the five- to six-hour ascent to that camp. About a half hour after we left, the Sherpas waved and hooted from on top of a loaded truck as it passed us on the gravel road.

"Don't worry, guys," Lakpa said. "They will be doing a lot of tough climbing higher up on the mountain."

Lakpa led us up the road for a mile or so, before we veered left into a rocky area through which several rushing streams ran. Apparently, "they" were not letting pedestrians go across several bridges that appeared to be under repair. At first, I thought we would have to ford the streams. But below the bridges, culverts had been placed and covered with dirt, allowing us to pass through without getting wet. We rejoined the gravel road for about a half mile past the unusable bridges, but then again departed the road and hiked the rest of the way on trails through the surrounding valley, frequently crossing braided streams of water without difficulty. The hiking was generally easy as we were slowly ascending upwards through a long grassy valley between high ridges on both sides. Every mile or so, we could see a military sentry post up on the ridges, a gentle reminder that we were still in Chinese-controlled Tibet.

Intermediate camp was nothing more than a small, relatively flat field in the middle of nowhere, at 17,700 feet. When we finally arrived, the Sherpas had set up our tents and were in the process of digging a two-foot-deep shithole calculated to contain the excrement of all of us for the next two days. There would be no well-defined slot above which to squat, just a hole to straddle.

Nasty!

And it got nastier and nastier over the next two days.

Not to be outdone, the yaks that would be used to transport our heavy gear and provisions up to the advanced base camp roamed the whole area, leaving yak dung everywhere. Though our tents had a layer of nylon and bed pads between us and the ground, the vestibule areas we had to crawl through to get into and out of the tents had dung residue all over the place.

Despite the less-than-hygienic conditions, I felt great on our climb up to the top of a nearby ridge at 19,100 feet the next day. Lakpa took a nice, slow pace and we took a relatively lengthy rest on a flatter "shoulder" about half of the way up, before ascending the very steep rock slope to the top of the ridge. I used the rest-step and cross-step methods to manage the stress on my knees and legs, and used pressure breathing almost continuously to get to the top.

"Nineteen-one," I announced to the group as I plopped down and reached for some water.

"I've got nineteen-oh-eight-eight," Jason replied, "but who's counting?"

"I'm counting every foot. Now all my lawyer friends owe $191 for the intern program. Upward and onward!"

Up to this point, which marked the high point of our acclimatization before reaching our advanced base camp home for the upper mountain climb, I could not have felt better about my chances of reaching the summit of Cho Oyu. I had pushed hard to stay up with Lakpa and the others over the last two climbs, but I had not exhausted myself…yet. And the descent back to intermediate camp was an enjoyable stroll. Alpine Ascents had done a masterful job of slowly but steadily building up our acclimatization so that we were still breathing almost normally at elevations of 18,000 and 19,000 feet.

That night we had a good meal, played some games of hearts, and got to bed early, as the next day's itinerary involved the long hike up to advanced base camp.

However, it would be a rough night for me.

Shortly after I went to bed, I was up again, heading to the shithole behind our tent. I barely got there before it let loose. Suffice it to say, diarrhea is no fun at almost 18,000 feet, but even worse when squatting over an open hole already filled with the waste of seven climbers over the last two days. Three more trips throughout the night did not seem to clear my system.

ANOTHER FIVE BIG MOUNTAINS AND TREKS

Ben, our lead guide, had convinced me to stop using Cipro prophylactically a few days earlier. I already regretted taking his advice. After the fourth trip to the shithole, I popped a pill and vowed not to go back off Cipro the rest of the trip.

But it was too late. At about 5:30 A.M. I felt a big heave from the bottom of my stomach to the top of my chest. Luckily, I stuck my head out into the vestibule area of our tent before projectile vomiting emptied the contents of my stomach onto the ground.

After things seemed to subside after about five heaves, I asked my tentmate Phil to let Ben know I was sick. Several minutes later Ben appeared outside our tent. He asked if I needed any Pepto Bismol. I declined. It was too late for that.

"Hang in there and drink a lot of fluids today," Ben said. "We're going up to advanced base camp today, so try to keep hydrated." Obviously, he had seen this show before and did not seem as worried about me as I was.

"Yeah, if I can keep it down," I replied, still trying to blow out all the food particles lodged in my nostrils and mucous membranes.

I should've never gone off Cipro!

A few hours later, after managing to nibble a few ginger snaps for breakfast, I fell in line behind the others with a half-full pack on my back. John from Colorado offered to carry my snacks and one of my water bottles to lighten the load. Two other climbers, Jason and Malcolm, stayed with me as I fell a bit behind the other climbers. My stomach was gurgling, and I felt like I could throw up again at any time.

Luckily the road was gradual. After thirty minutes or so, despite my illness, I worked into a slow but steady rhythm, which kept me within reach of the fellows up front. Ben was leading us this time, as Lakpa had to stay and organize the loading of the yaks for the trip up the mountain. I felt weak, gross, and nauseous, but knew I had to just keep going. I tried not to complain. The steady encouragement from Jason and Malcolm helped immensely.

After three hours of moderate climbing, we reached the end of the "road" and took a rest on a rock wall held in place by wiry mesh. Indeed, during the last two hours the "road" had deteriorated drastically and in places was non-existent, requiring us to cross very uneven murrain sections before returning to some semblance of a roadbed. Those detours were especially tough given my less-than-ideal gastrointestinal condition.

Gopal, our cook, and some loaded yaks passed us as we rested, heading up the hill behind us. I later learned that the Sherpas had led the main group of yaks across a shortcut through some rough murrain, cutting off the corner such that we never saw them as they went up the mountain.

The next section of the climb involved what looked like a steep and narrow ridge leading into the cloudy haze above us. Fortunately, I was feeling a bit better, and I kept down a bit of food before heading out. After a very steep climb up to the ridge, I was thankful that the "trail" up the crest of the ridge was more gradual than it looked from below. We worked our way up steadily through the rocks, fully expecting that we were nearing the advanced base camp. We could see Gopal and some yaks carrying provisions above us, seemingly stationary on a level area above us.

Finally, we are almost there!

Wrong!

When we reached the spot where we had seen Gopal, he was no longer there. No yaks were in sight. We kept trudging on.

After another fifteen minutes, we reached a point on the ridge and veered to our right, leading me to believe the advanced base camp would be just around the corner. But Ben kept marching on. Luckily, at this point, the "trail" was almost level and my nausea was manageable. Just as I was about to give up hope, the tops of multiple yellow tents came into view ahead and to our left.

"It must be the advanced base camp," I thought to myself.

"That's IMG's advanced base camp," Ben said, referring to the camp set up by International Mountain Guides, another guide group. "Our camp is a bit further in."

A bit further? A bit? What the…!

At least twenty minutes and three near-pukes later, we finally arrived at our advanced base camp, nestled in between mounds of murrain below the main trail on our right. A dining tent, a cook tent, and about seven or eight yellow tents were already set up. Each of us would have our own tent, providing some privacy and room to stash all our gear.

"Nobody should get into your tents for a while," Ben warned. "Stash your backpacks and meet in the dining tent for some warm juice and snacks. Don't lie down."

I followed his directions and soon was forcing down some juice and cookies in the dining tent with the others. However, my stomach was churning and I could not remain seated. I walked around a bit outside to try to relieve the nausea. The air at advanced base camp at 18,700 feet was thin but cool and crisp. And it was also starting to snow.

I retreated to my tent, lying down on the cushy foam pad they had supplied. I immediately began to retch. Soon I was vomiting uncontrollably again, into the back vestibule of the tent.

Great! How long is this going to last?

After this series of barfs, I think I finally emptied everything, either out the back or up the front. I took a second Cipro pill and a Tylenol and dozed off for a couple of hours.

When I woke up, I felt much better. I went back up to the dining tent where some of the guys were playing cards. I was starving. I wolfed down a couple of ginger snaps and crackers. Then I stopped. I was hungry, but I did not want to overload my still-fragile system.

Fortunately for me, with the help of the Cipro, my stomach bug lasted only 24 hours.

However, my problems were just beginning.

The next morning, I took my blood-pressure medicine, Ziac, a beta-blocker, which had the dual effect of lowering my blood pressure and placing a governor on my heartrate. My dosage had been reduced to one pill every two days per my primary care physician's instructions after he had seen me lose twenty-eight pounds over the last year training for the climb. My blood pressure had stayed down even though I had started to spread the medicine out in the months before the climb. My doctor's instructions were to limit the pills to one every two days on the mountain, reduce it to half a pill every two days when I returned for a week, cut it off completely for two weeks after that, and then come see if I could discontinue the drug. He warned that it would be dangerous to just suddenly cut off the drug without reasonable weaning.

Apparently, at 18,700 feet, Ziac works remarkably well...too well. Just before lunch I was walking into the dining tent when the lights in my brain went out. I turned sideways, knowing that I was blacking out. I lost consciousness only for a few seconds, but distinctly had a sense of floating without gravity and then hitting the ground hard on my right knee and right elbow. Luckily, I did not hit my head.

The next thing I knew, Malcolm and John, who had been sitting in the tent, were helping me up into a sitting position. I instantly regained consciousness and told them I was alright. Ben appeared from somewhere and asked me what happened.

"I just blacked out and went down...all of a sudden," I said. "It could be the blood-pressure pill I took this morning."

He immediately helped me up into a chair and pressed two of his fingers on my wrists.

"Do you normally have a pulse down here?" he asked. "I can't get any radial pulse."

"Normally I feel my pulse on the side of my neck at the jugular vein," I responded.

"Well, you need to have a pulse down at your wrists. Let me get a blood-pressure cuff and check where you are at. How long have you been taking these blood-pressure pills?"

"About three years—since my blood pressure spiked after my prostate issues. But we have been trying to wean off—and recently cut it to one pill every other day. I just took a pill about two hours ago."

A few minutes later, Ben returned with a blood-pressure cuff. After I stripped off my jacket and exposed my right arm, I could feel the cuff tighten around my bicep as he pumped it up. After a few tries, and some adjustments to the stethoscope, Ben announced that my blood pressure was below 80/60. "It's way too low," he said.

"Okay, no more high-blood pressure pills," I said.

"We'll need to check you every day to see if your levels come back up," Ben said. "You need to drink more fluids."

"The only thing is that my doctor said I should wean off the pills gradually and should not just cut them off."

"Well, until your blood pressure gets back above 100 systolic, I would advise you to stay off the pills."

"I agree. I want to be off them completely as soon as possible. But let's make sure the blood pressure does not go berserk in the opposite direction over the next few days."

The next day, my reading was 95/70, the next day after that it was 105/75, and then it moved to 110/80 by the third day. Fortunately for me, but unfortunately for my fellow climbers, several climbers in the group got the stomach bug while I was recovering from my blackout. So while I was recovering, I did not miss any further climbs up the mountain.

On the third day, I was cleared to climb again and the others were over their 24-hour bug. Time to go higher. Following Lakpa, we headed up the mountain through the rocky murrain alongside a glacial "river" of icy "fins" above the advanced base camp. There was no developed trail or path through the murrain, so the going was tough. We had to constantly pick out rocks to walk on, while trying to avoid icy sections hidden just beneath the surface. I wiped out on icy patches three or four times, grazing several fingers in the process. Two band-aids stopped the bleeding. But otherwise I did well.

We were carrying some of our heavier high-mountain gear (our ice axes, crampons, alpine harnesses, insulated boots, and forty-below sleeping bags), and, after a three-hour trek through the rocks and a final steep climb up a muddy section, we stashed them in large duffel bags near the base of an even-steeper scree hill. We were just below what Ben described as the "lake camp," but we saw no tents. My altimeter indicated we were at 19,800 feet altitude.

"A hundred ninety-eight dollars and counting," I said to myself, this time without announcing the elevation to the group.

Despite having carried a lot of weight on my back, and struggling a bit with the rocky and slippery footing, I was feeling much better than I had for the last four days. But I was too tired to join the chatting and banter among my fellow climbers.

Thankfully, despite being off Ziac for three days, on the trip up to the lake camp, I managed to keep my heartrate at reasonable levels even without any beta-blockers. I was content to stay off the meds so long as my blood-pressure levels stayed reasonably normal and my heartrate did not go through the roof.

It was a long, hard walk back down to advanced base camp, but with our packs almost empty, we made good time. I slept very well that night, expecting we would be going back up the mountain and all the way up to the 21,000-foot Camp One the next day. However, at breakfast, Ben announced that we would have another rest day, and he advised us to relax and stay off our legs. I was extremely disappointed about the delay as I had mentally geared up for the tough climb and felt great.

Damn, we hike when I am sick as a dog and then rest when I feel great!

Halfway through the morning, we learned that the main reason for the rest day was that Lakpa had himself come down with the stomach bug. The other Sherpas that day were not resting. They spent the day climbing up to Camp One, setting up tents and stashing provisions above. They also picked up our forty-below sleeping bags and some bed pads from our stash at the "lake camp" and carried them up to the next camp. They arrived back at advanced base camp before dark.

Thank God for Sherpas!

I only later learned that two of the Sherpas had climbed that day with the same stomach bug. They are incredible.

Our next step was to climb to Camp One at 21,000 feet. To get there we had to climb up through the glacial murrain to the "lake camp," along the same route we took two days earlier, then climb up and over about 1,200 feet of a very steep scree hill and into the permanently snow-covered areas. The trip through the murrain was easier the second time. This time I avoided any falls. We took a good rest at the bottom of the scree hill, but also added to our backpacks the boots, crampons, harnesses, and ice axes, which we had cached on our first trip up to the lake camp.

The added weight and the looseness of the scree on the next section made progress very slow. I was again directly behind Lakpa on the way up the scree hill. Even at a snail's pace, the climbing was brutal. There were no gentle switchbacks to work our way diagonally or zigzag up the hill…just essentially straight up. After about forty-five minutes, we had gone up only about five hundred vertical feet. Lakpa stopped and signaled for us to take a rest.

"Get some water and snacks," he said. "It gets steeper in the next section."

Shit. How can it get steeper? We're already almost sliding backwards.

Lakpa recognized we were struggling. After a brief discussion, he and Ben decided to lighten our loads by moving some of the harnesses and crampons to their own packs. They seemed to be able to handle just about any size load. This helped some, but over the next hour, we all struggled to keep moving upwards on increasingly steep scree slopes, one step at a time.

I was sucking wind as we went ever upwards. Jason was behind me encouraging me along, reminding me to "pressure" breathe. I was already "pressure" breathing constantly and working very hard to keep a steady pace, being sure to take rest steps to take the pressure off my calves as we ascended. So, this time his encouragement was more irritating than helpful.

I was going slow, but so was everyone else.

After another five hundred vertical feet or so, Lakpa gave us another rest and indicated that Camp One was just about thirty minutes away, beyond a curving path up through the snow to our right. That curving path turned out to be the steepest section we had yet encountered and was filled with loose rocks, snow, and scree. A fixed white rope had been placed along the left side of the "path." But without our ascenders or harnesses on, it was essentially useless. Instead we had to maneuver our way up through the loose rocks and snow, trying to steady ourselves with trekking poles. With only trekking boots and no crampons, I was sliding back on every third or fourth step. I was tired and frustrated, but determined not to stop despite my heartrate moving up into higher registers.

When we started out on the last section, Jason, Malcolm, Paul, and Keith quickly filled in behind Lakpa and I got in line behind Phil. We made good time for the first fifty or so yards, but then we hit slushy snow. The footing became more and more dicey. After concentrating solely on my own steps for the next ten minutes, I noticed that Lakpa and the first group of climbers had moved ahead, leaving Phil and me to struggle up the slope after them. Steve and Ben were somewhere behind us, but I did not look back. This was the first time I was unable to keep up with the leaders since my sickly climb to advanced base camp. But I knew that I could not stay up without pushing my now unregulated heartrate too high. So, I focused on just staying up with Phil. He was slipping and sliding on the snow and scree at about the same pace as me. But I give him credit. He was moving slowly, but kept going with resolute determination. I did the same, ignoring the strain on my legs and lungs.

About two-thirds of the way up the snowy, ladder-like "trail," I saw the first group disappear over the ridge above us.

Almost there, David. Keep your head down and just keep going. You're gonna make it!

Buoyed, I pressed forward, slowly gaining on Phil as we climbed the final third of this scree hell. My breathing and the stress on my legs reached a climax as I approached the last fifteen feet before the top of the ridge. Those final few yards seemed to last forever as I took it one step at a time, with three "pressure" breaths in between each step. It was a brutal end to a five-hour climb from advanced base camp.

As I reached the top of the ridge, I crossed over into a completely new world...nothing but snow and lots of it, with drop-offs to the right and left. Camp One was nestled on a narrow ridge on a shoulder of the mountain, with steep white slopes above it, all with fixed ropes. Yellow tents were scattered in rows in front of, below, and to the left of us, as many groups had already set up camp. From this point on, it would be full mountaineering with specially insulated boots, crampons, ice axes, fixed ropes, and harnesses with carabiners and ascenders to lock onto the fixed ropes.

Alpine Ascents' set of tents already had been set up by the Sherpas. To get to them, we had to go down and up some snow slopes ahead of us on a narrow ridge with a cornice to avoid on the left and a sheer rocky drop-off on the right. I followed Phil over to the tents along a well-trampled path in the snow, removed my backpack, and plopped down on it to rest. I didn't move for at least fifteen minutes. Then I grabbed some water and a Snickers bar and pulled out my forty-below parka. The sun was moving behind some clouds and the temperature was dropping quickly.

Then it sunk in. We were at 21,000 feet—six hundred feet higher than the summit of Denali—meaning we were at a higher altitude than anywhere in North America. However, we were still nowhere close to the summit of Cho Oyu, which remained over 5,000 feet above us. It was the second highest I had ever been and the real climb was just starting!

That evening, we had hot chocolate and a boiled packet of some sort of chicken "stew" for dinner, while huddled in our tents. It was not terrible, but clearly was not up to the standards of Gopal's cooking back down at advanced base camp. I managed to eat most of it, then supplemented the meal with another one of my Snickers bars.

As night approached, the temperature dropped precipitously. Going outside, except possibly to take a dump, was not recommended. However, inside the tent was comfortable, especially with my legs buried in my forty-below sleeping bag.

Before going to bed, I borrowed Phil's satellite phone and called my wife.

"Hey, gorgeous," I said, surprising her with the call.

"Hey, handsome," she responded. "Are you doing okay? You sound tired."

"No, I'm doing great. I'm calling you from Camp One, 21,000 feet. Tough climb to get up here, but I feel good. Looking forward to going higher tomorrow—up to the ice cliff."

"Okay," she said. "Be safe and don't do anything stupid."

"No problem," I replied. "We're on track to go for the summit in about a week. It's getting exciting now that we are finally up on the higher part of the mountain. Anyway, I've got to go...on Phil's satellite phone so I don't want to use up his battery."

"Okay, I love you."

"I love you, too," I responded as I hung up and handed the satellite phone back to Phil.

Although after thirty-two years of marriage, my response confirming my love for my wife had become almost automatic, it was true. And being away for almost a month in a far-off land and being high up a big mountain only reinforced my feelings for her. It is true that "absence makes the heart grow fonder." Absence, along with the risks inherent with high-altitude climbing, accentuates that fondness and those heartfelt feelings. Despite the great camaraderie among my fellow climbers, I desperately missed her.

That night, in accordance with Ben's admonition to stay hydrated, I positioned one of my large Nalgene water bottles close by, encased in a red insulated cover, and stashed down in one of my trekking boots. I figured that would keep it warm enough for a few midnight sips. And for the first few times when I awakened, the water was cold, but very pourable. Later, in the early morning hours, the water inside the bottle began to ice over, so I had to crack the thin layer of ice on the top before taking a sip. By morning, most of the remaining water was filled with crystalized ice. It was still drinkable, but was close to developing a solid block of ice. I never checked the temperature, but suffice it to say, that night was damned cold. All through the night, I could hear the snow and icy precipitation hitting the tent canvas, creating almost an igloo effect.

And all night long, I awoke to find clusters of caked-up blood deep in my nostrils. The Kleenex tissues were getting redder and redder with each blow of my nose. I began to wonder if I would advance to full-blown nosebleeds over the next few days.

The sun rose gloriously the next morning, heating up the entire area. From inside the tent, we kicked accumulated snow off the sides of the tent and began peeling off some of the layers that had kept us warm through the night. I could hear other climbers stirring from the nearby line of tents and then heard them laugh and walk around outside. The jingle of crampons, carabiners, and ascenders let me know that other groups would be going up the fixed ropes ahead of us that day.

"Breakfast in ten!" Ben announced from the guide's tent, about five feet behind us.

This time, they were serving bacon and pancakes…yum!

After breakfast, Ben announced that instead of just going up to the ice cliff and taking a good look at it as previously planned, we would be climbing the ice cliff and stashing gear at "Camp One and a Half," meaning that instead of climbing up to the ice cliff at about 22,000 feet with a light daypack with just snacks, water, a warm layer, and our outer shell jackets, we would be carrying a much-heavier pack with gear and provisions as we worked our way up to the ice cliff and climbed it.

This was an unexpected and last-minute change in the plan. And frankly, I did not like it. I had enough of a struggle to make it up to Camp One with a heavy pack, and was looking forward to having a much lighter pack as we got used to working with the fixed ropes, crampons, and ascenders on the climb up to the ice cliff. Now we would have to carry just about as much weight as we did the day before.

Nevertheless, the guides dictated the program and the schedule, and we had no choice but to comply.

I barely had my crampons adjusted on my new Everest GTX Millet boots and my harness and attachments organized around my waist when Ben and Lakpa announced we were ready to head up the mountain. By then the sun had warmed up the entire area and I realized that I had overdressed on my lower body, with Long Johns underneath and my inner shell, waterproof pants on top. I quickly loosened some Velcro along the sides of the pants to create some ventilation, but I did not have time to go back and change into lighter trekking pants.

Lakpa started out while I was still adjusting my pants, and, with the warmth of the sun, I forgot to put on my gloves. Rather than slip in right behind Lakpa in my customary fashion, by the time I joined the others, I was behind everyone but Keith and Ben.

Steve was nowhere to be seen, as he had developed a very bad cough since arriving at Camp One and was showing clear signs of HAPE—high altitude pulmonary edema—a swelling of the lungs. The guides had put him on two liters of oxygen with a portable mask through the night, but his condition was not improving. So, he was staying behind and would take a "rest" day on oxygen.

My tentmate, Phil, was also nursing a cough and showing some beginning signs of HAPE, at least according to Ben. Phil did not agree with the diagnosis and told me he felt good enough to move up higher on the mountain.

About halfway up the first steep snow slope, Lakpa looked back down the fixed line and saw that I was not wearing any gloves. He immediately ordered me to stop and put some on. Malcolm, who was in front of me, paused to pull my gloves out of the top zippered section of my pack. As I put them on, he then moved quickly up the slope. I felt somewhat silly for not having them on already, but conditions were so warm I did not think I needed them yet.

To try to keep up with the leaders, who were already cresting the top of the first slope, I probably attempted to move a bit too fast. I had not gotten totally adjusted to my new boots or to walking in the crampons, as we had not yet used them on the whole trip or done any practice runs in them after arriving at Camp One. Plus, I had not used an ascender since my climb of Mt. Vinson in Antarctica eight years prior. So, my effort up the first slope was not exactly efficient. I could feel my heartrate zooming upwards. But once I reached the top of the first slope and rested as I transitioned my ascender and safety carabiner to the next fixed rope, my heartrate recovered.

I pushed on.

I felt a bit more efficient on the next steep section. But my heartrate was again zooming up, even though I did not feel I was exerting myself that much. Once I reached the top of that section I looked at my Garmin and saw that my heartrate was at 185. Not good. But again, it went back down as soon as I stopped to rest. It was then that I remembered that I had been off my blood-pressure medicine with the beta-blockers for over five days. I no longer had the governor on my heartrate that I had become accustomed to for the last three years.

However, I did not come all this way to give up with a little raised heartrate.

I pushed up one more section. This time, when I got to the top, I was breathing so hard that I could not stop gasping for air. My heartrate was up to 190. Worse yet, it was not coming down. After hunching over in a stationary position for about three minutes, it was still at 170. I could feel my heart pounding inside my chest, not recovering like it normally does.

Come on, David, relax and breathe!

By then Keith and Ben had caught up with me. The rest of the group had gone over a crest, down a slight dip, and were waiting at the bottom of what looked like an even-steeper and higher section of fixed rope.

But my heartrate did not come down and I could not relax my system.

At that point, I lost confidence in my body's ability to handle the physical stress necessary to keep going up. I realized I would be risking a heart attack if I went much further. Without the ability to control my heartrate, I could not summit this mountain.

Not and come back alive.

"Are you okay?" Ben asked. "What's going on?"

"I'm done," I responded weakly.

"What's going on?" he asked again.

"I can barely breathe and my heartrate is completely out of control. It's going bonkers."

"You seem to be okay now."

"Yeah, barely. After three minutes' rest. But without my beta-blockers, I can't control my heartrate."

"Your beta-blockers? Why aren't you taking them?"

"They were in the blood-pressure meds."

"Hmmm…," he mumbled.

By now, Lakpa had backtracked to where we were standing to find out what was going on. I repeated the information to him.

"David, you're a strong climber," Lakpa said. "You've done well so far. Can you at least try to make it up this next hill? Then we can check on you at the top and make a decision."

"I'm sorry, Lakpa. I've made the decision. It's just too much of a risk. I know my body and it's not working right. I'm done."

"If he's done, I'm done, too," Keith said. "I've been waiting for someone else to drop out so that I don't have to pay the entire cost of leaving early."

Keith's decision had nothing to do with his climbing ability or his fitness to continue. Rather, while on the trip, his wife's father had died and her mother had taken ill, so he was anxious to get home to Mississippi as soon as possible. But he knew that leaving by himself would be very expensive if he had to pay for a driver and guide and the logistics to get back to Lhasa by himself. So, he jumped at the opportunity to leave when I announced I was done.

"Okay," Ben said. "But just to be clear, this is your decision and both of you need to know that if you turn back today, your expedition is over. You cannot change your mind tomorrow or the next day. We'll get you back to advanced base camp and arrange for you to get back to Lhasa. It's gonna be expensive."

"Is there any way I can stay at advanced base camp, and stay a part of the team until everyone else summits?" I asked.

"No. Once you are done, you're done," Ben said. "We've got to look after the rest of the guys and AAI does not let us leave someone without a guide, even at advanced base camp by themselves. No, if you turn back now, then that's it."

"Then that's it."

I checked my altimeter: 21,233 feet. No summit, but I had reached a pretty high "peak."

Almost a thousand feet higher than the top of Denali! So why did I feel so bad?

"Okay," Lakpa said. "Ben will go back down to Camp One with you to make sure you get there safe, and you must stay in the tents or right next to them the rest of the day until we get back. Steve is down there, too. Do not go anywhere else. Do you understand?"

Keith and I nodded.

The decision having been made, Lakpa headed back to rejoin the group at the bottom of the next steep slope, and Ben directed us to head down the fixed ropes towards Camp One. He followed us until we headed down the last steep section to the camp. As soon as we waved, indicating we were off the fixed rope and back to the camp, he headed up the mountain to rejoin the others.

My expedition, just like that, was ended, not more than an hour after heading out that morning. I felt simultaneously embarrassed and relieved. What started out as a day full of optimism had ended in full-fledged disappointment. I was embarrassed that I had managed to climb only a little over two hundred vertical feet before having to turn around that day. But I was relieved because I had been fighting off the nagging feeling that the cards just were not in it for me ever since I blacked out five days earlier.

I hated the beta-blockers, as they had held me back on my training climbs back in the States, but I knew they were a safety net for me, keeping my heartrate under control as we climbed steadily higher. Without them, I just wasn't sure that my heart would be able to withstand the pressure and exertion a mountain of this caliber would require.

Too many high-altitude climbers have died from heart failure. Indeed, though I did not know it at the time, a legendary climber, Conrad Anker, who discovered Mallory's long-lost body on Everest and led the acclaimed Meru climb that was made into an outstanding movie, recently suffered a heart attack at age 56, on a Nepal peak at less than 20,000 feet. He barely survived the medical evacuation. So, taking risks with uncertain heart situations at high altitudes is not advised, no matter the skill or experience of the climber.

Having abandoned the climb, there was nothing to do but wait throughout the day. I talked to Keith at length about what had just happened, trying to justify my decision and already second-guessing myself. Due to the strong sun, it was warm enough to sit outside the tents and watch as other groups went up or came down the slopes above the camp. So we had plenty of time to talk outside.

At some point in the afternoon, a guy Jason and Keith knew from a prior climb descended to the camp from above. We had met him back at the hotel in Shigatse, two weeks earlier. He indicated that he and his fellow climber had just returned from stashing gear up at Camp Two at 23,000+ feet. Keith asked him about the conditions higher up. He gave some vague responses about the going being tough and the climb being steep, but not much more detail. Apparently, no one had yet put in the fixed ropes above Camp Two, so there was no opportunity to go further at this point.

After about a half-hour break, the fellow and his Australian-sounding climbing partner headed down, returning to advanced base camp, chattering away as if they were on a Sunday-afternoon stroll.

After they left, I asked Keith to take a few photos of me holding a placard related to the Summer Law Intern Program for which I was raising money on this climb. I tried not to show my disappointment as he snapped three or four shots. They came out beautifully. Nothing like a perfect color photo with snow, tents, and a huge drop-off behind me to bring back for the publicity shots and articles about the program after the fact!

Around 2:30 P.M., Lakpa, Jason, John, and Malcolm arrived back at Camp One. They looked tired, but seemed to be in good spirits. They confirmed that they had successfully scaled the ice cliff and left a cache of gear up at Camp 1.5. Otherwise, they were not very talkative. They concentrated on getting rehydrated and resting from the effort.

After a while, Malcolm stuck his legs out of his tent and sat up in the entrance. Steve was still sleeping inside on oxygen.

"Where's Phil?" I asked.

"He's coming down with Ben," Malcolm said. "It may be a while. He's suffering."

"Shit. Did he make it up the ice cliff?"

"Yes, but he was seeing things and getting a bit crazy up there."

"I hope he's alright," I said. I was a bit worried about Phil's condition before he went up that day, but now I was concerned about his safety. "He's been fighting a cough for a couple of days."

"Yeah, I think he'll make it, but he may be done after today. What the hell happened to you this morning?"

"Couldn't control my heartrate—it was going bonkers. I'm off my beta-blockers without the blood-pressure meds, so I just decided I couldn't take the risk. And I didn't want to hold you guys back. Looks like you guys did well today."

"Yeah, but 'well' is a relative word," he said with a shrug of his shoulders. "We survived it, but it's a whole different world up there."

"Well, congratulations on making it up and back. It'll probably be easier the next time. I'm just disappointed that I won't be joining you guys."

About an hour and a half later, we saw Ben's figure appear at the top of the snow slope above us. He quickly glided down the slope to our tents.

"Where's Phil?" I asked.

"He's right behind me. Should be here in a couple of minutes."

"Is he alright?" I asked.

"Yeah, but he was struggling today. It may be the end of the road for him as well."

"I'm sorry that I had to turn back, but glad the other guys made it okay."

"No problem, David. At least you know your own limitations."

Just then, I got a glimpse of Phil stumbling along at the top of the slope. I watched nervously as he slowly worked his way down the fixed rope, swaying from side to side and almost falling at least half a dozen times.

It was painful to watch.

When he finally reached the tents, Phil could hardly talk. He looked like he had taken a beating and had just survived.

"Well done, Phil. Are you okay, buddy?" I asked, knowing that he was probably not okay.

"Just gotta rest," he mumbled. "Get water and rest."

We helped him discard his crampons and harness, and he crawled into the tent. He took a long gulp of water and then lay down. Within minutes, he was asleep. I crawled into the tent with him, just to make sure that he was breathing properly, then left him alone to sleep off the exhaustion.

Later that evening, after another boiled package dinner, huddled inside our forty-below sleeping bags, Phil and I discussed the events of the day. He wondered what had happened to me that caused me to turn around. I told him.

"Are you sure you can't keep going?" he asked. "Can't you go back on the blood-pressure meds?"

"I could, I guess, but then I could black out at any time without warning if it does the same thing to me."

"So, you're done?" he asked.

"Yeah. What about you? How was the ice cliff and how hard was it just to get up there to it?"

"It was tough. A lot of steep sections. I was wiped out by the time we got to the ice cliff."

"But I heard you made it up to the top of the cliff."

"Yeah—barely. Lakpa went up first—made it look easy. He dropped some ropes down. Jason went up. He had a couple of tough spots, but he went over the top pretty quick also. Malcolm did it as well. They disappeared so I could not see them anymore. Then I went, and it was crazy.

The ropes are all over the place and my feet kept sliding. I was dangling and screaming for help, but I couldn't see them above me. I kept pulling up with my arms and trying to get some traction, but my feet kept sliding out. I kept yelling for help. I don't know how I did it, but I finally made it up and they dragged me over the top. My arms were dead. Then John and Ben were up there. I don't remember much else."

"Wow! So how are you feeling now? Are you gonna go higher?" I asked.

"I don't know. I don't know if I can do that again. What do you think?" He coughed gruffly several times and took a sip of water.

"Hey, I can't tell you what to do. That's your decision. But if you're just tired and feel like you can recover by tomorrow, I'd advise you to wait until the morning to make a decision."

"So, what's the story with Steve and Keith?"

"They're done," I told him. "Keith turned around with me, mainly because he needs to get home to be with his wife, since her dad died and her mother is now sick. Steve's on oxygen and never came out of his tent the whole day. Ben says he has HAPE. So, three of us are definitely going down and leaving whenever they can get transportation for us."

"Ben thinks I have HAPE, too. But I don't think so—it's just a cough," he replied. "Are you sure you're done?" he asked me again.

"Yeah, I'm afraid so. I just don't feel like I can take the risk. My heartrate was completely out of control today. So, what are you thinking?"

"I don't know. Part of me tells me to keep going and part says, no, you've had enough. I don't want to hold the others back and I don't want to have to leave later, on my own."

Four or five more rumbling coughs sounded like they came from deep in his chest.

"I feel like I'm letting you down by not staying," I said. "But I'm just not comfortable with my situation right now. It's too risky. You don't sound too great with that cough of yours. But please don't make your decision based on the other three of us leaving. It's got to be your decision. Maybe you should think about it overnight."

"Yeah. Let me call my family before I go to bed. I'll make a decision in the morning."

Phil then got on his satellite phone and his wife answered.

"Hi, what's going on with you?" Phil asked her, coughing at the end of his question.

"Phil, are you alright? You sound terrible," she responded.

Phil cleared his throat. "I'm fine, just a little tough climbing today. I'm great. Nothing to worry about."

"Are you sure?" I could tell she knew him well and could sense his distress even over a satellite phone from 10,000 miles away.

"I'm good," Phil responded, then changed the subject. "So how are you and the kids? What's going on there?"

Phil spent the next twenty minutes talking with his kids and wife, as if it was just another day on the mountain. No details about the ice cliff or his troubles making it back to the camp. No hint that he was exhausted or thinking about leaving the mountain.

But that was probably best. If he was going to continue the climb, there was no reason to worry his wife or get her involved in the decision from afar. He had a tough decision to make.

His cough was worsening as he finally fell asleep but constantly turned restlessly that night.

In contrast, having made my decision earlier in the day, I slept like a baby, nestled inside my Mountain Hardware high-altitude sleeping bag at 21,000 feet, without a worry in the world.

In the morning, Phil announced that he had decided to leave the climb as well. So, in the span of less than twenty-four hours, the climbing team dropped from seven to three—just like that.

I could sense a bit of frustration on the faces of Ben and Lakpa. They had done a great job of acclimatizing us to the elements and the elevation, and through no fault of their own, over half of the team was packing it in.

Instead of possibly moving up to Camp Two for one night more of high-mountain acclimatization, the whole team would now descend back to advanced base camp and rest for another day while logistics were arranged for the four of us to hike out and meet a van and driver near intermediate camp.

I felt good on the descent from Camp One. Going down by the white fixed rope on the scree-filled side of the mountain was tough, especially since I was using my hiking poles and Steve, in front of me, was swaying back and forth, holding onto the rope. He was still on oxygen and looked like he could collapse at any time. Whenever he swayed to the left, the rope came across my right thigh causing me to readjust my right hiking pole and almost causing me to lose my balance. Though I was carrying a full backpack with all my gear, which took two trips to take up, I was much more worried about him than me.

We made it one-third of the way down and out of the snowy scree before taking a break. Below us, working its way up, was a team of Chinese climbers, dozens of them. The first few, who were probably guides, moved up to where we were quickly, showing no strain. The next half dozen did well also, breathing hard, but quickly recovering just beyond us. The last twenty of the Chinese climbers probably looked just like we had two days before, struggling with every step upwards, gasping for breath by the time they reached the rest stop. The last two were about ten minutes behind the rest and looked like they would not make it. But, with shouts of encouragement from their peers, they slowly got there.

God only knows whether they would make it all the way up to Camp One. Or beyond.

The rest of the way down was not a piece of cake. Footing on the down-sloping, hard-packed scree was still treacherous. But within another twenty to twenty-five minutes, we were at our "cache" location near the lake camp. After a short breather, we attacked the final steep downslope to the glacial murrain, making good time and warming up as the sun was starting to rise in the sky. Only Steve and Phil seemed to be dragging as we went back down.

Once we reached the murrain, Ben suggested that we split into a fast and a "less-fast" group to get back to the advanced base camp. Jason, John, and Malcolm quickly volunteered for the fast group. After looking at Steve and Phil, I also said I was feeling good and would try to keep up with the fast group. Despite having decided to turn around, I still felt like I could keep up with the leaders, at least now that we were back on more level ground.

"I think it would be better for you to go in the second group, David," Ben said authoritatively. "Let's go, guys."

The tenor of his voice made it clear there would be no negotiation.

And just like that, Ben, Jason, John, and Malcolm were gone, quickly disappearing over a ridge of gray rocks.

The men had been separated from the boys, so to speak. From that point on, it was the summit team and the evacuation team.

I felt like a scumbag.

The trip back to advanced base camp was agonizingly slow. Lakpa led us down, and I remained two steps behind him all the way. Even with the full backpack, I felt fresh and energetic. Keith stayed close with us, but Steve and Phil seemed to be fading by the minute. We waited for them to catch up at least ten times, with Lakpa constantly checking on Steve and reminding him to keep his oxygen mask on.

Whatever problems I had with my heartrate were not a factor on the downhill climb. I grew more and more impatient as we approached the camp and had to wait again for Phil and Steve. Lakpa insisted, properly, that we all should arrive at the camp together. So, we plodded along at a snail's pace the rest of the way. Jason, Malcolm, and John had been there so long when we arrived that they had gotten showers and were already playing cards in the dining tent. For the first time since we had been on the trip, there was no one there to greet us as we returned from a long hike.

"Well done, David," I said to myself, disheartened by the turn of events, but glad to be back in the relatively safe environs of advanced base camp.

For much of the rest of the day, I began to have second thoughts.

Come on, David. Maybe you should just go back on the blood-pressure medications and beta-blockers and make one more attempt at the top of the mountain!

It wasn't that bad, David. If Malcolm and John can do it, surely you can, too!

Don't be a wimp, David. You crushed it today. Suck it up and get back in the fast group!

As tempting as it was to reverse my decision, I kept thinking of my wife and kids and my retirement plans. I also still had residual pain on my right elbow and knee from when I blacked out six days prior. As I rubbed the sore spots, I realized more and more that I had made the correct decision. Still, part of me wanted to tell Ben and Lakpa that I had changed my mind.

I'm not a quitter.

When I broached the subject with Ben that evening, he quickly responded.

"No can do," he said. "When we told you that if you turned around up there, your expedition was over, we meant it. We can't afford to have someone who is half-in and half-out up on the mountain with us. It wouldn't be fair to the others. Plus, we've already arranged for transportation, hotels, and plane tickets back to Kathmandu for four people. Nope, it's the end of the line, David. It's probably better this way anyway."

"Yeah, of course you're right," I said. "I felt great coming down today, but that's all downhill. I don't want to go back on the pills and I don't have complete confidence that I won't have the same heartrate problems if I were to go up again. I know my own limitations and it's best that I don't risk it."

I almost convinced myself. At any rate, Ben did not give me any choice but to honor my decision.

Phil also had second thoughts. But ultimately, we would have been stupid to reverse course. The mountain had warned us not to continue. And with a mountain this big, we were wise to listen.

Even departing is not easy on a mountain like Cho Oyu. We could not leave until porters had been arranged to carry our duffel bags and gear back down to intermediate camp. Payment was based on weight, and I was running out of cash, so I threw away extra food, batteries, and any other useless items in the garbage sacks at the dining tents and packed up my backpack pretty much to the hilt before stuffing the rest of the gear in my North Face duffels.

Still, it would cost me $150 for a porter to carry my two duffels. To make matters worse, it snowed overnight, dropping about four inches of snow on the rocky trails down the mountain. It continued to snow as we set out.

Ben and Lakpa must have drawn straws and Lakpa lost, so he had to lead us out of there. He would have to retrace his steps (all the way from the Chinese base camp, as it turns out) later that day.

As was the case two days earlier, Keith and I stayed right behind Lakpa as he masterfully picked out the snow-covered trail down the mountain ridge and back to the road. Steve, who was still using oxygen, and Phil, who felt the need to stay back with Steve, trailed behind us, turning a three-hour hike out into over four hours. Despite my full pack, I kept a good pace, always staying closely behind or beside Lakpa. Once on the road, we had plenty of time to talk casually, and even more time while waiting for Steve and Phil to catch up.

Not once did Lakpa criticize me for turning back, despite my own misgivings about the decision, which I shared with him.

"Better to be safe," was all he would say. "Better to be safe."

But that said it all. He was a man of few words. But his words usually carried a lot of weight.

Surprisingly, a significant portion of the "descent" down the road was uphill. We gradually were dropping down in elevation, but at one point we found ourselves climbing switchbacks up to a higher road and then working our way upward along that road for twenty or thirty minutes, before descending again.

Several times we passed Chinese soldiers patrolling the area. They looked like they were teenagers, but their firearms looked menacing. Lakpa greeted them each time and there was no trouble. Why they were there is still a mystery to me.

It seemed like forever before we finally turned a corner and saw a van pulled off at a side spur of sorts just above the intermediate camp. There was construction going on all around the area and so the small junction area had lots of activity. The van was much smaller than the one we had traveled in with the whole group weeks earlier, and it quickly became apparent that our gear would not fit behind the back seat. Eventually everything was stuffed in, but Phil and I both had to sit on the left half of the back seat, with gear bags stacked to the ceiling on the other half.

Lakpa stayed with us all the way down to the Chinese base camp, where we had a few minutes to change into dry clothes and get some water and snacks. We said our goodbyes to Lakpa and watched as he scurried around to find a truck or motorcycle ride back up to intermediate camp. He would have to hike back up to advanced base camp that same day.

All in an ordinary day for the best Sherpa in the world!

It was just as long a day for us. Stuffed into the van for another eight hours, we arrived in Shigatse at dusk, barely in time for some rather nasty soup for dinner. The next day, we traveled another seven hours to Lhasa, stopping at several questionable roadside cafés on the way. By the time we arrived at Lhasa, I was nauseous again, my stomach churning and my spirits waning. This time our hotel was very near the center of town, near the central monastery and where the narrow streets were filled with little shops of wares and souvenirs. We had a small room off a very cute courtyard and would be there for two nights, as the first available flight out of Lhasa to Kathmandu was in two days.

The next day, between my waves of nausea, I managed to go shopping for about thirty minutes, finding a few items for my wife and friends. But I skipped the sightseeing trips taken by Phil and Keith. Basically, I slept uncomfortably in my bed, except for hourly visits to the commode.

God, I hate Tibetan food! It just messes with my system!

Somehow through the change of plane tickets, we ended up in first class on the flight from Lhasa back to Kathmandu. That was the good news. The bad news was that the plane got within ten minutes of landing in Kathmandu and abruptly turned around and headed back to Lhasa. They said it was because of a torrential rainstorm in Kathmandu, but the skies looked clear to me when we turned around.

Once back at the Lhasa Airport, we were treated as prisoners under house arrest. Since we had already passed through visa control to get on the plane, we had no valid visa to enter China on our return. Military police escorted us into the departure-gate area, where we waited for about three hours, hoping that the plane would be refueled and we could still get to Kathmandu that evening.

However, the plane was going nowhere. Instead, we had to retrieve all our bags that had been checked in and load them on a series of four or five large buses. However, because Phil had been on a separate group visa from the one Keith, Steve, and I were on, he was pulled aside and taken into a security room near the visa checkpoint in the airport. We had no choice but to leave him behind and get on one of the buses. We did manage to snag his gear bags and make sure they stayed with us.

There was not enough room for the baggage under the bus, so the overhead racks and walkways inside the bus ended up being crammed with suitcases and backpacks, such that we were literally packed in like sardines. Up in the front of the bus was a military officer responsible for making sure no one wandered off and everyone was accounted for.

When we left the airport, Phil was still nowhere to be seen.

About an hour later, the five buses pulled up in front of an older, deserted hotel in a compound behind walls. There, we were escorted into a large reception area. The lines were already twelve-deep at the reservation desk. It looked like a hopeless wait, but Steve managed to get the individual attention of a supervisor. The three of us got assigned rooms within about thirty minutes after we provided passports, identification cards, and boarding passes for review and copying, along with a $20 deposit for something that was never fully explained. They did tell us we would get our papers and deposit back in the morning.

When we left for our rooms, the lines were still at least ten-deep.

With no sign of Phil, we stacked his bags up in a corner, and would check on them later. Dinner was supposed to be served at 7 P.M., which was over an hour away. When we came back down to the lobby before dinner, Phil had arrived, with a full police escort. We greeted him and got him his bags. But he told us they were housing him in a separate section of the hotel under security, so he could not join us.

What a nightmare!

The next nightmare was the meal they served us for dinner. I can't even explain what it was they were serving. What looked like potatoes was certainly not potatoes. The soup had a strange flavor that eliminated any appetite after the first bite. There were no drinks, no meat of any sort, and very little of any substance in any of the serving containers.

Breakfast was not much better. They had some pinkish little sausages that looked like Vienna sausages, but tasted like poop. Next to those was some porridge-looking, glue-like mush that tasted like it looked. I grabbed two hardboiled eggs and a couple of peanuts, only to find that one of the eggs was almost raw. The other was edible but had a questionable taste to it. I had to eat something. The only good thing about breakfast was that Phil had been temporarily released from his confinement. He sat down with us as we consumed the awful meal before returning to his "handlers."

About two hours and another crammed bus ride later, we fought our way into the Lhasa Airport international departure terminal once again. As we left the bus, we noticed Phil being escorted in ahead of everyone, with his escorts now lugging all his bags behind him. He zipped through the checkpoints and disappeared around the corner, leaving us to fight our way through the crowds just to get inside the terminal.

After clearing the temperature checkpoint and the x-ray machine, we then had to wait for over an hour to have new boarding passes issued and our bags checked.

Why they couldn't just use the same bag-check tags as we had the day before is beyond me.

We finally cleared the baggage-check line with all our bags approved and tagged and headed over to the passport control. Just as I was about to reach the passport check officer, another officer came running over from the baggage check-in area and motioned me out of the line.

"Red North Face bag is yours, Mr. Shufer?"

"Yes, what's the problem?" I asked.

"Come with me, sir."

"What is the problem?" I asked again.

"You must come now—back to baggage check!" he said, as another officer approached.

"Okay, okay," I said.

I did not say, "Don't wet your panties." But I thought it.

Over at the baggage check, they pulled out one of my duffels.

"You have batteries in this bag?" an official asked me.

"I don't think so."

The official pointed to an object on the x-ray machine. "Open bag, sir," he said.

"Okay, no problem." I looked over to the passport control and saw that Steve and Keith had made it through and were no longer in sight.

Shit! Am I ever gonna get out of China?

I dug through my bag and could not find any loose batteries. I knew that I had thrown out all my extra batteries back at advance base camp to lighten my load.

"Help yourself," I said to the man. "I don't know what you're seeing, but I don't think there are any batteries in here."

He dug in and after a few minutes pulled out the ultraviolet steri-pen used to kill bacteria in our water bottles, which I had completely forgot about.

I opened it for him and it had four AA lithium batteries inside.

Damn, how did I forget that? Now they're gonna take it and it cost almost $100.

"No problem," he said, putting the steri-pen with batteries back in the bag. "You may go to passport control."

"What, after all that, you are not taking the batteries?"

"It's okay. No problem," he said again.

I realized that I should just shut up and move on. But I hung around just long enough to see my bag taken off the machine and put onto the departure conveyor belt. Then I hustled through passport control and joined my friends. Phil had already been relaxing there for about two hours, his "handlers" getting him some snacks and water for the wait.

"Wow, how did you turn this all around into the VIP treatment?" I asked.

"You just have to know how to deal with these guys," Phil replied with a slight smirk on his face.

Three hours later, we landed in Kathmandu, breathed in the heavy, smog-filled air, and thanked our lucky stars that we got out of China alive!

But whatever bug had plagued my GI system left China with me. It was not resolved until over two weeks after I arrived back in Atlanta. My sick body was physically back home, but my mind was still floating somewhere in Tibet for a couple of weeks.

After I returned, I followed John, Malcolm, and Jason's climb to the summit through the cybercast postings on AAI's website. After a very dicey climb to Camp Two in a raging snowstorm and a return to advanced base camp for a final rest, all three of them made it to the summit from Camp Two on a beautiful, clear day. Apparently, they never set up any Camp Three.

I was envious of them when I saw their summit photos with Everest and Lhotse shining over their shoulders in the background. I had dreamed of that photo for myself for ten months. But they were the strongest and most prepared climbers in the group. They persevered through all the acclimatization hikes, the stomach bug, the cold, the heat, the snow conditions, and the incredible altitude involved in climbing Cho Oyu.

On a business trip to Seattle for a deposition in summer 2017, I had dinner with Malcolm. Apparently, the rest of the climb on Cho Oyu was not as smooth as it appeared on the cybercasts. There was a mix-up on summit day, when fixed ropes had not been set up above Camp Three. Then John caught a crampon on an ice bridge and dropped down into a crevasse at over 25,000 feet in elevation, resulting in a time-consuming rescue. And the trip through the band of rocks near the summit plateau was a "brutal" climb, worse than the ice cliff. But Malcolm, John, and Jason worked their way through the problems with Ben and Lakpa's help. In May 2017, both Malcolm and John also reached the top of Everest with Ben taking them to the top and Lakpa running their base-camp operations.

I am highly disappointed in my own performance on Cho Oyu, but I am excited for the success of the team. I only wish I could have been there with Jason, John, Malcolm, Ben, and Lakpa on that glorious, clear day at the top of Cho Oyu.

Afterword

After his unsuccessful climb of Cho Oyu, the author has decided to limit his future climbs to doable 14,000ers in Colorado and perhaps another attempt to climb Mt. Blanc in the Alps. Treks in Patagonia, other parts of Nepal, and Northern India are also possibilities. Cho Oyu was supposed to be a substitute for Everest given its proximity and height, but the author is pleased that it at least served as a substitute for Denali, since at 21,233 feet elevation on Cho Oyu, the author climbed almost a thousand feet higher than Denali's summit before making the decision to turn around. Of course, his wife's veto of Everest and Denali remain steadfast and are even more firmly entrenched after the author's Cho Oyu experience.

Being the oldest climber on most of the author's recent major mountains climbs has been a challenge. Watching 34-year-old studs march up steep slopes without breaking into a sweat and trying to keep up without slowing everyone down has become more and more difficult with each passing year. The author's climbing hero, Sherpa Lakpa Rita, now in his early fifties, has decided that seventeen summits of Everest is enough for him, even though physically he could certainly still do more. But age affects everyone, mentally and physically, even the best mountaineers.

The author remembers vividly just how athletic he was in his late twenties and early thirties, playing soccer, running 10Ks, and taking on any challenge. He recalls how his physical condition went to pot once he reached age forty and stopped playing competitive soccer. Training for mountain climbs starting at age forty-four postponed the inevitable aging process. He wishes he had started his mountaineering career earlier. Yet, even in his forties, the author could keep up on some difficult mountains. Clearly, the author peaked (pun intended) at age fifty when he reached his highest height at the summit of Aconcagua, just under 23,000 feet in elevation. But now, another ten years later, he struggles to keep up with the most serious climbers, no matter how hard he trains.

The mind is willing but the body does not always cooperate. High blood pressure is difficult to cure. Medications can cause dizziness and uncertainty, or in the case of beta-blockers, can hold a climber back. That sometimes has the benefit of moderating the heartrate to avoid disastrous heart failure or attack, but also is detrimental to the climber's ability to push it to the limit. Getting the right equipment and the right guides is the easy part. Stopping the aging process and eliminating medical or other health issues are virtually impossible. Since the Cho Oyu expedition, the author climbed two more 14,000ers in Colorado in August 2017, (Mt. Bierstadt and Mt. Yale) but underwent two more prostate-related surgeries in the fall of 2017, and another in Spring 2018, making further high-altitude climbs unlikely.

So, for this "regular-guy" author, retirement is just around the corner and his sights are focused on comparatively "regular" 14,000ers, which can usually be climbed in a single day. With luck and dedication, the author still will climb a few modest peaks every year for another ten years. Meanwhile, he intends to work diligently on his golf game at lovely Kiawah Island just south of Charleston, South Carolina, where he and his wife have bought a home. The Ryder Cup Ocean Course is calling his name.

And the elevation there is almost zero!

Index

Aconcagua, Argentina, 3, 12, 14, 23-25, 42-45, 73, 114, 139, 166, 171-172, 178
Advanced Base Camp (Cho Oyu), 206-211, 226
Aguas Calientes (Machu Picchu Town), Peru, 122, 151, 153-155
Alejandro (Wayki Trek Guide), 129-131, 133-134, 136-147, 149-151, 153, 158
Alma, Colorado, 177, 201
Alpine Ascents International, 2-3, 12-13, 22-26, 31, 35, 38, 41, 54, 82, 90, 95, 166, 174, 183, 185, 190, 213, 219, 232
Ama Dablam View Hotel, Nepal, 69
Appalachian Trail, Georgia, 172
Aquille du Tour, France, 169
Arkaquah Trail, Georgia, 172
Art Loeb Trail, North Carolina, 172
Atlanta, Georgia, 38-40, 99, 173, 182-183, 232
Atlanta Bar Association Summer Law Internship Program, 202
Bartram Trail, Georgia, 172
Ben Jones, 184, 188-189, 197, 199-212, 215-219, 221, 223-228, 233
Beijeng, China, 194, 198
Black Balsam Mountain, North Carolina, 172
Bogmati River, Kathmandu, 46
Brahma Petra Grand Hotel, Lhasa, China, 191
Brasstown Bald, Georgia, 164, 172
Breckenridge, Colorado, 173-174
Callao Airport, Lima, Peru, 122, 127
Camp One (21,000 Foot Camp – Cho Oyu), 213-217, 219, 221, 223, 225
Chamonix, France, 169
Chinese Base Camp (Cho Oyu), 200-203, 228
Cho Oyu, 67, 163-233

Cold Mountain, North Carolina, 172
Colorado Trail, Colorado, 178, 181
Conrad Anker, 220
Cusco, Peru, 122, 126-131, 134, 150-151, 154-155, 158-160
David Morton, 54, 95
Dead Woman's Pass (Warmiwanusca), Inca Trail, 136-138, 140, 143-144, 170
Denali/McKinley, Alaska, 1, 38, 163, 166, 171, 214
Dengboche, Nepal, 74, 88, 91
Denver, Colorado, 173, 181
Diamox, 73-74
Disappointment Cleaver, Mt. Rainier, 16-17, 19, 29-31
Doha, Qatar, 181-182
Dudh Kosi River, Nepal, 50, 52, 55
Eric Remza, 12, 24
Everest Base Camp Trek, 37-97, 168, 183, 191
Fuji Mountain Guides, 99
Gopal, 47, 72, 84-85, 201, 207, 214
Gorek Shep, Nepal, 76, 82-88, 90, 169
Gotemba, Japan, 101
Goyko Lakes, Nepal, 67, 81
Grand Canyon, Arizona, 92, 116, 170
Grayson Schaefer, 54
Haltoo Hotel, Tingri, China, 198
Hamid International Airport, Qatar, 181-182
Hiroshima, Japan, 119
Huayna Picchu, 152
Inca Trail/Machu Picchu, 121-161, 165
Ingraham Glacier, Mt. Rainier, 12, 15, 28, 30
Intermediate Camp (Cho Oyu), 204-206, 228-229
International Mountain Guides, 207
Intipata, Inca Trail, 148-149
Island Peak, Nepal, 74, 91

John Muir Camp and Huts, Mt. Rainier, 3, 5, 7, 9, 13-15, 18-19, 25-28, 34
Jon Krakauer, 78
K-2, 163
Kathmandu, Nepal, 38-39, 41-49, 95-97, 168, 182-183, 186-188, 190, 193, 227, 229, 232
Keio Plaza Hotel, Tokyo, Japan, 99
Kennesaw Mountain, Georgia, 164
Khumbu Glacier, Nepal, 79-80, 84
Khumbu Ice Fall, Nepal, 79, 84
Khumbu Valley, Nepal, 48, 54, 61, 70, 72, 82, 169
Khumjung, Nepal, 68-70, 87, 91
Khunde, Nepal, 69
Kilimanjaro, 3, 23, 25, 41, 63, 139, 163, 166, 169, 171, 203
Kyoto, Japan, 100, 119
Kyushu, Japan, 119
Lhasa, Tibet (Western China), 188-190, 195, 218-219, 229
Lima, Peru, 122-124, 126-127
Llaqtapata, Inca Trail, 135
Lobuche, Nepal, 79, 82, 87
Lorje Bridge, Nepal, 55, 94
Lukla, Nepal, 37, 48-50, 67, 92-95
Machu Picchu, Peru, 121-122, 128, 131, 135, 146, 148, 151-155, 159, 161, 165, 170
Mallory, 220
Marriott Mountain Resort, Breckenridge, Colorado, 175
Maytaq Hotel, Cusco, Peru, 128-129, 158
Melissa Arnot, 54, 80-82, 89, 95
Meru Monastery, Lhasa, China, 191
Miraflores, Lima, Peru, 123-125, 127
Monkey Palace, Kathmandu, 45
Monjo, Nepal, 55, 92, 94
Mont Blanc, France, 163, 169
Moray Ruins, Peru, 156-157
Mt. Ama Dablam, Nepal, 54, 60, 69, 91, 93
Mt. Antero, Colorado, 173, 177-181
Mt. Baker, Washington, 2, 5, 22

Mt. Bross, Colorado, 168, 177
Mt. Cameron, Colorado, 168, 177
Mt. Cholotse, Nepal, 77-78
Mt. Columbia, Colorado, 177
Mt. Cotopaxi, Equador, 35
Mt. Democrat, Colorado, 168
Mt. Elbrus, Russia, 3, 23, 139, 166, 187
Mt. Everest, Nepal, 1, 14, 28, 38, 42, 48, 54-55, 60-62, 70-73, 76-87, 90, 92, 163, 166, 169, 171, 174, 185, 188, 197-199, 202-203, 233
Mt. Fuji, Japan, 99-119, 163, 170
Mt. Gongla, Nepal, 37, 49
Mt. Harvard, Colorado, 177
Mt. Kala Pattar, Nepal, 76-77, 82-83, 88-91, 169
Mt. Kantega, Nepal, 62, 91
Mt. Koscuiszko, Australia, 166
Mt. Lhotse, Nepal, 56, 60, 71-73, 233
Mt. Lincoln, Colorado, 168, 177
Mt. Lobuche East, Nepal, 81-82
Mt. Machu Picchu, Peru, 148-149, 151-152
Mt. Makulu, Nepal, 74, 91
Mt. Nuptse, Nepal, 56, 60, 71, 73, 84
Mt. Princeton, Colorado, 177
Mt. Pumori, Nepal, 79, 82, 88
Mt. Rainier, Washington, 1-35, 38, 42, 163, 166-167, 173, 178
Mt. Salkantay, Peru, 146
Mt. Shavano, Colorado, 177
Mt. Tebegauche, Colorado, 177
Mt. Thamserku, Nepal, 55, 62, 91
Mt. Whitney, California, 2, 166
Mt. Veronica, Peru, 139, 146
Mt. Vinson, Antarctica, 166, 217
Mt. Yale, Colorado, 177
Namche Bazaar, Nepal, 55, 57-58, 61, 67-70, 91-93
Narita Airport, Tokyo, Japan, 99
Nasqually Glacier, Mt. Rainier, 5, 14
National Geographic, 40, 55, 72, 121, 152
Nima (Sherpa), 57, 201-202
Okinawa, Japan, 101, 119

INDEX

Ollantaytambo, Peru, 122, 133, 139, 151, 155, 158
Panorama Lodge, Namche Bazaar, Nepal, 58
Paradise, Mt. Rainier, 4, 9, 14-15, 18
Periche, Nepal, 72-74, 77, 79, 91
Phakding, Nepal, 51, 53-54, 94
Phil Erschler, 19
Phortse, Nepal, 91-92
Phuyuptamarca, Inca Trail, 148
Pico de Orizaba, Mexico, 12, 23, 166
Potala Palace, Lhasa, China, 191-193, 197
Punta Arenas, Chile, 166
Quandary Peak, Colorado, 173-176, 178
Rabun's Bald, Georgia, 172
Radisson Hotel, Miraflores, Lima, Peru, 123, 127
Rainier National Park, Washington, 11
RMI, 4
Runkurakay, Inca Trail, 145
Runku Raqay Pass, Inca Trail, 146
Sacred Valley, Peru, 122, 130, 133, 161
SA International, 122
Sagarmatha National Park, Nepal, 59
Saksaywamam ("Sexy Woman"), Cusco, Peru, 159
Salida, Colorado, 173, 177
Salkantay Route, Machu Picchu, Peru, 121
Sarah Montgomery, 14, 17, 19, 42-44, 54, 58, 63, 67, 69, 75-76, 79-82, 88, 90
Sayacmarca, Inca Trail, 146
Scott Fischer, 78
Seattle, Washington, 1-3, 11-13, 18, 22, 26, 35, 38, 233
Seoul, Korea, 39-40, 44
Sera Monastery, Lhasa, China, 193-194
Sherpa Cammie Rita, 201
Sherpa Lakpa Gelu, 14, 17, 27-34
Sherpa Lakpa Rita, 14, 24, 42-47, 51, 54-56, 59-63, 67-72, 74-78, 80, 83-87, 89-92, 94-96, 184, 188, 191, 195-206, 210-212, 216, 218-222, 224, 226-229, 233
Shigatse, China, 195, 220, 229
Shining Rock, North Carolina, 172
Stonehenge, 159
Subash (Sherpa), 57
Subashiri Trail, Mt. Fuji, 100-102, 115, 117
Sun Gate (Inti Punku), Inca Trail/Machu Picchu, 151-152, 154
Sunrise Lodge, Phakding, Nepal, 52
Sun Temple, Cusco, Peru, 129, 160
Taboche, Nepal, 77
Tabuche Peak, Nepal, 62
Tengboche, Nepal, 70-71, 91, 93
Tennant Mountain, North Carolina, 172
Tenzing-Hillary Airport, Lukla, Nepal, 37
Thame, Nepal, 61-63, 68
Thamo, Nepal, 62
Tingri, China, 197-200
Tokyo, Japan, 99, 101, 170
Urubamba, Peru, 133
Urubamba River, Peru, 133, 155
Wayki Treks (Inca Trail/Machu Picchu), 130, 143
Whitaker Café, Mt. Rainier, 4-5
White Mountain, Colorado, 178
Vern Tejas, 24, 166
Yak & Yeti Hotel, Kathmandu, Nepal, 42, 184, 188-189